May 1970

5.36

OF GARDENS
AND GARDENERS

By the same Author

*

STRAWBERRY GROWING COMPLETE:
GRAPES UNDER CLOCHES
MELONS UNDER CLOCHES

OF GARDENS AND GARDENERS

EDWARD HYAMS

South Brunswick and New York:
A. S. Barnes and Company

 First American edition published 1969 by A. S. Barnes and Company, Inc., Cranbury, New Jersey 08512.

Library of Congress Catalogue Card Number: 71-83389

SBN 498 07482 X

Printed in the United States of America

CONTENTS

PREFACE

The disorder of this book is a by-product of the way in which it was written—at random, from time to time, and when the particular subject interested me.

When I came, at the publisher's request, to collect these notes and essays into a volume, the question of order presented itself: I decided to ignore it. It would have been possible to group the essays under various heads, more or less contrived. But this is a bedside book, intended to be picked at, not read from cover to cover. I hope, therefore, that I shall be forgiven for interspersing accounts of plants with accounts of gardens, of alien garden styles, or of gardening people.

The only justification I needed for including a piece in this book was that it interested me.

E.H.

ACKNOWLEDGEMENTS

Thanks are due to the following publishers and authors for permission to quote from the works listed:
Italian Gardens by Georgina Masson (Thames and Hudson International Ltd.); *The Living Garden* by Sir Edward Salisbury (G. Bell & Sons Ltd.); *Pilgrimage for Plants* by Frank Kingdon-Ward (George G. Harrap & Co. Ltd.); *Gardens of China* by Osvald Siren (The Ronald Press Company, New York); *Japanese Gardens* by Jiro Harada (The Studio Ltd., *now* Studio Vista Ltd., London).

'TO GARDEN . . . .'

The verb 'to garden' has only a very broad general meaning; it means different things in different places and classes. Some of the meanings attributed to it cut right across national and even continental frontiers, being the same for a particular class all over the world. For example, to the English farm labourer, the Chinese peasant, the Italian peasant, the South American peasant, the African or Indian villager, 'to garden' means to grow vegetables to eat, and perhaps a little fruit. To the majority of English middle-class gardeners the verb really means 'to grow flowers'. The English are good at plants and bad at garden design which no longer interests them very much; they adopt one of half a dozen conventional plans in the layout of their gardens but their object is to have as many flowers as possible, and a lawn. To those Italians and French who are socially above the vegetable gardener and have not been too much influenced by English gardening, the verb 'to garden' implies, as it were, an act of architecture. The best Italian gardens, and the best French gardens are, in their different ways, extensions of the house, works of architecture in which some live plants become as much part of the builder's raw material as are stone or brick. The modern American garden is a play place decorated with plants; it does not exist for art's sake or the sake of flowers; in spirit it is Italianate or French rather than English.

Three peoples have, in their time, made gardening into one of the fine arts for a short period of time: the Chinese; the Japanese; and the English. Perhaps, I am not yet sure, it will be possible to add a fourth to this list, the Brazilians, if the tropical gardens of Burle Marx give rise to a school of garden art.

The distinction I make here is as follows: the garden as a work of fine art is made to look at, as a picture is painted, and, like a picture, to make a certain impression or set of impressions on the beholder. It was in that spirit that the landscape gardens of China were made; they were literally picturesque, they were the work of *paysageistes* who instead of using paint used rocks, trees and other plants, water and a little masonry. Even though one went into and walked in such a garden, whereas one cannot get inside a work by, for example, Poussin, the purity of the art is not impaired for one was not supposed to do anything once one was in, but only to contemplate the work and let it act upon the spirit. How does this differ from the great Italian or French gardens? Radically, for those gardens were intended to be, and clearly are, summer rooms, a part of the house which happens not to be under a roof, places to converse in, make love in, play games in; in short, places for the carrying on of social intercourse. If any reader doubts the value of the comparison between painting and landscape gardening, there is this point in support of it, (and one could cite others): a *trompe l'oeil* perspective was achieved by the Chinese garden landscape artists by concentrating the heavier foliaged trees in the foreground, those with lighter leaves in the middle plain, and those with light, feathery and glaucous foliage in the distance. By this, among other means, vistas were drawn out and impressive distances simulated within a little space.

The Japanese had gardens of both kinds, gardens which were Chinese in spirit; and social intercourse gardens, those in which musical parties were held, or the tea ceremony made fashionable by the great tea masters who built special gardens for that ceremony. But the Japanese also carried the garden as a work of fine art very much further than any other people. They began to do so, apparently, under the influence of Chinese painting, the black-and-white drawing or wash drawing of the Southern Sung. This simply means, of course, that they, too, created pure art landscapes using stone, water and plants instead of paints or inks. But they subsequently went much further. At first a few flowers were allowed in the picture garden; but as the art progressed the growing of flowers was relegated to flower nurseries, and flowers were wholly excluded from the garden. At the end of the process was the so-called *dry landscape* garden of the Zen Buddhist monasteries—in short, pure abstract gardening. No plants of any kind were used, only two materials, sand and stones, unless the most important element, space, be considered, as probably it should be in this context, a third material.

The English came much later to gardening as a fine art. So much so that some critics have insisted that they derived the art from the Chinese. I have dealt elsewhere with this theory and it does not hold water: the earliest of the English landscape gardens of the eighteenth century were too early to have been influenced by the first work which describes Chinese gardens for English readers and which was not published until the last decade of the century. No, the English created their garden art in the same spirit and with very much the same kind of feeling as the Chinese but independently of them: similar influences in the two cultures must have been at work, for example, love of nature. of the country tamed, gentlemanliness, wealth in the hands of men of taste; that kind of thing.

Fortunately the greatest of the English works of art in this field, as well as many other and less than perfect works, still exist. In Hoare's Stourhead we possess a garden which is as much and as manifestly a work of fine art as any painting by Poussin or by any of the seventeenth and eighteenth century *paysageistes* of France and Italy. It is to look at and to be moved by, not to play in, nor to grow flowers in. It is true that because Hoare's evergreens have been replaced by such flowering shrubs as rhododendrons and camellias, it is necessary to visit the garden late in summer or in the winter to see it as that great artist, the banker Hoare, made it.

THE MOUTAN

If I had to answer the absurd question: What is the most beautiful flower you have ever seen, I should opt for the moutan. Although I am not sure that the name covers the whole subgenus of the woody paeonies, it is preferable as a name to 'tree-paeony'; for the plants are, of course, nothing like trees. The moutans are shrubs, and although they may sometimes grow gaunt and tall, they are never even remotely tree-sized.

To the best of my belief nobody knows how long the moutan has been in cultivation. But since it has only been seen wild in western China—and that very, very rarely—and since it is documented as a garden plant in Chinese garden literature at least as early as the sixth century of our era, and perhaps earlier, it was presumably domesticated by the Chinese. An early sixth-century reference to it places its origin in Szechuan and Shensi. Reginald Farrer found it wild in Kansu (see below). There had obviously been a great deal of cultivated propagation and selection of good varieties before that date: the *Moutan Poo** lists thirty garden varieties grown in the eighth and ninth centuries; and a little later very fine ones exchanged hands at fabulous prices, as high as one hundred ounces of gold for a single plant. It would seem that there must have been a sort of moutan bonanza in eighth-century China rather like the tulip bonanza in Holland nearly a thousand years later, or the 'Easter Lily' bonanza in the United States in the nineteen-thirties.

The moutan was introduced into Japan in the year 734 or thereabouts. The results were splendid for:

* *King Flower Book.*

'This race of imcomparably great gardeners put their mark upon the plant. Varieties of more exquisite beauty of line, of clearer colouring, with flowers of lighter weight which held themselves beautifully presented upon the bush took place of the heavier, larger Chinese flowers of more muddled petalage.'

(M. Hayworth-Booth. *The Moutan.* Constable)

The moutan reached England and was planted at Kew in 1789, after Sir Joseph Banks had asked a physician of the East India Company to get him a plant of it: he himself had only heard of it through a Dutch source. After that there were more introductions, all the early ones were from China. Not until 1802 did a plant which turned out later to be the type, reach England. This is the moutan with enormous semi-double white flowers which have a maroon blotch at the base of each petal. I am not sure that it is not more beautiful than any of the garden hybrids, glorious though some of them are; certainly I have always preferred it.

By the end of the nineteenth century not only did we have many scores of varieties growing in hundreds of gardens, but there were some remarkable old plants established here and there. The original Kew plant had grown to be eight feet high and ten across by 1842 when it was destroyed to make way for a new building. It need not have been; but it was not then realized that moutans, however old and large, can be moved without doing them any harm. Some of the moutan plants imported in 1802 had, less than thirty years later, reached an immense size: one is described (in 1826) as seven feet high, forty feet in circumference and bearing up to 600 flowers. There were other great plants still later in the century.

In that much admired style which I have never been able to enjoy, Reginald Farrer describes his discovery of the wild moutan, a century and a quarter after the first introduction of cultivars, in his *On the Eaves of the World.* He is sitting on a hillside, resting, above the village called Fu-erh-gai where he was to spend the night.

'So I sat at last and rested, gazing down the steep loess track to the little village at my feet, so comfortable and pleasant-looking in its grove of poplars, till my eye was caught by certain white objects further along the hillside, that were clearly too big by far to be flowers, yet must certainly be investigated if only to find out what clots of white wool, or yet whiter paper, surely could be doing in the wild coppice, perked up here and there above the small fry of little barberries and so forth. Probably they had some religious meaning. I would see.

'Through the foaming shadows of the copse I plunged, and soon was holding my breath with growing excitement as I neared my goal and it became more and more certain that I was setting my eyes on *Paeonia Moutan* as a wild plant. The event itself justified enthusiasm, but all considerations of botanical geography vanish from one's mind in the first contemplation of that amazing flower, the most overpoweringly superb of hardy shrubs.'

Moutans are not difficult to grow. For one thing which is very important in much of Britain, they are perfectly tolerant of chalk and other limestone soils, while growing equally well and even rather better in peaty, acid soils. For another thing they are very hardy indeed. They do have one demerit. They begin to burgeon very early in the year, as do the herbaceous paeonies, and this exposes the very beautiful young foliage to destruction by spring frosts. Much of this danger can be avoided, in those parts of the country and those low-lying gardens where it is serious, by so siting the moutan plants that they do not receive any morning sun until eleven o'clock or even noon. For if lightly frozen foliage has a chance to thaw very slowly the bursting of tissue cells, which does the harm, may be avoided: whereas if the sun strikes the leaves when they are still frozen, rapid thawing bursts the leaf cells and the leaves are destroyed.

Not all 'tree-paeonies' are truly moutans. *Paeonia delavayi*, *P. ludlowii* and *P. lutea* are not, though as parents of some magnificent hybrids they have contributed to the making of many new garden moutans.

The moutan itself is *P. suffruticosa* and whether you grow the type, in the superior form called 'Rock's Variety', or the newer cultivars, there is one thing to remember: they hate a damp atmosphere and are subject to fungus disease which can even make them ungrowable in some parts of the country; expose them to wind, never try to shelter them excepting from morning sun. And, secondly, when you receive a young plant, plant it deep, not shallow: it will have been made by grafting the variety you want on to a piece of herbaceous paeony root, and until you get it on its own, scion root, it will not grow as it should, so the graft scar must be deep enough below the soil surface to leave room for those scion roots to grow.

ARUMS

In most of Britain arum lilies, callas as the Americans call them, *Richardias*, or more correctly, *Zantedeschias* in botanical Latin, are greenhouse plants, or at least they are so considered. In practice certain selected forms of the common white arum lily, *Z. aethiopica* can, with a little extra care, be established out of doors in the south and west. One rather curious and usually successful practice is to plant them at the bottom of a pond so that the roots are protected from frost whatever happens; for although the pond may freeze over in cold weather, it is extremely unusual in Britain for a pond to freeze through to the bottom.

I had not even known that there were arums in any colour but white when, walking one day through Berne in Switzerland, I saw crimson arums in the window of a florist's shop. I crossed the road and went into the shop and asked the girl whether the flowers had been dyed in some way. She replied that they had not, they were 'really' that colour. I was in a hurry, short of money, and it never crossed my mind that there would be any difficulty in discovering the origin of those flowers. I got from the girl the name of the grower and at a later date wrote to him from London; the letter returned to me after many weeks; the addressee could not be found. It was, in short, what we used to call 'one of those things'. But at least it aroused my interest in the genus.

The whole genus is confined to South Africa in nature and most of the species seem to prefer marshes to dry land. My first experience with it was with the white *Z. aethiopica* in two or three of its garden forms; these survived and flowered well in Devonshire but could not be over-wintered in Kent. The most interesting experience I have had with this plant was when some of the flowers set seed which was fully grown but still green by the end of the autumn; I brought a head of seed into the house and, in a dry kitchen, it ripened to pale orange. This seed was then sown under glass in a sample of the new Levington Compost which the makers had just sent me. I should think every seed must have germinated and made a good plant; there is, in short, not the least difficulty in growing arums from seed.

From an English nursery I next had some rhizomes of *Z. elliottiana*, a very handsome arum from the Transvaal which bears its six-inch golden-yellow spathes on two- to three-foot stalks. Although it is commonly reckoned a warmhouse plant it flowers freely in southern and western English gardens, and moreover survives most winters in the open and would, I should think, survive any winter if it were well littered with bracken or straw before the cold weather sets in. An outstanding quality of this species is the high gloss on the spathe colour. It is most effective when grown with *Z. aethiopica*. The two cross readily, and some seedlings are more substantial and have bigger spathes than the parents, but the colour is rarely so rich. Another yellow-flowered arum which I obtained from South Africa and grew for a year or two is called *Z. melanoleuca*, but its pale yellow spathe does not match *elliottiana* for either colour or form. A third yellow-flowered arum is *Z. sprengeri* which I also had from South Africa. It is a dwarfer species than the others I have mentioned, flowering at about eighteen inches and having a small spathe which is sometimes bright yellow but tends to be a rather wishy-washy sulphur colour. It comes from the Transvaal and it ought to be as hardy as *elliottiana* but I found I could not keep it for very long.

The most exciting arum I had from my South African nursery, however, was *Z. rehmannii*. As I understood it to be variable in the matter of colour, I bought quite a lot of rhizomes and tried them in various parts of the garden and also in pots under glass. They are from Natal and I expected them to be tender. But some of the plants survived many winters, notably where they were among very dwarf shrubs and so in protected soil. They have rather narrow lanceolate leaves, less arrow-head shaped than most of these aroids, about a foot tall and the best plants produced flowers with a bright rose-pink spathe; in others the colour was poor, a sort of pink-washed greenish-white; and one plant had flowers of a hideous purplish-brownish red. But *Zantedeschia rehmannii* must have been the source of those crimson hybrids I had seen in Switzerland.

I do know of one source of arums which had spathes in colours ranging through all the yellows to orange and scarlet and finally crimson as well as others with much more peculiar colours including violet. But to the best of my knowledge (which is, however, very imperfect), the whole of this race of hybrids was lost as soon as found. During the late 'twenties and 'thirties of the century a Japanese geneticist working in California decided to make use of the eight species of Zantedeschia in the practical work on which his theorizing would be based. This meant crossing and back crossing using all eight species. And it was in his seedlings that the extraordinary range of spathe colour was obtained. I came across an account of his work, printed with colour plates in Tokio, and set about trying to discover what had happened to the plants. It seems that the scientist in question did not think of them as new garden plants, but simply as the results of his genetical experiments; so far as I could discover no rhizomes were ever distributed; their creator went back to Japan; his plot of land was sold and ploughed for some other purpose.*

Nevertheless, it seems probable that his hybrid arums were not the only ones in the world. There is no difficulty in crossing between the species; and there is the evidence of those crimson flowers in that Berne florist's shop.

Among the roots and seeds I had from South Africa at the same time as the arums, was that of an aroid which was not a *Zantedeschia* but whose genus I never did discover. It was the only black, or very nearly black, flower I have ever grown, and strikingly beautiful. It was a dwarf plant with a long and beautifully shaped spathe the inside of which was a mahogany-purple so very deep that where the inward curving form of the spathe kept the surface in shade, it was a rich black; the texture was velvet. The spadix, too, was velvety black. I lost this plant through carelessness after a few years but it is one which I shall certainly try to grow again at some time in the future.

* *Intercrossing among Pink Calla, White Spotted Calla and Yellow Calla* by Ryôhitsu Shibuya (Tokio 1956). Since this was written I have seen many-coloured arums, including a violet one, in Australian gardens.

SOME CHILEANS

The gardener who has never gardened in the west country or in Ireland or South-West Scotland, is rarely familiar with the Chilean flowering shrubs which can be grown in Britain and which are as beautiful as they are curious and interesting in form and flower.

I discovered them first in Irish gardens, then found some of them in Cornish and Devonshire gardens, and finally came to growing some of them myself.

I was driving along a road in West Ireland when, topping a wall front and to the left of me there appeared the head of a small, bushy tree of very stiff growth and very dark green foliage which was decorated with many thousands of rosy-crimson lantern shaped flowers. I had never seen the plant before and in my excitement almost wrecked the car by running off the road and nearly into a bank. On closer inspection the merits of the shrub were revealed as even greater than they had at first appeared, for the enchanting flowers, hanging gracefully each on its own long stalk, seemed to be made of the finest candle-wax; their texture and substance were remarkable.

This was the Chilean shrub *Crinodendron hookerianum* (or *Tricuspidaria lanceolata*, or some other combination of these four names). I have grown it since, but it is very marginal in gardens north-east of Cornwall, excepting on the south-west coast of Scotland. It is at its best in our latitude in the Irish gardens and at its magnificent finest at Mount Usher, County Wicklow, where groups of it are well over twenty feet tall and as much or more through. The species needs a moist, peaty, woodland type of soil, or a deep and rich loam on the acid side of neutral; I believe it to be quite intolerant of limestone soils. It prefers a half shaded site and it should be exposed to the warm rains of the south-west, screened from the cold winds of the north-east. In England it is usually a bush, in Ireland a small tree, again bushy and sometimes clad to the ground with foliage. It is an evergreen, of course, with tough, lanceolate, very dark green leaves. The flower buds, on their rather long, curving pedicels, appear in autumn and hang waiting for the spring throughout the winter, a serious weakness in any but the warmest parts of the country for they are very apt to be destroyed by frost.

Crinodendron is easily grown from cuttings in a close case or under mist and, where it can be grown, should be, for there is no northern hemisphere shrub at all like it.

Of the four species of the genus Eucryphia two are Chilean, and those two the best; they also provide the best hybrid for our gardens. I have grown all of them. This, once again, is a genus which does much better in the extreme south-west of England and Scotland, and still better in Ireland, than anywhere else in Britain. From the behaviour of Chilean shrubs and trees in Irish gardens it seemed to me that the conditions in those gardens must be very much like those in the neighbourhood of Valdivia and the island of Chiloë, the Chilean provinces from which so many fine plants have been introduced. I have since been there and found I was right.

Eucryphia glutinosa is a shrub in England, a tree to twenty-five feet or more in Ireland or the warmest gardens of our own south-west. It is reasonably hardy, for although it may sometimes be an evergreen in favourable conditions, it is a deciduous species in cold climates; it does quite well even in the south-east on condition that there is no lime in the soil, for this is an acid-soil plant. The leaves are pinnate, with from three to five ovate leaflets. Their colour is a medium green with a fine greyish sheen and in autumn before falling they turn a vivid flame-red or, in some soils, golden yellow. Once the shrub reaches maturity it flowers profusely—I have often seen specimens completely covered with flowers. These are borne, two or three inches across, like single white roses with a great boss of prominent golden stamens. Flowering time is August/September. This Eucryphia is very easily grown from cuttings under glass.

There is, at Castlewellan in County Down, Northern Ireland, a remarkable double avenue of Eucryphias including this one and among the *E. glutinosa* specimens some are double-flowered; but as is so often the case, much of the beauty of the flowers is lost in doubling, and the single-flowered type is much to be preferred.

The second Chilean Eucryphia is an even handsomer plant than *glutinosa*; but this, *Eucryphia cordifolia*, is much less hardy; on the other hand it is evergreen wherever it is grown, and it is tolerant of chalk and other limestone soils. In its native Valdivia, in some Irish gardens and notably at Mount Usher, and even in Devonshire gardens whose climate is favoured by a suitable fall of the land or the near neighbourhood of the sea, it attains about thirty feet; old specimens, although usually more or less fastigiate in shape, are often as much as ten feet through; and at Mount Usher groups of three or four make enormous boskages. The leaves in this case are not pinnate but simple, heart-shaped, dark dull green, and leathery. The flowers of this Eucryphia are even finer than those of *E. glutinosa*. White, two inches across, beautifully cupped and with a great centre of bristling golden stamens, they are borne on old specimens in such abundance that the foliage is almost hidden. They are very attractive to bees and in Valdivia *Eucryphia cordifolia* honey is greatly valued.

One of the English gardens in which both these Chilean Eucryphias were first well established was Nymans. In 1915 or thereabouts a chance seedling of Eucryphia which was found there by the gardeners and grown on, turned out to be a hybrid between the two species; it is true that some botanists held that it was not a hybrid, but a particularly vigorous form of *E.*

glutinosa to which it bears more resemblance than to the other one. On this point, however, W. J. Bean, at that time Curator of the Royal Botanic Gardens, Kew, had this to say:

'Some doubt has been expressed as to whether it is really a hybrid or only a vigorous form of *E. glutinosa*. It undoubtedly resembles that species more than *cordifolia* yet the presence of undivided leaves, the greater size and firmer texture of the foliage in general, as well as the genuinely evergreen character, seems undoubtedly to indicate the influence of the latter. It first flowered in Col. F. Stern's chalk garden at Highdown near Worthing, in September 1922 and its success there is regarded as due to the *cordifolia* influence, for whilst that species grows well in chalky soil, *E. glutinosa* is a failure there.'

(*Trees and Shrubs Hardy in the British Isles*)

At all events, this new Eucryphia was called, at first *E. nymansensis* but is now more correctly called *E* × 'Nymansay' since it is a cultivar whose hybrid nature is no longer in doubt.

Mitraria coccinea, a gesneriad, is another Chilean evergreen and likewise from the province of Valdivia and the island of Chiloë. It is a very easy plant to grow in warm, moist, peaty, south-western gardens, but useless in the colder east. However, I recently discovered another way to grow it when I saw it in the plant room of a friend's apartment in New York. It seemed not to object to the poor light and was both growing and flowering freely; it may, perhaps, become established as a house plant where it can be kept sufficiently humid. In the open garden it must have shade and it must have a measure of shelter from the cold quarters; and it needs a deep peaty soil to do well. It is either a climbing or clambering plant, or it is quite prostrate, covering a bank or tree stump. It has small, tough, oval leaves which are shiny, and is an evergreen. The underside of the leaves is more or less glaucous. The flowers open in May: they are carried on longish pedicels, and consist of a one-inch tubular corolla, narrower at the mouth than half way up its length from which point it narrows again, so that it is urn-shaped. This corolla is orange-scarlet and it has golden anthers protruding from the mouth. The flowers are plentifully borne and the plant in full flower is very striking without being among the most spectacular.

ORIGIN OF BOTANICAL GARDENS

The oldest Botanical Garden in Europe, that is a garden of plants arranged for scientific study in some kind of systematic order, is at Padua, in Italy. It was started in 1545. What was the origin of the idea? Was it a by-product of the Renaissance spirit and one evidence of the rebirth of the sciences? It was not, certainly, borrowed from the ancients who seem never to have made such gardens and whose study of plants was never very systematic.*

Rereading Prescott's History of the *Conquest of Mexico*, I came across a passage which gives a hint of the possibly American origin of such gardens: I shall quote rather more than the necessary paragraph because the one preceding it contains a point of unusual interest which has, it is true, nothing to do with our subject here:

'Among the most important articles of husbandry, we may notice the banana, whose facility of cultivation and exuberant returns are so fatal to habits of systematic and hardy industry.

* Theophrastus is the exception.

Another celebrated plant was the cacao, the fruit of which furnished the chocolate,—from the Mexican *chocolatl*, now so common a beverage throughout Europe. The vanilla, confined to a small district of the sea-coast, was used for the same purposes, of flavouring their food and drink, as with us. The great staple of the country, as, indeed, of the American continent, was maize, or Indian corn, which grew freely along the valleys, and up the steep sides of the Cordilleras to the high level of the table-land. The Aztecs were as curious in its preparation, and as well instructed in its manifold uses, as the most expert New England housewife. Its gigantic stalks, in these equinoctial regions, afford a saccharine matter, not found to the same extent in northern latitudes, and supplied the natives with sugar little inferior to that of the cane itself, which was not introduced among them until after the Conquest. But the miracle of nature was the great Mexican aloe, or *maguey*, whose clustering pyramids of flowers, towering above their dark coronals of leaves, were seen sprinkled over many a broad acre of the table-land. As we have already noticed, its bruised leaves afforded a paste from which paper was manufactured, its juice was fermented into an intoxicating beverage, *pulque*, of which the natives, to this day, are excessively fond; its leaves further supplied an impenetrable thatch for the more humble dwellings; thread, of which coarse stuffs were made, and strong cords, were drawn from its tough and twisted fibres; pins and needles were made of the thorns at the extremity of its leaves; and the root, when properly cooked, was converted into a palatable and nutritious food. The *agave*, in short, was meat, drink, clothing and writing materials for the Aztec! Surely, never did Nature enclose in so compact a form so many of the elements of human comfort and civilization!

'It would be obviously out of place to enumerate in these pages all the varieties of plants, many of them of medicinal virtue, which have been introduced from Mexico into Europe.

Still less can I attempt a catalogue of its flowers, which, with their variegated and gaudy colours, form the greatest attraction of our greenhouses. The opposite climates embraced within the narrow latitude of New Spain have given to it, probably, the richest and most diversified flora to be found in any country on the globe. These different products were systematically arranged by the Aztecs, who understood their properties and collected them into nurseries, more extensive than any then existing in the Old World. It is not improbable that they suggested the idea of those "gardens of plants" which were introduced into Europe not many years after the Conquest.'

Prescott is certainly wrong about one point: the flora of what he calls New Spain is not 'the richest and most diversified in the world;' that of Western Asia is more so, and especially of Western China. And he is surely wrong about the banana; it seems perfectly clear that it was introduced to the Americas from South-East Asia; Vavilov* gives only one determined source, Indo-Malaya; and Prescott himself admits in a footnote that the great naturalist Hernandez does not even mention it in his 'copious catalogue' of New World plants. But he may well have been right about the idea of systematic botanical gardens coming from Mexico.

It does seem that the Texucan and Mexican emperors made and were fond of gardens of all kinds. From sixteenth-century Spanish sources Prescott gives some description of the great Texucan emperor Nezahualcoyotl's palaces, including the gardens:

'They led through long arcades and through intricate labyrinths of shrubbery, into gardens where baths and sparkling fountains were overshadowed by tall groves of cedar and cypress. The

* N. I. Vavilov: *Origin, Variation, Immunity and Breeding of Cultivated Plants.* In Chester's translation. New York 1951.

basins of water were well stocked with fish of various kinds, and the aviaries with birds glowing in all the gaudy plumage of the tropics . . .'

There is no American native cedar, but Central America has a wealth of lovely conifers, including cypresses. When Mexico had become the leading power in Anahuac, the Aztec monarchs seem even to have improved on the Texucan model. Montezuma's garden sounds, from the description derived from Hernandez and others, to have been both a garden of plants and a menagerie of the kind which certainly did not exist in Europe at that time:

'There were, also, edifices appropriated to objects of quite another kind. One of these was an immense aviary, in which birds of splendid plumage were assembled from all parts of the empire. Here was the scarlet cardinal, the golden pheasant, the endless parrot tribe with their rainbow hues (the royal green predominant), and that miniature miracle of nature, the humming-bird, which delights to revel among the honeysuckle bowers of Mexico. Three hundred attendants had charge of this aviary, who made themselves acquainted with the appropriate food of its inmates, oftentimes procured at great cost, and in the moulting season were careful to collect the beautiful plumage, which, with its many-coloured tints, furnished the materials for the Aztec painter.

'A separate building was reserved for the fierce birds of prey; the voracious vulture tribes and eagles of enormous size, whose home was in the snowy solitudes of the Andes. No less than five hundred turkeys, the cheapest meat in Mexico were allowed for the daily consumption of these tyrants of the feathered race.

'Adjoining this aviary was a menagerie of wild animals, gathered from the mountain forests, and even from the remote swamps of the *tierra caliente*. The resemblance of the different species to those in the Old World, with which no one of them, however, was identical, led to a perpetual confusion in the nomenclature of the Spaniards, as it has since done in that of better-instructed naturalists. The collection was still further swelled by a great number of reptiles and serpents remarkable for their size and venomous qualities, among which the Spaniards beheld the fiery little animal "with the castanents in his tail", the terror of the American wilderness. The serpents were confined in long cages lined with down or feathers, or in troughs of mud and water. The beasts and birds of prey were provided with apartments large enough to allow of their moving about, and secured by a strong lattice-work, through which light and air were freely admitted. The whole was placed under the charge of numerous keepers, who acquainted themselves with the habits of their prisoners and provided for their comfort and cleanliness. With what deep interest would the enlightened naturalist of that day—an Oviedo or a Martyr, for example—have surveyed this magnificent collection, in which the various tribes which roamed over the Western wilderness, the unknown races of an unknown world, were brought into one view! How would they have delighted to study the peculiarities of these new species, compared with those of their own hemisphere, and thus have risen to some comprehension of the general laws by which Nature acts in all her works! The rude followers of Cortes did not trouble themselves with such refined speculations. They gazed on the spectacle with a vague curiosity not unmixed with awe; and, as they listened to the wild cries of the ferocious animals and the hissings of the serpents, they almost fancied themselves in the infernal regions.

'I must not omit to notice a strange collection of human monsters, dwarfs, and other unfortunate persons in whose organization Nature had capriciously deviated from her regular laws. Such hideous anomalies were regarded by the Aztecs as a suitable appendage of state. It is even said they were in some cases the result of artificial means, employed by unnatural parents desirous to secure a provision for their offspring by thus qualifying them for a place in the royal museum.

'Extensive gardens were spread out around these buildings, filled with fragrant shrubs and flowers, and especially with medicinal plants. No country has afforded more numerous species of these last than New Spain; and their virtues were perfectly understood by the Aztecs, with whom medical botany may be said to have been studied as a science. Amidst this labyrinth of sweet-scented groves and shrubberies, fountains of pure water might be seen throwing up their sparkling jets and scattering refreshing dews over the blossoms. Ten large tanks, well stocked with fish, afforded a retreat on their margins to various tribes of water-fowl, whose habits were so carefully consulted that some of these ponds were of salt water, as that which they most loved to frequent. A tessellated pavement of marble enclosed the ample basins, which were overhung by light and fanciful pavilions, that admitted the perfumed breezes of the gardens, and offered a grateful shelter to the monarch and his mistresses in the sultry heats of summer.'

These Mexican gardens were already well known to the Conquerors by the middle of the third decade of the sixteenth century. The Paduan botanic garden was established, as we have seen, in 1545. It does not seem to me impossible that it was, indeed, from the Texucans and Aztecs that Europeans had the idea of gardens of plants; and that, at many removes, we owe the pleasures of Kew to the great princes of the Central American civilization.

GOLDEN RAY LILIES

Of all the true lilies in the world, by which, I mean species of the genera Lilium, Cardiocrinum and Nomocharis, the most magnificent are surely the lilies of Japan, and of these the most spectacular is the Golden Ray Lily.

It strikes me as curious that *Lilium auratum*, the Golden Ray Lily, does not seem to have been known either in England (or Europe) until Veitch, the great nurseryman, showed it in 1869; or the United States where, in the same year, it flowered for Francis Parkman of Boston, an amateur who had imported bulbs from Japan. It may be that the release of this most magnificent of bulb plants to the rest of the world had to await the fall of the Shogunate with its policy of total isolation, and the establishment of the new Empire. But after all the Dutch, most advanced of European gardeners and especially interested in bulbous plants, had been the one people who had managed to trade with the Japanese and to obtain permission for their merchant seamen to land and work there—at the price, according to the jealous nationals of less enterprising countries, of trampling on the crucifix.*

However, as far as we know, we have not had this lily for more than about one century. There are two distinct types, which is not unusual in plants with a wide altitude range: L. *auratum* var. *praecox* is a high altitude lily, perhaps one can even call it an 'alpine' type, with a stem which though very strong is thin and not more than about four feet tall, often less. It will probably bear from one to four flowers per stem, flat, open bowls, rather starry, up to a foot in diameter, ivory white lightly speckled with gold and with a golden ray to each petal.

* A libel propagated by, among others, Swift.

(Lilies have no true petals, but the word is convenient since this is not a botanical work). The other type, var. *platyphyllum*, a name descriptive of the broader leaves, can attain twelve feet in height and carry as many as twenty-five or even thirty flowers of the same kind but not more than eight or nine inches in diameter.

An important point, in view of the belief even among expert lily men that crimson colour in a lily of this kind means that it is a hybrid with *L. speciosum* as the other parent, is made by Jan de Graaff, greatest of lily men, in more than one publication:

'The flowers range in colour from ivory-white with only a few golden specks, to almost solid carmine red, a variation which has given rise to the erroneous belief that such highly coloured lilies are of hybrid origin.'

This is borne out by the observations in the wild of the plant collectors, notably Wilson; and by experiments with thousands of bulbs straight from the Japanese mountains and grown in Oregon as breeding material.

Provided the soil be free from lime, and especially from chalk, which this lily will not tolerate, there is no difficulty whatever in growing it. *L. auratum* gave me far less trouble when I began to grow it than, for example, many of the Chinese trumpet lilies and most American native lilies. In a few years good clumps were well established, and although no plant of mine ever attained twelve feet, nine feet was reached and eight was common. But I believe I succeeded with this lily because I rejected the advice of English lily pundits and followed only that of Jan de Graaff. It was he who told me on no account to plant the bulbs at nine or ten inches, as commonly recommended, but at not more than six inches. Most English lily growers will tell you not to give lilies, and certainly not this lily, farmyard manure. De Graaff, on the other hand writes:

'. . . contrary to the opinion expressed in many books, this lily is a gross feeder and needs a rich soil. Incorporated with the soil some time before planting, old well-rotted cow manure and a generous mulching with compost and rich leafmould are most beneficial.'

Thus grown, he says, *L. auratum* lilies will yield an abundant increase; and that was exactly my experience.

Yet failure with this lily was more common than success for so many years that gardeners still have the impression that it is very difficult and miffish. The explanation is, again, to be found in de Graff's enormous experience and practical knowledge of the plant. Between 1862 and 1912 all auratum lily bulbs from Japan came from the wild and were simply dug up, packed and shipped. They were healthy, or most of them were. But as soon as, after 1912, the Japanese began to produce bulbs commercially for export:

'. . . the larger concentration of lilies on their farms, together with the total absence of any protection against the spread of virus disease, soon caused a widespread infection of the bulbs. Removing the roots before shipping the bulbs, facilitated packing and handling and lowered the weight and hence the shipping costs, but certainly did not help to improve the quality of the stock nor its adaptability to our gardens.'

For gardeners the lesson is very clear: buy only bulbs of seedling stock, for virus disease is not transmitted through the seed. And refuse to buy bulbs which have had the roots removed.

These roots below the bulb serve to anchor it and to feed it; they do not support the growth of the leaf-and-flower stem. That is attended to by the stem roots which grow from the base of the growing flower stem. It was the fact that Golden Ray lilies are stem-rooting which led to the conclusion that they have to be planted at nine or even twelve inches deep; in fact, however, since the richest layer of top soil is on top, the six-inch depth recommended by de Graaff is not only successful in practice but is correct in theory.

One more quotation from Jan de Graaff on the subject of this glorious species:

'Several colour types have been segregated, such as *L. auratum* var. *rubro-vittatum*, with deep crimson stripes. There are ivory-coloured types known as *L. auratum* var. *virginale* and one called *pictum* in which the flower is heavily spotted with crimson. These so-called varieties are colour variations selected from seedling auratums. The differences have been accentuated by further crossing of selected and desirable types. Such lilies are not of hybrid character and merely represent selected strains of greater or lesser uniformity.'

Pure ivory, gold striped, crimson or speckled, Golden Ray lilies are beyond comparison the most splendid of all the non-woody plants and, of all the myriads which grow from bulbs, at once the most spectacular and the most moving in their beauty.

FLOWERS OF BARILOCHE

Ever since I received from a correspondent in San Carlos de Bariloche a small brochure entitled *Flores de Bariloche* and published by the Editorial Libreria Naumann, I was determined to go to that small, high town on the mountain frontier between Argentina and Chile; in due course I did so.

This charming little book is about the flowers of Bariloche, the descriptions being by Mr Konrad Naumann, and the wellrinted paintings by Miss Jean Winterhalter. The Prologue which explains the antecedents of the work says that it contains nly '*una infima parte de las bellezas florales de la zona . . .*' What follows is why even this 'very small part' of the flora of Bariloche, which is at such an altitude that many of its plants re suitable for English gardens, must attract any English ardener.

The first plant illustrated is *Embothrium coccineum.* The most nteresting detail given about it, from my point of view is: *Tronco: hasta 2 m. de altura y 30 cm. de diametro.* In short this beautiful little tree grows no bigger on its native hills than in the ardens of Devonshire, and not nearly so big as in Irish gardens nd some others of the western seaboard. It is at its most remarkable in the woodland part of the great Mount Congreve arden in County Waterford, where some of the oldest plants ave attained almost thirty feet and a great fulness. In copious ermilion flower these trees are like forest fires. In Ireland they ot only set plenty of seed but seed themselves very freely, so that n the Mount Congreve woods it is possible to find scores of fine eedling embothriums. But this tree is not only at home in the oft climate of Ireland; it is hardy a great deal further east and orth; and there is no reason why it should not be so; Bariloche s, in its higher parts, a winter sports resort.

Why then, have we never seen the second plant of the Naumann-Winterhalter booklet in this country, not even, I think, at Kew. *Phrygilantus tetrandrus, Quintral del Alamo* in the vernacular, is a mistletoe of the Andes, or at all events it is a member of the family *Loranthaceae* and is parasitic on trees. But this Andean mistletoe has very spectacular red flowers rather like hose of our honeysuckles. It is notable that many, perhaps a majority of the flowers of those parts are vividly red but are scentless: their business is not to attract bees but humming-birds, nd for this they need to be vividly obvious. In parts of Bariloche he flower of the quintral provides, with its nectar, the only food of the *picaflora* and it is that minute bird which distributes the pollen. The handsome leaves, more or less heart-shaped, are deciduous. There can be little doubt that the plant would be hardy in parts of Britain but whether it would acccpt our native or introduced trees as host plants, I do not know. It would be worth trying in one of the great Irish gardens. I was there at the wrong season to collect seed but perhaps the seed, in its sticky berry like our mistletoe, would germinate here.

Next, a pretty little orange-flowered and blue berried barberry, *Berberis buxifolia*. It was introduced to Britain in 1826 by the naturalist Anderson who was attached to the Admiralty survey ship commanded by Captain King and commissioned to survey the Magellan Straits. It has flourished in Britain ever since. Another and much finer and even more familiar barberry comes from the same region and from other parts of Patagonia, *B. darwinii*, *El Michay* in the booklet. Gardeners who have this in their shrubbery or border may like to know that in its native land this barberry is valued because the flowers—yes, flowers, not fruit—are edible, having a sharp acid taste comparable with that of lemon juice.

Fragaria chiloensis, ancestor of all our large-fruited strawberries, is depicted beautifully by Miss Winterhalter, as native to Bariloche. It is followed by a pretty pink-flowered vetch but perhaps the flower is too small to make introduction worth while. The majority of the Bariloche plants I have yet mentioned until this point have been successfully introduced here. Then why, again, do we not have *El arrayan*, *Myrceugenia apiculata*? It is a rare and very curious plant by Mr Naumann's account; and a very attractive one, myrtle-like as one would expect, by Miss Winterhalter's painting. There are very few plants so limited in their range for it is confined to a single site of about thirty acres on the Quetrihue peninsula in lake Nahuel Huapi. The curious treescape composed by the *arrayanes*, remarkable for the twisted, diverse and fanciful shapes of the plants, inspired the decor of Walt Disney's *Bambi*; subtract Disney's sentimentalizing and you have, obviously, a very curious kind of wood. The plant is a tree which takes several hundred years to attain a height of thirty or forty feet, but in that time produces its extremely elaborate and fantastic ramification. The beauty of trunks and branches is enhanced by the bark colour which is maroon; of the whole tree by the covering foam of pure white flowers in late spring, and by the masses of purple berries in late summer, berries which are edible although, as Mr Naumann says, *no muy gustoso*. Why do we not grow this fascinating plant?

There is, later in the booklet, a superb portrait of *Fuchsia coccinea* with purple petals and scarlet sepals like so many of our cultivars: with that one we are very familiar in our gardens. Next to it comes *Desfontainea spinosa*, a shrub which is quite common in English West Country and Irish gardens; people who are not botanists, seeing it in flower for the first time, are very surprised to see what looks like a holly bush covered with orange flowers. *Calceolaria* we are familiar with also, and we have species of *Mimulus* as attractive as the Andean ones. *Ourisia coccinea* is in many English gardens; in its native Andes it is being widely destroyed by the advance of man's works, and already in the region of Bariloche is only to be found at 600 feet above the level of Lake Nahuel Huapi. *Mitraria coccinea* is another of the Bariloche natives depicted by Miss Winterhalter; no wonder it is so hardy in our own gardens; and great wonder that it is not much more commonly grown in them.

My failure with one of the most interesting of the plants depicted and described in the booklet is explained now that I have read what Mr Naumann says of it: Although it is hardy I have repeatedly lost *Asteranthera ovata*, a prostrate sub-shrub which has magnificent scarlet flowers. It is difficult to keep it wet enough in a low-rainfall country like England; I found it growing in almost marshy conditions and 100 inches of rain; for the rest, growing at the foot of trees and shrubs, it can do with very little daylight. It might make a good house plant if it could be kept wet enough.

I come, having missed some out, to the most spectacular plant in the book; and there is an odd little mystery about it. This is *Mutisia decurrens*, of the *Compositae*, a climbing daisy which was long ago introduced to Britain and which, although hardy, was lost and never reintroduced. Why?

Mutisia decurrens is now very rare, both in Bariloche and elsewhere; and if it is as difficult to keep in cultivation as it seems to be, it may even become extinct. I saw it many years ago on the trellised wall of an English house and it was magnificent; it had withstood 20° of frost. But it has since died. The reasons for its growing scarcity in the wild are the usual ones. The lovely 3-inch orange, scarlet or rose-pink daisy flowers are gathered for their beauty and so never allowed to make seed; and the plants are dug up by gardeners but do not survive awkward and amateurish handling.

This mutisia is a strong, tough-stemmed climber to twenty feet or more, a woodland plant using trees for support and holding on by tendrils growing from the tips of the leaves. In good sunlight, it ramifies freely and flowers abundantly. The seeds, as in the case of so many composites, are feathered; they are also, alas, for the most part infertile, and none of the seed I collected has germinated either at Kew or at Wye College.

Yes. there are a lot of reasons to visit San Carlos de Bariloche.

IRISH-ITALIANATE

The opposing extremes in European gardening are to be found in, on the one hand, the Italian garden, on the other the Irish

The Irish garden is itself, at its best, the extreme case of the English woodland paradise garden, surpassed in England only by one or two superlative cases such as Bodnant and Nymans. The Italian garden is never a garden of plants; it is, as I have said already, a drawing-room out of doors.

The term 'Italian' is used so loosely that it is of little more than very general significance: used pedantically it means a garden of more or less elaborately laid out clipped box, a sort of embroidery done with evergreens. Used geographically, it has to include, on the one hand, the simple and lovely series of 'garden rooms' composing a good Tuscan garden such as that of the Villa Capponi in Florence; on the other, the magnificence, the Renaissance panache of such grand gardens as those of several Villas Medici, or the Villa d'Este. Yet although the old Tuscan gardens are very simple and reflect in their simplicity the austere spirit of the Tuscan people, while the Roman and Renaissance gardens are very elaborate and reflect the exuberance of the Latin joy in fine living, these two kinds of gardens have this in common, that they are conceived and made as settings for human activities and are incomplete until there are people walking, talking, thinking, reading, or playing games inside them. The Irish gardens, at the other extreme, are not beautiful frames but beautiful pictures; in them it is the trees, shrubs and flowers which count, not the people; and it is almost the case that the people are the servants of the plants.

This, of course, is only true of the extreme cases; there are gardens in which the two styles meet and mingle. Now there is nothing very surprising in finding Italianate features in an Irish garden like Ilnacullin in the Bay of Glengariff; nor in the fact that there is much in the layout of the great garden of Birr Castle which is derived from Italy. Italy was for so long the tutor and mentor of all Europe in the arts, that that is just what one would expect to find. But it is perhaps more surprising to find a touch of Irish romanticism in an Italian garden; I do not mean simply an English or Irish woodland garden growing in Italy—there is a fine one in the Villa Taranto and there are others, since the mania for English gardens has long been raging all over Europe. No; I mean an essentially Italianate garden touched with Anglo-Irish nature-poetry.

The garden of the Villa San' Remigio is just such a case, however.

This garden is in Pallanza next door to that of the Villa Taranto and it belongs to the Countess Bonacossa. The garden has been well-described by Georgina Masson in her admirable *Italian Gardens* as '. . . a fascinating by-product of the Italian garden tradition—the romantic conception of a classical garden.' When I visited it and heard the Countess Bonacossa talk about the making of it I realized that this was the kind of garden I should love to make, although I should never be able to do so on such a grand scale: in it the two traditions which all Englishmen of education respect and between which they are pulled, have been reconciled: the austere boney tradition of Mediterranean classicism; and the lyrical, lush tradition of North European romanticism.

Early in the last century an Irish gentleman named Browne and his two daughters were travelling by carriage through Italy and were delayed at Pallanza on Lake Maggiore—where the climate is soft and humid in spring, summer and autumn—by a break-down to their carriage which took several days to repair. The two Browne girls walked up to the top of the hill where the ancient and tiny church of San Remigio, said to be the oldest surviving Christian church in Italy, commanded magnificent views over the lake and of the mountains on the far side. They were so delighted with this hilltop that they persuaded their father to buy it. They built a house there and began to make a garden. But the real makers of the garden as it is now were the Contessa Bonacossa's parents, the *marchese* and *marchesa* della Valle di Casanova; and notably the *marchesa*.

Sophie della Valle di Casanova was a considerable artist. The garden which she was chiefly responsible for making (and even the detail of the carving of the balustrades and the curve of the stairways is her own design), is in essence Italian, for example in its firm plan, in the use of 'garden rooms' (that is to say densely hedged or walled enclosures leading into each other), in the use of several different levels with terraces to command wide views, in the use of statuary and stone stairways of formal design; this is a Tuscan garden with a Renaissance touch of grandeur, and there is even a typically Tuscan *giardino segreto* on a tiny terrace by the ancient San Remigio chapel. But in the riches of the plant material used; in the relationship of one garden to the next; in the merging of the formal into the semi-wild; in the deliberate contrivance of expectation followed by surprise, this is a romantic, an Anglo-Irish garden. To quote Georgina Masson again:

'. . . it is a dream world. Italy and the Mediterranean as the northerner images it, not as it really is. Thus classical goddesses drive their chariots through pools surrounded by romantic woodland and lily ponds mirror the reflections of distant snowy peaks.'

This is to say that the San Remigio garden is less a work of architecture in the Italian gardening manner; and despite its Italian detail, more a work of picturesque art in the Anglo-Irish manner. As Miss Masson says, it is not pure Mediterranean, but Mediterranean as the North European imagination, manifest in minds as widely separated as those of Anne Radcliffe and Goethe have conceived it for centuries.

One remarkable feature of the garden seems to me to emphasize and demonstrate that it does indeed represent the coming together of two styles and might, therefore, be a model for future garden makers if there ever are any on such a scale again. One aspect of the garden is a series of terraces stepped one above the other on a very steep hillside. The gardens of each terrace are differently charming; one of them is the Horse Fountain garden, that of the classical goddesses in their chariot. The terraces are carried by vaults on pillars forming arcades, so that under each one there is a sort of long and rather dark artificial grotto or cavern. And these were used by the *marchesa* Sophie not in the Italian manner at all; she turned them into lush, damp ferneries. It has not been possible to maintain them as once they were, with hanging baskets of orchids and other flowering exotics, but they are still delightful.

The union of classical and romantic gardening is perfectly accomplished at San Remigio; there is no feeling of incongruity; the two great styles are not just thrown together. The Italian is penetrated by the Anglo-Hibernian, the Anglo-Hibernian by the Italian; I know nowhere where the possibilities of horticultural syncretism are better demonstrated.

SOME AUSTRALIAN PLANTS

Just as the Australian animals are peculiar—being apt in some cases to lay eggs but suckle their young for instance—so a lot of Australian plants are not quite like the plants of the other worlds. For example, whereas the spectacular parts of European and Asiatic flowers are the petals or petal-like organs, that is the perianth segments, it is often the case that in Australian plants the spectacular organs are the stamens and there are no petals. This is the case, for example again, with the true *Acacias* (the mimosas of the florist). But the most striking case is that of the *Callistemons*.

It is not surprising that the Callistemons are not more common in English gardens, for they are not hardy excepting in the west and extreme south. Species which have been grown under glass at Kew can be grown in the open only south-west of Dorsetshire; or in the part of Scotland immediately about Glasgow; or almost anywhere in Ireland excepting the midlands. But they are rewarding shrubs where they can be grown. Fountain-like in habit, for they send up a number of outward curving main stems from the ground, they have lanceolate leaves which are a tender bronze red in youth, evergreen and often glaucous in maturity; and flowers which are like nothing we are familiar with in the northern hemisphere. These flowers are 'bottle-brushes', that is cylindrical inflorescences composed of stamens arranged like the spokes of many close-packed wheels about the growing stems so that the flowers, and later the seeds, are left behind as the shoots grow. Thus, on an old shrub, all the main growing stems have cylindrical groups of old seed capsules, which are woody and last for many years, at intervals all along their length.

The inflorescences themselves are very curious as well as being pretty. In those *Callistemons* which I have grown, having raised them from seed—*C. rigidus, C. puniceus* and others—they are in some shade of red, often very vivid, being composed of hundreds of one to one and a half inch stamens which are crimson, carmine or vermillion, arranged cylindrically about the growing stem, usually from two to to three inches in diameter. Nor is the flower the only beauty of these Australian shrubs; the leaves, although a dull green at maturity, are very colourful in youth, crimson in some species, bronze-red in others.

In the genus *Melaleuca*, also Australian, whereas the forms of leaf and flower are the same, both organs are usually much smaller, the leaves often almost linear, the bottle-brush flowers tiny, although not as small as in the case of some acacias.

One of the most attractive Australian shrubs or small trees which will flourish in the warmer British gardens is the Tasmanian *Telopea truncata*. This belongs to the family of the *Proteas*, like the South American *Embothriums*, a family whose centre is in South Africa. It is very like an embothrium but perhaps hardier than any of them, since it comes from a lower latitude. Yet whereas embothriums are not uncommon in Britain the telopeas are very rare in our gardens; and the only garden I know where there are some really fine specimens are Castlewellan in Northern Ireland, and the Slieve Donard nursery in the same country.

Myosotidium nobile is the New Zealand forget-me-not. It is a magnificent perennial in those warm, moist, peaty gardens which can grow it. At the base, close to the soil, is a rosette of thick, bright green, fleshy leaves rather like those of a primitive cabbage (or, for example, a *Bergenia*); from this grows a flower stem up to three feet tall. The flowers are a vivid blue. It is, as its specific name implies, a noble plant; but, climate apart, it is difficult to grow. In nature it grows very near to the sea, so near that it is perhaps washed by sea-water at high tides. A very distinguished English gardener, a West Country nobleman, having been given some roots of this splendid antipodean forget-me-not, was told by the donor that it would only grow well if some rotten fish were buried under its roots. Being a man who believed in doing awkward jobs for himself, he went into a well-known multiple fishmonger's in his county town and asked if they had any rotten fish for sale, a nice demonstration of the simple-mindedness of the very rich. In practice, fishmeal does quite as well.

The best of the Australian flowering plants will not grow here at all; it is too cold for them. But several of the true *Acacias* can be grown in suitable parts of the country. The hardiest, and one of the best is *Acacia dealbata*, the commonest florist's 'mimosa' (the true *Mimosas* are all tropical and many of them are 'sensitive' plants). I have seen fine specimens of this as far north and east as Hampshire. In my own garden this species grew at an astonishing rate, attaining about thirty feet in four years. Its glaucous and finely divided foliage was pretty, but it was very slow to flower. A gardening acquaintance of mine, Dr Barker of East Portlemouth, near Salcombe in Devon, who has grown about twenty species of *Acacia*, told me that none of them flower young and that although at first he had thought there were some acacias which were very shy flowering, and others which flowered freely, he came to the conclusion after much experience of this genus that all of them would flower if one waited long enough.

I have two memories of *Acacia dealbata* in our climate—I exclude from such reminiscences the south of France where these trees are perfectly at home: in the last year of the war I was sent on loan to the Free French Navy and my ship was based on Brest; the town had been more or less destroyed by the Germans and Americans for their different reasons (so very indifferent to the people of Brest); but the old 'mimosas' were still flourishing and they cheered an otherwise cheerless winter. The other memory of this species is of the fine trained plant on the wall of Dartington Hall, a tree which rarely fails to flower between the 20th December and 20th January, and is often in flower by Christmas.

PEACHES

The late Justin Brooke was the most remarkable fruit-grower I ever met. In his Suffolk orchards he not only succeeded with a wide range of apples and pears, but with figs and peaches.

PEACHES

Peaches succeed in England not only on walls—though in my experience they are easier and more fruitful that way—but in the open. Yet thousands of gardeners have found that they can get no crop off peach trees in the open orchard or garden. The fact is, the trees must have exactly the right conditions.

The Peach is a West Asiatic plant which was introduced to European cultivation by the Romans and may have reached England in their time. It is, of course, ruggedly hardy. Unfortunately it cannot be taken for granted that a tree or any other plant will flourish with us simply because it can stand much lower temperatures than those we experience in an average English winter. For if the Peach, like many other exotics in our gardens, can stand very cold winters, it must have very hot summers. If it does not, two things happen; the wood fails to ripen and therefore to make flower bud; and, being still green it is killed back by frost. I am quite certain that much of the die-back of new wood which we always get on peaches here when they are grown fully exposed, is not really caused by the bacterial disease commonly blamed for it, but simply by the freezing, during winter, of green wood. If this were not so then die-back would be as bad on wall-trained peach trees as on those in the open, which it never is. And there would be some die-back on trees under glass, whereas I have never seen any, and I have grown peaches fully exposed, on walls, and under glass for many years.

This fruit succeeds far better in the east than in the west of England because although the winters are harder, the summers are hotter and the sunshine clearer. It succeeds much better on clay soils than on lighter soils, and on limestone than on acid soils. Justin Brooke was able to give it the conditions it required, and accordingly he got crops which very few other growers seem able to achieve. On the occasions when I went to his orchards and talked with him as he showed me round, I learned a great deal from him. He believed that the one peach which is really good in our eastern climate, and which yields fruit of the highest quality, is 'Peregrine'; I have grown this in the open, on walls and under glass and it very rarely fails. It is a mid-season variety of medium size, perfect shape, delicious flavour and perfume. It never suffers from that splitting of the stone which mars some, especially some early varieties. Brooke had other rules for peach growing: he would not hear of grafting peaches on to plum stocks, the conventional practice; he thought that the only right stock for peach was peach, and in his nurseries the peaches were always grafted on to peach seedlings. Among the advantages of this method is one very great one: there is no suckering. Suckering is always more or less a problem with peach trees grafted on plum stocks.

Brooke also liked to see a plantation of peach trees grassed down as soon as possible. He thought the trees grew more healthily and bore more fruit with their roots under sod than in cultivated ground. The grass, of course, has to be kept short and the cuttings must never be carried away, the mowing is done without a catching box on the mower and often enough to make sure that the mowings shall be short and light enough to be left to rot slowly into the ground without untidiness or damage to the growing grass.

It is always necessary to hand-pollinate peaches under glass. I tried doing without this, and got no fruit or very little. But you can overdo it: I watched an amateur gardener pollinating peach trees in his greenhouse last year and was amused to see that he was treating every single flower, a very tedious operation and one which was simply making future work for himself; he was ensuring such a 'set' of fruit that the work of thinning would be very much heavier than it need have been. It is sufficient to pollinate one flower in five; and by distributing the work evenly over the tree thinning of the fruit will be much easier later.

It is not necessary to hand-pollinate peaches out of doors,

whether on walls or exposed. Although they flower early it is not so early in the year that there are no pollinating insects at work. Hive bees, it is true, are not very reliable if the weather is cool or wet; but wild bees are not so touchy about the weather, and although the population of wild bees has been seriously reduced by insecticides, still there seem to be enough in most gardens to get the fruit set.

On walls and under glass it is best to thin peaches in two operations; first when the fruitlets are the size of a shilling; and again when those you have left are the size of a walnut. It is difficult to force oneself to remove as many fruits as one should for the best results. The finest wall or greenhouse fruit is produced by leaving only one peach for every square foot of surface covered by the trained tree. I very rarely did the job so thoroughly and with something like twice as many fruits left on, that is one for every six square inches, I got fruit of adequate size and excellent quality.

APRICOTS

Apricots are a mystery to me; in Justin Brooke's orchards I have seen the apricot trees weighed down with an abundance of fine fruit. Not only have I never succeeded in getting a single apricot on any tree of mine, but it is usual to come across gardeners with the same complaint. Very often the trees, even mature trees, never flower at all; or, if they flower, no fruit is set. Failure to flower may perhaps be caused by the coolness of our summers; failure to set fruit by the fact that apricots flower so very early that there are few pollinators about or the weather is too cold for the flowers to mature those organs on which the formation of fruit depends.

This earliness of the apricot, in flower and in fruit if you ever get any, is reflected in the name: Dioscorides says that although the Greeks called the apricot *Armeniaca* after the name of the country it came from, they later called it *proikarpos* with reference to its earliness. The Romans Latinized the word, getting *praecoqua* (cf. precocious). Most of the European peoples took this Latin name for the fruit, but meanwhile it had acquired the prefix *a*. This was because North Europe seems to have had the fruit and name not in classical times from the Romans, but in the Middle Ages, from the Arabs. And this is traceable as follows: the Arabs took the Latin name *praecoqua*, Arabized it to *barquq*; add the prefixed article *al*, and you get *albarquq*. The nearest to this in any European tongue is the Spanish *albericoque* from which it is perhaps safe to guess that the fruit itself, and the name, came into Northern Europe, or rather returned there after the chaos of the early Middle Ages, by way of Moorish Spain; the North Italians call the fruit *albercocco*, which, again, is near the Arabic. In France, England and Germany there is more corruption of the word to *abricot, apricot, aprikose*. One final and very curious point; the South Italians and Sicilians call this fruit *Meliacca*. That seems to be a corruption of Armeniaca. It looks as if the South Italian Greeks retained the older name for the fruit which the metropolitan Greeks had dropped. It is not unusual for old words to be retained by colonial offshoots of a metropolis; the English of the United States retains more old English words than the English of England.

But call it what you like and spell it as you will, I shall be grateful to you if you can tell me how to get crops of apricots.

AN EASY ORCHID

Most amateur gardeners treat the whole Orchid genus with excessive respect, and orchid-growing as a mysterious art which only the experienced professional can fairly aspire to. There are actually two very different kinds of orchids which are easy to grow: one is a group of sub-tropical exotics of which the magnificent *Cymbidiums* are typical; the other is a small group of hardy American ground orchids, notably two 'slipper' orchids, which are native to the woods of the eastern United States. The first group is the one I want to write about here.

Cymbidiums are greenhouse, but not hothouse, plants. More exactly, they are plants which can very well stand winter temperatures as low as 45°F. although they do in fact do better if the winter temperature can be maintained not lower than 50°. In practice this means that they can be grown in an ordinary greenhouse provided that there is some source of heat available to maintain that temperature during cold spells, but that on many winter days no heating will be required. It is very easy and not very dear to fit an amateur's greenhouse with sufficient of the special heating tubes made for the purpose, and to have them controlled by a thermostat set at 50. If you do this, however, insist on a rod-type thermostat; I have found the other kind unreliable in greenhouse conditions. In summer the cymbidiums, provided they are lightly shaded from direct sunshine during the middle of the day, enjoy spells of sub-tropical heat but what they then require is high humidity. In such conditions they grow fast and build up reserves for future performance.

For the benefit of those who do not know these orchids by name, they are plants with pseudo-bulbs, strap-shaped leaves from eighteen inches to three feet long, and flowers in sprays on tall, strong stems, from six to fifteen flowers per spray. The flowers are large, about three inches across or thereabouts, and they vary in colour from white through a large part of the typical orchid spectrum. In short, they are very beautiful and, like so many orchids, almost incredibly long lasting whether on the plant, where they often look as fresh and new after eight weeks in bloom as when they first opened their buds; or cut and kept in water.

They are not fussy about soil, or not as fussy as many exotic orchids; they can be grown in a mixture of very coarse and fibrous loam, peat and chopped sphagnum moss. If you have ferns in your garden or live near to a source of bracken, coarsely chopped dead fern mixed with the soil is a good idea. The mixture should be made open and porous by also mixing in a fair proportion of very coarse silver-sand. If ordinary pots are used, then from time to time you will either have to move the whole plant into a larger pot; or remove some of the back-bulbs and grow them on to make new plants, replanting the newest part of the orchid in the original pot. If, in the course of such operations, any of the fleshy, white roots are broken they should be cut off cleanly with a sharp knife; any root which shows signs of decay should be removed at the same time and in the same way. When replanting cymbidiums remember the way in which they increase: allow room for development of new pseudobulbs, whence the flowers will spring, in the direction away from the old back-bulbs.

It is possible to grow cymbidiums in the open border of the greenhouse, provided the soil mixture is correct; or in very large containers, such as deep wooden cases, or tubs. In that case the plant need not be disturbed for many years; it can be allowed to grow very large, and will in time bear a great many sprays of flowers. By far the most impressive cymbidiums I have ever seen were grown in that way and not in ordinary pots, plants with leaves over a yard long and flower sprays bearing twelve or more flowers. These cymbidiums were given a very deep and very coarsely fibrous soil, and they were also provided with a great deal of water. But, of course, the drainage was perfect. They were kept up to 50° in the winter, and in the summer allowed temperatures as high as 90° but in very high humidity and under some fairly heavy shading. The grower in question, an amateur who knew far more about his plants than many professionals, did not believe in heavy shading excepting during the greatest heats of summer; he thought that cymbidiums would flower more freely if given plenty of light at times when it could do them no harm.

Flowering of cymbidiums is from about mid-winter until May. For those who grow a sufficient number there is often a good market for the flowers which fetch very high prices; it is not unusual for a single spray to sell for three to five pounds. As for buying the plants, if you buy named varieties of flowering size then they are quite dear, though not as dear as many other orchids; but the good orchid nurseries often sell unflowered seedlings two years short of flowering size, or thereabouts, and these are not dear, are sure to be good and may—it is a gamble—turn out to be very fine ones worthy of naming, and of propagation.

WINTER FLOWERS

A lot of gardeners prefer not to bother with winter flowers. In the colder parts of Britain that may well be wise; for although many flowering shrubs bloom in winter and can look enchanting against the stark background of leafless trees and shaggy lawns, the flowers themselves are not as hardy as the shrubs and are frequently ruined by frost. But not always and not all of them and to me it has always seemed well worth while to plant some shrubs for winter colour and fragrance.

For my taste the best of all winter flowering shrubs is the Chinese Witch-hazel, *Hamamelis mollis.* Its growth, once established (and it can be touchy at first), is fast, stiff, more or less erect, until a large and much branched bush has been formed. It flowers in mid-winter on the naked wood, the flowers having maroon calices and bright yellow strap-shaped petals. They are very fragrant. With this witch-hazel it is pleasant to have the red-flowered *H. japonica*, though perhaps just 'red' is hardly the word for its curious brownish-orange flowers. It is, by the way, also a very good shrub for autumn leaf colour. Establishing these two and getting them to grow away at once is a matter of careful planting. Whatever their soil tolerance once established, there is no doubt that they like a lot of moist peat at the roots when first planted.

The winter-flowering *Viburnums* should be planted in a group with these witch-hazels. Although the species *V. fragrans* is good, the cultivar *V. bodnantense* is better, and its variety 'Dawn' is best; the buds are coral-red, the flowers white and very sweetly and strongly scented. In his book *Colour in the winter garden* (Phoenix House), Mr Graham Thomas has an account of a winter-flowering Viburnum which I have not yet grown, *V. foetans*:

'. . . the half-evergreen *V. foetans* with stiff drooping bunches of similar [to *V. fragrans*] flowers in creamy white borne on smooth, fat twigs. Like the others its flowering period is long. . . . Good accounts of *V. foetans* have reached me from Edinburgh where it has formed a large, rounded bush, flowers freely, and is not harmed in the bud by frost.'

A favourite winter-flowering tree, with me, is *Prunus subhirtella autumnalis*. This cherry sometimes begins to flower in November but there are later forms. The flowers begin white but mature a soft rose-pink; they are very copiously borne and the tree itself, though large when it is old, is of a light, open, pleasing shape, with a broad head. There is a pink form, the variety *rosea* which sometimes flowers in late winter, but often not until early spring. I saw one flowering at the same time as and beside a *Cornus mas* which was one firm cloud of pale gold. They went very well together but cannot be relied on to flower at the same time.

Arbutus unedo is one of the best winter-flowering evergreens. I wonder why it flowers and ripens its handsome fruits so late in Britain. There is a part of the Maritime Alps *maquis* which I know rather well where this arbutus is the dominant plant over a vast area; the flowers and fruits are at their best in late October, whereas in England they are very fine in December. The best display is of flowers and fruit together, the lily-of-the-valley like flowers the colour of pearls, the fruits scarlet. The fruits, which give the plant its vernacular name of Strawberry Tree, are in fact edible, but they have little taste and are dry and rather sticky, not at all agreeable. The spread of *Arbutus unedo* throughout the Mediterranean region was much assisted in the past by its importance, to the ancients, as a winter fodder for cattle in grassless countries. Although an *Erica* it is a limestone plant (as, indeed, are several other *Ericas*) and grows well in chalk.

Chimonanthus praecox and its variety *luteus* are far too well known and loved to need description here. It has the strongest scent of all. It is often complained that this shrub is very shy-flowering, or will not flower at all. It is a matter of age: I have never known a young plant which did flower nor an old one which did not. Moreover one too often sees this plant growing in shade, where it cannot really ripen its wood and make flower bud; it should be in full sun, and preferably on a south wall because if fully exposed there is danger of the flowers being ruined by quick thawing after over-night freezing.

Mahonia bealei has the most magnificent foliage of any winter-flowering evergreen. The leaves may be eighteen inches long, they are pinnate with many leaflets, and the shape of these leaflets is itself interesting. The massive and burly growth of this shrub makes it a wonderfully 'architectural' plant. The inflorescences are clusters of nine-inch racemes of deep yellow flowers individually like berberis flowers. They are erect but fan outwards to form a most handsome fountain-like display. *Mahonia japonica* is a gaunter plant and its foliage is not so handsome, but the drooping racemes of primrose yellow flowers are sweet scented. Best of all, for leaf shape and the vividly chrome-yellow foot long flower racemes, is *M. lomariifolia*; moreover it flowers in mid-winter, often at Christmas. But it is not hardy enough for the average climate of Britain. However, there is a hybrid of which it is one parent, the splendid *Mahonia* x 'Charity' which is hardy, looks like *M. bealei* but has the *lomariifolia* flower colour.

AUTUMN FLAME

I have seen New England turn scarlet and gold in autumn. The most vivid of the colours is supplied by the genus *Rhus* including the 'Poison Ivy' *R. toxicodendron*, the Stag's Horn Sumach, *R. typhina* which is the dominant shrub over large areas of country; and the subtlest colours are provided by the maples. In Britain none of the North American shrubs and trees are absolutely reliable when it comes to providing autumn colour. But there is a small Japanese tree, perfectly hardy in the average climate of Britain, which is not only reliable in its colour change, making that change whether the summer has been hot and dry, hot and wet or cool and wet, but whose vivid crimson-scarlet is the most spectacular by far of all the autumn leaf colours I have ever seen.

Disanthus cercidifolius is a member of the *Hamamelidaceae*. It may be a shrub, eight feet or so tall and spreading broad; but as a rule it is a small tree to about twelve or perhaps fifteen feet, taller than it is broad, with rather erect branches densely clad in leaves which are very like those of the Judas Tree in shape, but are green instead of being glaucous. Or at least, there is much less blue in the green than in the case of the Judas Tree. I have never seen this tree flower, but it does have flowers in the leaf axils, small, dark purple, starry and with an unpleasant smell. Here is what W. J. Bean (*Shrubs and Trees Hardy in the British Isles*) has to say about it:

'Native of Japan; introduced about 1893, not yet well known in gardens. I saw it in flower in Mr H. W. Grigg's garden at Crown Hill, near Plymouth, in October 1916 but it is not attractive in bloom. We know it however to possess one excellent quality: its foliage—handsome and Judas-tree like in form—turns in autumn to one of the loveliest claret reds suffused with orange. No new shrub is, indeed, more beautiful in this respect. It is rather tender when young but appears quite hardy after a few years. . . .'

The tree is seen at its best in the climate of south-west Ireland where it grows larger than it commonly does elsewhere and where its colouring in autumn is exceptionally rich. The best specimens I have seen are at Anne's Grove in County Cork. I have some young plants from that great garden given me by the late Mr Richard Grove Annesley. The form seemed a particularly good one especially for leaf size and for the particular red of the leaves in autumn. As other gardeners wanted young plants of it, I tried it from cuttings and found that they rooted without difficulty.

ALMONDS AT AYACATA

I have never had good almonds from English grown trees. I used to get the nuts forming well enough on even quite young almond trees in Kent, but the fruit was worthless, that is the kernels, the actual almonds; they were small and never developed to their proper size or if they did they were very bitter. Almonds are worth growing for their beauty early in spring, but hardly with a crop of nuts in mind. But at the time when I was trying to grow almonds for their nuts I was told by at least three considerable pundits that to have good fruit you must grow only the white-flowered kinds, and that those which yield good nuts never have pink flowers. I have since seen this stated for a fact in two different books by authors of repute.

It is nonsense. It may be that specialists can associate a particular form and colour of flower with a certain quality of nut. But broadly speaking there is no connection at all between flower colour and good fruits. I know this because of the almond trees I saw in flower at Ayacata in Grand Canary; and later in Sicily. Ayacata is a pretty little town high in the mountains of Grand Canary and it lives off its almond groves. They are very beautiful indeed in the months of January and February when they flower. The trees are planted on the slopes of the surrounding mountains for as far as one can see, and as they are not planted in regular rows, but (for a good reason) apparently at random, they form a sort of forest of almond trees rather than an orchard. The reason for this random planting is that there is hardly any soil, the mountains, of a lovely soft grey stone without grass, are badly eroded. Wherever a boulder or group of boulders holds a pocket of soil, the people plant another almond tree, and once the trees are established they seem to grow quite well on naked stone, or almost. Now the flower colour of these immensely fruitful trees, some of which are old and gnarled, half blasted by lightning or time, varies from white through every shade of rose pink, to maroon. They must, I think, be fairly primitive trees, for there is no attempt to propagate by grafting, seedlings are raised and planted for their own fruit and not as rootstocks.

The almond, *Prunus amygdalus*, comes from Afghanistan, Azerbaijan and Mesopotamia. The tree seems to have been diffused from its original home by way of the Punjab, where it is very ancient in cultivation but not found wild. But the Greeks had their almonds—'Pontic Nuts' at first, and not distinguished from other kinds of nuts—from the Lydians. In Cato's list of trees worth planting for fruit the almond appears as *nux Graeca*. It could have meant anything or nothing to us, but it happens that Columella explains that the trees called *nux Graeca* bear the nuts called *amygdale*.

Like the peach, only more so, the almond needs hotter summers than we can give it; and if it gets them it can stand the severest cold of winter. Like the peach, again, it is better on limestone than on acid soils, and likes heavy clays more than light soils.

As any housewife knows the best almonds come either from Jordan or from the province of Valencia in Spain. Both were Islamic countries and it is to their ancient population that they owe their almond trees. Although, no doubt, there was some spread of almond trees through the Roman Empire from the

Italian centre, a latter and second diffusion of these trees occurred under Arab auspices. It is not known exactly when almonds were first planted here but they had become common-place by the sixteenth century. But the nuts from English almond trees can never have been much good excepting when three hot summers followed each other in succession, something which happens very rarely.

LIME AND LIME-HATERS

It is fact that all plants without exception need calcium in the soil. Without it they cannot grow healthily; it is the material they make some of their hard parts of, for example, the shells of seeds. On the other hand, as every gardener also knows, there is a large group of plants which are known as lime-haters and which cannot be grown successfully in soils which have much lime, whether in the form of chalk or some other limestone. As it happens, one of the most beautiful and spectacular genera we can grow in gardens, *Rhododendron*, is calcifuge—lime-hating. Moreover camellias do not like much lime although they are less sensitive than rhododendrons; and there are many other such genera, often among the finest garden plants, such as *Lilium auratum*.

Why does lime, which is essential to all plants not excluding the calcifuges, poison some plants? The answer is that it does not. It is an absolutely essential ingredient of any fertile soil. But there is another element which is equally necessary although only in trace quantities, iron. Calcium combines so readily with salts of iron, and in such a way as to make them unusable by plants, that plants which are less able to get their ration of iron because of the presence of calcium, suffer from a deficiency disease in consequence: chlorosis. The lime does not, then, poison the so-called lime-hating plants; it harms them at second hand by inhibiting their intake of iron.

Gardeners used to try to remedy this by dressing the soil with large quantities of some suitable salt of iron. This usually had no effect whatever; it seemed a good and logical idea, but all that happened was that the iron was denied to the plants as fast as it was fed to them, by being at once joined with calcium in an unassimilable compound.

The gardener's problem is not to get rid of the lime, an impossibility in any case other than very locally; but to get iron to the plants despite the lime. This has been possible for some time now. Without going into an explanation of what exactly a chelate of iron is (an explanation I am not competent to give anyway), it can be said that chelated salts of iron are salts in which the iron molecules are so firmly held by the molecules of some other element with which it is joined to make a compound, that the calcium in the soil cannot get the iron away from its partner, or can do so only relatively slowly, thus giving such plants as Rhododendrons and other calcifuge *Ericas* a chance to get a measure of iron into themselves.

There was a theory that the trouble with calcifuge plants was not that they could not get iron out of the soil in the presence of lime above a certain level, but that they could not use the iron in the rising sap if there was too much calcium also in the sap. But the success of chelated iron in making calcifuge plants grow in limey soils seems to me to prove that the trouble is in the soil and not inside the plant. Not that the first chelates were very good; the effect of using them was hardly more than the effect of using ordinary salts of iron. But eventually Swiss chemists produced a chelate so rigid that the calcium could do nothing with it. It is the one commercially known as Sequestrene Iron.

The effect of using this Sequestrene on plants suffering from lime-induced chlorosis is quite magical. My own experience of it has been with camellias; plants which were so yellow that there was hardly any real green to be seen, turned deep, lustrous green in a matter of three weeks and began to grow vigorously, which they had never done before.

Does this mean that chalk gardeners can now grow rhododendrons? It may mean just that, technically, but it would be a silly thing for them to do; there are quite enough lime-loving shrubs and there is no doubt that it still remains better to grow what likes your soil, than what does not.

TI TREES

I first saw *Leptospermum scoparium* in flower on the island of Tresco where, in one part of the woods outside the garden proper, this New Zealand species has naturalized itself so that hundreds of seedling Ti Trees spring up each year. The type, if not its varieties, is hardy enough to grow in the south of England and along the warmer seaboard. Occasionally we get a very severe winter and the *Leptospermums* may then be killed; but one has only to keep some young plants from cuttings under glass or a few seedlings, in hand, to be able to replace such casualties, and their growth is so fast that the loss is not serious.

The genus is remarkable for its delicacy of form; the slender, lightly branched little trees are covered with the tiny evergreen leaves and from a distance look misty, more like the work of a *pointilliste* painter than of nature. The flowers are borne in such number that the whole tree is covered with them. In the type they are white, myriads of half inch single roses—such is the shape. I prefer this type to the coloured varieties, but certainly the cultivar 'Nicholsii' with its crimson flowers is more spectacular. It is also much more tender, succumbing to cold which does not harm the type plants. In the Tresco woods I saw what were, I suppose, forms intermediate between these two, with flowers in various shades of pink. We actually owe 'Nicholsii' to the great Tresco gardening family, for it was Captain Dorrien-Smith who introduced it from New Zealand in 1908. What seems to have been lost is a very fine cultivar named 'Eximium' which had much larger flowers and which was given an Award of Merit by the R.H.S. in 1938. But it is as nothing by comparison with the superb cultivars which I saw in the Christchurch Botanic Garden in New Zealand, none of which have yet reached Britain.

The hardiest *Leptospermum* is a very dwarf rock-garden plant with a very long name, *L. scoparium nicholsii nanum.* It is an enchanting plant, not more than six inches high with minute bronze-red-green foliage, a very dense habit of growth and carmine flowers in abundance. Presumably this is a high mountain form; at all events it stands far more frost than any of the tall ones.

I was given some plants of *Leptospermum pubescens* by a famous Scottish gardener. It differs from *scoparium* in the hairiness of its twigs, the silkiness of its leaves and it is even more upright in habit. The flowers are white. This species is supposed to be hardier than *scoparium* and perhaps it may be; for my part I never had either of them damaged in Devonshire.

MINIATURES

Miniature shrubs fascinate me, plants which have all the hard woodiness and stiff twigginess of trees or shrubs but are only a few inches high. One in particular was a great source of pleasure during the years when I managed to keep it alive, but it is far from being an easy plant: this is *Daphne petraea.* It is a minute evergreen shrub with rather gnarled looking trunk and branches when old, not more than four inches tall as a rule. It is native in the south Tyrolean mountains where it grows between stones or in rocky clefts, often on perpendicular cliff faces, fully exposed to the sun. The densely packed, minute, pointed little leaves are dark green, hard and leathery. The curious thing is that this tiniest of the Daphnes has the largest flowers of the genus. My own two specimens, grown at first between two stones beside a path but later moved into a pan of limestone chips and peaty loam, used to cover themselves, in June, with vividly pink and fragrant flowers over one-third of an inch in diameter across the open lobes. The flowers grow terminally in clusters of four.

Half the difficulty with this plant is perhaps due to the way in which nurseries propagate it. I suppose it is very difficult if not impossible from cuttings (in any case there would be very little material), and terribly slow from seed (which would probably be hard to come by anyway). The method is to graft on to *Daphne laureola.* The stock tends to grow out of its own accord as if the tiny scion did not give it enough outlet for its energy, and this has to be carefully watched for. But it is in every way so difficult a plant in cultivation that successful cultivators of *Daphne petraea* are very few. Bean says—'Its most successful cultivator was the late Mr Reginald Farrer who used to show little bushes in pots at the Temple Show in London almost covered with blossom.'

It is worth struggling with and it is a shrub I shall certainly try to grow again one day.

Much easier and no less charming is the miniature rhododendron, *R. impeditum*. It is a dense and twiggy, full and rounded evergreen bush between six inches to a foot tall and about as much through. The shoots in youth and the underside of the leaves are covered with minute scales which give the surfaces a silvery-grey look, but the upper sides of mature leaves are bright green. These leaves are oval and not more than three eighths of an inch long by quarter of an inch wide; this is their greatest size, for they are quite often smaller. The flowers, borne in clusters of two or three and carried on upright stalks at the ends of leafy shoots, are about an inch across, flattish bowls in shape, and in colour a pale purple, but this is variable and in some specimens I have had quite a rich purple colour. This rhododendron, like so many of the best of its large genus, is Chinese and was introduced by Forrest in 1911. There is another miniature, also Chinese, which is very like it, *R. intricatum*, which is likewise about a foot tall at maturity but remains smaller than that for many years. It has the same minute leaves; the flowers are borne in rather the same way but are smaller, and in colour a pale lilac. Both these little rhododendrons are ruggedly hardy and grow healthily in well-drained gritty peat with ample moisture.

There are several and perhaps many dwarf barberries, but not many real miniatures. *Berberis buxifolia* var. *nana* from the Andes seldom exceeds eighteen inches in height and is evergreen, with orange flowers and blue berries. Some of the *B.* x *irwinii* cultivars are miniatures: 'Corallina Compacta' long remains under six inches, very dense and close in habit, with masses of coral flower buds opening orange; another of the same complex is 'Gracilis Nana'. The cultivar 'Minor' of *B. thunbergii* is usually about a foot tall and through. There are perhaps others, but these are the ones which I know. They have the true qualities of a miniature, that is all their parts are in proportion to each other.

I have already described the tiny *Leptospermum scoparium nicholsii nana* which properly belongs here. Another shrublet which gave me much delight is *Daboecia azorica*. When I planted it I expected it to be about a foot tall, but in fact it always remained a low mat of tiny, dense linear leaves of a very rich green and it never grew more than four inches tall. The flower colour is superior to that of the other daboecias, being a true and glowing red. The flowers are borne on two-inch racemose stems held erect above the foliage, about a dozen or fewer per raceme. Like others of its kind, this *Daboecia* needs a gritty, peaty soil quite free from lime, and ample moisture above good sharp drainage. I found it difficult to increase by cuttings but very easy to layer. It is presumably not very hardy but never took any harm in my Devonshire garden.

Hebe pimeleoides is a New Zealand shrub from the alps of South Island, and much hardier than most of its kind, possibly one of the few shrubby veronicas absolutely hardy in the average climate of Britain. It is more or less prostrate, sending out its tough, woody little branches parallel with the soil and either on it or an inch or two above it. In time the plants form dense little mats of their oval, very glaucous foliage and in season, the two-inch cylindrical spikes of purplish blue flowers which stand erect. I had a form with white and blue flowers; and the variety *glauco-coerulea* had bluer flowers and bluer foliage.

There is a little-known and little-grown miniature myrtle which, although it comes from South America is native so far south, both about the Straits of Magellan and in the Falkland Islands, that it is perfectly hardy. Its name is *Myrtus nummularia* and when I finally succeeded in getting a plant of it I found it as pleasing as I expected it to be from descriptions I had read. It is prostrate in habit, forming a dense and twisting mass of woody branches very near to and parallel with the soil. The tiny, pointed leaves, under quarter of an inch long and about half as wide, are glossy bright green and like all myrtles this is an evergreen. The carriage and presentation of the flowers is admirable: they are borne on short, stout stalks so as to facc the sky, and they are white, quarter of an inch wide, cupped and with bright yellow centres. The fruit is very decorative, a quite large, oval, bright pink berry.

SOME TULIPS

I have never been interested in and am incapable of writing about the great hybrid, garden tulips. I do not mean to condemn them or anything foolish like that; but one cannot be interested in every kind of garden plant and that particular kind has never made any appeal to me whatsoever. But the botanical species tulips are quite another matter. I have grown a number of them and easily understand the charm they had for the Persian, Turkish and other Near Eastern gardeners before we ever started to grow them here. I like the way in which, if they relish the soil and climate of your garden, they will settle down and become native to the place, spreading to form very large clumps and reappearing year after year without all the trouble of lifting and replanting the bulbs.

The most spectacular wild tulip is, I suppose, *Tulipa fosteriana*. Flowering quite early in April, the one foot stems carry the huge flowers without flinching: the flowers are at their best when they open, whereas in the big cultivar tulips the flowers seem to me to be spoiled once they pass the stage half way between the bud and being full blown. Fully open, *T. fosteriana* is a ten-inch star of vivid glossy crimson-scarlet about a centre of almost black anthers. I have grown a number of forms of this tulip and found that the taller kinds such as 'Red Emperor' and 'Madame Lefeber' are a nuisance, being too tall to carry their immense heads, especially in windy April. The dwarfer forms are therefore better, and a very good one is called 'Princeps'.

T. fosteriana comes from the region about Samarkand and Bokhara, and so does *T. eichleri* which has scarlet flowers half the size of *T. fosteriana*. The flowers are very elegant in bud, being waisted. But open, they are spectacular, the glossy scarlet perianth segments displaying the black blotch at the base, that blotch outlined with a fine yellow line.

A tulip which almost went native in a garden I had in Kent, was *T. clusiana*, an Asiatic tulip naturalized all over Mediterranean Europe. It is quite different from the two above, in no way spectacular or showy, but very elegant, carrying its striped white and red flowers on stems so slender that the flowers droop a little. There was another tulip which spread well in the same Kentish garden, forming large clumps of flowers which diminished in size from the centre to the periphery of the clump. I daresay these clumps should have been lifted and the bulb increment replanted, but I left them alone to behave like wild plants. The tulip was *T. kaufmanniana*, the Water-lily Tulip. My *kaufmanniana* flowers were usually about six inches tall, had large flowers which were buff yellow marked with crimson. In bright sunshine they would open to the full width and even reflex their petals, an exquisite sight.

One of the botanical species tulips which I planted was *T. turkestanica* but it is more of a curiosity than a real beauty. There are from three to as many as seven flower heads to each stem; they are greenish white and although when they open wide and look starry they are quite pretty, their only real merit in the garden is that they flower in February or early March.

The Turkish *T. sprengeri* will naturalize in English gardens and it flowers about the end of May, doing very well in full sun but tolerating shade. The flowers have eighteen-inch stalks which are amply stout enough to carry the heads, composed of two- to three-inch perianth segments and very globular in form. The colour is a rich mahogany.

It seemed to me reasonable to try to naturalize the native, or at least very anciently naturalized, English tulip in my garden. *T. silvestris* which I have found wild once or twice in several parts of Europe. The stems are slender and sometimes over a foot tall and hardly strong enough to hold the flower upright, so that the heads, at least in bud, droop elegantly. The colour is a clear yellow. What happened to this tulip in my garden was that the plants spread underground and produced a great deal of leaf but very little flower and in some years they had no flowers at all.

FREESIAS

Some years ago I visited three large greenhouses planted to freesias, at Wye College—which, for the benefit of those gardeners who do not know the names of the institutions which do so much for the advancement of horticultural learning, is the agricultural and horticultural college of London University. As freesias are cut for market as soon as they show colour, only a few flowers were fully open, but enough to demonstrate the wonderful colour range—from snow-white, through cream and rich butter-yellow, orange and crimson, not to mention the mauves and blues; the exquisite form; and the splendid substance and erect habit of these modern freesias.

FREESIAS

This genus provides an excellent example of what man can do in improving on nature. It is confined to South Africa and *Freesia refracta*, which grows in long grass, flowers in spring and in summer receives a fierce baking from the sun, was introduced into cultivation about 150 years ago. The flowers are yellow with a few lines of violet, but there are varieties with pure white or with bright yellow flowers. The fragrance is not found in all varieties. In 1898 a species with pink flowers was found and named *F. armstrongii.* And this is the raw material with which, by crossing, horticulturalists have produced the kind of flowers I saw at Wye . . . and which you can buy at any good florist's in January and February; and which, moreover, you can with a little trouble grow for yourself.

The first work of hybridizing was done at Kew; it was taken up by Dr Ragioneri in Italy, by Lutz and others in Germany, by van Tubergens in Holland, and in England by several gifted amateur plant breeders, notably Mr C. H. Dalrymple whose freesia houses in the skirts of the New Forest were one of the pleasures of my wartime leaves from the Navy. The Danes were foremost in developing the commercial growing of freesias for the market; and the Dutch have become outstanding in propagation of the genus, so that it is from Holland that we get the best freesia seed and the best freesia corms.

If you grow freesias from seed, you cannot grow named varieties: from a good seed-mixture you will get white, yellow, red and blue flowers, but they will blossom unevenly and will show some diversity of habit. The seed is sown in April, and the seedlings should be pricked into five-inch pots, three or four to a pot, or into deep boxes, the soil being a good compost—J.I. potting compost will do very well. Better still, avoid pricking out by sowing the seed very thinly in the pots or boxes, and thinning out the seedlings. Germination is improved by 'chitting'—in this case, soaking the seed in warm water until rootlets begin to appear. The pots or boxes can be kept outside the greenhouse and in a fairly cool place throughout the summer, moved into the greenhouse in September. Freesias in their native land are spring flowers; so they not only do not want much heat, but great heat will spoil the flower crop. These seedling freesias will flower in October and November. The temperature of the house should not exceed 50°F. by more than 1 or 2°. It will be obvious from the above that the whole operation can equally well be done in a suitably deep cold frame or pit, provided that really cold weather does not set in early.

Named varieties, producing flowers of greater substance with better stalks, finer fragrance and richer colours, are grown from corms. In the early days of freesia growing, gardeners often failed because their corms remained obstinately dormant; this was because they had been stored cool, whereas their resting season at home is high summer; suppliers of corms now store them at 80°F. They should be planted in September, in pots or boxes of manageable size, as above, and kept outside in frames which can be shaded and kept free of early frosts, until they begin to show growth. They should not be watered until growth does appear, and then only sparingly. Great care is necessary in giving only a minimum of water until the plants are in flower, when they can be watered more freely. As growth appears, the pots or boxes are removed to the greenhouse and there a temperature of 50°F. should be maintained. In October and November, and even in December, this will often be produced, and even exceeded, by the sun on the glass, without any artificial heating. But heat will be needed to maintain the temperature of the house in January and February—freesias will not succeed in an entirely unheated house as a rule. However, this does not mean that unless you have a house with a boiler and water-pipes, you can not grow freesias. Electrical devices for heating small greenhouses are not ruinously dear; and much cheaper, at least to run, are blue-flame paraffin stoves.

When flowering, whether of seedlings or of corm plants, is

over, it is still necessary to give the plants some attention unless you want to buy new corms every year, and make no use of the corms produced by your seedlings. First, as to the seedlings, probably not all will be worth keeping as permanent stock; it is well worth while to mark the best plants—for flower size, flower substance, length and sturdiness of stalk, colour and fragrance—during the flowering season. These are your selection, and the rest can be scrapped. Those retained, and your named varieties from corms, should still be carefully watered and discreetly fed until the leaves begin to die down.

If you are to avoid dormancy troubles, you must then do one of two things; either move the pots and boxes into a cold frame so that they can be exposed, under glass and unwatered, to the full summer sun until they are wanted again in September, when they will need a period of relative cool before starting into growth again; or the corms must be lifted and stored at a very high temperature and a humidity adequate to save them from desiccation. The ordinary gardener has no means of producing these conditions, although probably something could be done by using polythene bags and the family airing cupboard.

An extremely important point in the cultivation of freesias is support. On its native heath the stalk is held up by surrounding long grass. If given no support, freesias invariably flop, and if they are allowed to do this, they cease to grow and will never recover; subsequent straightening will be useless. The pots and boxes should be provided with a number of eighteen-inch canes. In pots the freesias can be individually tied as they grow—loosely, of course. In boxes a sort of net of strings can be woven into the canes, at all levels to the top of the canes, so that the plants are bound to grow into and through it. Where freesias are being grown on a larger scale, for example, in beds in the greenhouse, by far the best support is provided by large mesh fishnet fastened at the ends and sides to stout bamboo canes. These canes, in their turn, are tied or clipped to upright canes driven very firmly in the ground, and from time to time the whole net is raised further up these uprights, so that the support given to the plants is raised in level as they grow and need it further from the ground.

Finally, here is a list of the best named varieties: there are, of course, other fine ones, but this list will give the gardener a range of colours, good strong stems, large and well-formed flowers, and plenty of fragrance. 'Golden Yellow' is the best of the yellows, richly scented and with a fine compact head of large, strong flowers; 'Robin Hood', crimson with a white throat; 'Blue Ribbon', lobelia-blue with a white throat; 'Carlo Carlee', creamy-yellow; 'Princess Markjke', orange-red; 'Sapphire', mauve; and 'Snow Queen', the best of the whites. All red freesias are apt to be smaller and not quite so fine as the other colours, owing to the fact that *F. armstrongii*, source of the red hybrids, is a small and rather puny species. Also, for a reason I have not discovered, it is more difficult to grow good white freesias than yellows or blues, although *refracta alba* is a white which occurs in the wild.

I have said nothing about the summer-flowering freesias called 'Paradise' freesias. For these, the corms should be planted in May. But, for me, the freesia is a mid-winter flower for embellishing the house, and not a border plant at all.

LESS COMMON BULBS

When I receive a bulb catalogue I am apt to skip the major sections which one knows almost by heart, the border tulips, the daffodils, the hyacinths, pleasant and desirable though they all are, and turn at once to the last few pages where one can usually find a sort of miscellaneous section dealing with bulbs of plants which not everyone grows. This is not for snobbish reasons, but because it is in that section where you find bulbous plants which have not as yet received much attention from the plant-breeders and which retain a great deal of their original simplicity and distinction. I admire the work of the plant-breeders, but in many cases it has gone too far. The enormous daffodils, for example, in hundreds of varieties, now available to the gardener, are magnificent flowers, especially for the house; but are they really as attractive as, for instance, the Angel's Tears, *Narcissus triandrus*? Do they really look as well, in a garden of normal size, as *N. pseudo-narcissus*, our own wild daffodil of the Lake District and a few other favoured places?

One of the bulb flowers whose neglect is incomprehensible to me, is *Camassia cusickii.* The bulbs themselves are a pleasure to handle, huge things, weighing up to half a pound each, although, as a rule, rather less than that. These bulbs should be planted in November or thereabouts, but they can certainly be planted later. Mine were planted three inches deep in a mixed border of shrubs, bulbs and a few herbaceous perennials.

This species of camassia produces a large number of long, glaucous, wavy leaves about twelve to eighteen inches long and at the centre of this mass of foliage a long sturdy stem which may reach three feet and will be covered for a great part of its length with pale or lavender blue flowers about one and a half inches in diameter. There may be as many as 100 of these. It is a stately and very beautiful plant, so that gardeners familiar only with *C. esculenta*, itself well worth growing, are apt to be surprised at its quality. One of the reasons for its relative unpopularity may be that its bulbs, like those of the whole genus, do not increase by offsets. However, camassias set seed and ripen it and, I am told, though I have not tried it, that the seeds sown out of doors germinate readily and although seedlings take four years to flower, this is a cheap and easy way of getting a large number of the plants.

Comparable for stateliness and distinction with *C. cusickii*, but flowering in late summer or early autumn instead of in the spring and early summer, is that mysteriously neglected beauty, *Galtonia*.

In flower *G. candicans* looks like nothing so much as a gigantic white bluebell. The long, narrow leaves bend gracefully outwards, and from their midst rises a stem to between three and four feet topped by a raceme one foot long of pure white bluebell flowers, each well over one inch long, and fragrant. The flowering stem of *G. candicans* may even attain to six feet so that the bulbs should be planted well back in a mixed border, or a group of them may be planted alone, in grass. The genus is South African, like so many good garden plants, but it is perfectly hardy. Whether the bulbs increase by offsets, I do not know, not having grown this plant long enough. (The R.H.S. *Dictionary* is silent on the subject.) But seed capsules ripen on plants in an English garden, and the seeds germinate. The genus includes two other species *G. clavata* and *G. princeps*, neither as good as *candicans*. It is not necessary, or even desirable, to plant *Galtonia* bulbs in the autumn; early spring is better.

A couple of years ago I planted, for the first time in my gardening life, bulbs of *Erythronium dens-canis* which are known as 'dog's-tooth' violets, which they do not in the least resemble. I was delighted with the result. Erythroniums are rock-garden plants, but one good place for them is a border-retaining stone wall, just between soil and stone. Or they can be naturalized, like hardy cyclamen, under a tree or shrub. Like the best of the cyclamen species, erythroniums have very ornamental leaves, not, indeed, marbled with silver, but curiously and attractively blotched with brown. The flowers, more like cyclamen than violets, are either a curious pinkish-purple colour, or white, or both. The whole plant does not exceed six inches in height. The bulbs do best if planted quite soon after flowering as the leaves begin to die and they should be set at least three inches deep. As far as I know only the one, Old World species, *dens-canis*, is available to gardeners, but there are other species, all of them North American: *E. americanum* has violet leaf-markings, and yellow flowers; *E. californicum*, white and purple flowers, and there are others with yellow and orange, violet, lilac, and lavender flowers.

The rootstock of the genus ixia, which is of the iris family, is not a bulb but a corm. In at least one corner of the British Isles this South African beauty, the African corn lily, has gone wild, or at least naturalized itself quite happily. But this is a quite exceptionally favoured spot, and ixias are probably not perfectly hardy everywhere in Britain. The usual recommendation is to plant the corms in November and cover the place with bracken or some other warm litter as protection against really hard frost. In the south-west this is not necessary.

Ixias flower in June. They produce long narrow sword-like leaves and flower stems from twelve to eighteen inches long; they are rather reminiscent of Kaffir lilies, but the colour range is much wider. Each flowering stem has a spike of from four to a dozen starry flowers in red, pink, orange, blue, yellow, almost all the colours of the rainbow. The colour depends on the species, but the species are so closely related that one does not buy the corms by species, with some exceptions, but simply as ixias. Outstanding among the species is *I. viridiflora*, one of our rather few green-flowered plants. The flower spikes in this species are very well furnished, and as the numerous flowers, close-clustered, stand out well above the foliage, their greenness is far more striking than in the case of other green-flowered plants, especially if this species be planted with other, multi-coloured ixias. It is, however, not easy to get this one.

To most gardeners, the name gladiolus means a huge, massive, florists' flower, perhaps best relegated to the kitchen-garden for cutting, since it never looks well in a border. But what about the species gladioli? These plants have a grace which the hybrids have lost, and look perfectly well among other plants in border and shrubberies. A particularly easy one is the European *G. byzantinus.* Plant a few corms where they can remain undisturbed and form a clump; in a few years you will have every year a most impressive 'stand' of tall, red flowers and enough new corms to create a score of fresh clumps. A most rewarding plant.

SOME GARDENERS

It is not true that all gardeners are agreeable people but I have not yet met one who was both a good gardener and a bore, although I suppose most of us may be to people who are not interested in the subject.

The last professional gardener of the old school whom I knew at all well, and perhaps he was the last of that kind still engaged in running a great garden until his sudden death in his early sixties, was Jonathan Johnson, who was head gardener of Dartington Hall Gardens. He did not like to be called head gardener; he had, though he was a sensible, able and amiable man very good at his job, been affected by the fashion for high sounding euphemisms and he liked to be addressed as the Superintendent of Gardens, a title which has now become the rule at Dartington Hall. His manner with strangers who tried to patronize him or who did not pay him the kind of respect he thought due to him, was pompous and people were apt to laugh at him behind his back. But with people whom he knew he was simple and friendly and his vast knowledge of plants and gardens, and his long experience were at the service of anyone who liked to ask for advice.

As a gardener he had absolutely no side, none of that professional tendency to mystification, to making what was simple and straightforward seem difficult and obscure. Like all men who are really good at gardening he had endless enthusiasm and he never stopped working. Long before or after working hours he was about the gardens, often with his shotgun under one arm to protect the buds of shrubs and trees from bullfinches or to see the boys under his care—it was he who started the horticultural training scheme at Dartington, which has since become increasingly important—had done their work properly. If he conducted you round the garden you were quite certain to miss nothing worth seeing. One was always taken to visit certain plants or groups of plants he was particularly attached to, for example a group of three very well grown *Magnolia stellata* which he had raised from cuttings. He was a clever propagator, using the older methods; I sometimes thought that he felt that newer methods, for example mist propagation, were a sort of cheating, setting real skill at nought. But he was not stupid about this and always used scientific techniques in the end.

The two gardeners who made the greatest impression on me, both for their horticultural learning and skill, and one for the sweetness of his nature, were both Irishmen: the late John Walpole; and the late Richard Grove Annesley. I did not get to know either of them until they were in their eighties. Walpole was at that time the owner of Mount Usher which has passed to his son Robert Walpole, who must be the sixth generation of Walpoles to maintain, continue making and caring for, that magnificent garden. I went to see him twice while I was writing a book on Irish gardens and both times he took me round the whole twenty or more acres, never at a loss for the history and natural history of a plant or a planting. He was quite able to outwalk men half his age and seemed never to be tired. His manner was direct and authoritative, and seemed to me a proper expression of his short, stocky figure, massive grey head, and determined, stumping gait. He always gave credit to those gardeners who had guided him or helped him and took to himself only a very modest measure for the beauties and rarities of Mount Usher.

He was quickly responsive to enthusiasm about his garden or his favourite plants, but I had a feeling that it would be a great mistake, with him, to make a statement without being very sure of one's facts or to pretend to know more about a genus than one did. He had a sardonic eye and a dry sense of humour which went very well with his austere Quaker beliefs and manners. When, by letter, he invited me to luncheon on the occasion of my first visit, I was much struck with the fact that he put into the letter his hope that I would not mind there being no wine or other alcohol; and that though I was welcome to smoke if I wanted to, he never had tobacco in the house.

He was most generous with plants—for example he gave me a rare and beautiful variegated *Pittosporum* with tricolour leaves—but he liked to feel sure that he was giving plants to people who would and could grow them properly and would not let them die.

Richard Grove Annesley of Annes Grove in County Cork was not only one of the half dozen greatest gardeners of his time, he was one of the sweetest natured and most courteous men I have ever known. When I went to see his garden I put up at an hotel in the nearest town; I telephoned him to make an appointment and he insisted on my moving into the house in such terms that I could not possibly refuse. I stayed five days, and even that was hardly enough time in which to see the garden in detail, for although laid out in definite divisions, woodland, formal garden, bank garden, water garden and so forth, it was so richly furnished with such a vast range of fine plants that a month would hardly have been enough time for it. Moreover one day was taken out to go to Ilnacullin, or Garinish Island in Glengariff Bay. Although Mr Annesley was still able to drive his car, he was not up to a long and difficult drive. So I drove him to Garinish and we spent the best part of the day in another of Ireland's finest gardens, and one which Annesley had helped the Bryces and Harold Peto to stock.

Mr Annesley knew his garden plant by plant. He did not always come out with me all the days I spent in it but when I came in to lunch or dinner he would ask after particular plants in remote parts of the garden, and give me their history; and he was one of those men whose shop talk is always interesting, if shop talk is the right word in this context. He was remarkable for the diffidence with which he put forward any theory about plants or gardening; and if, having given an opinion, someone else disputed it, he would withdraw at once as if his own opinion was worthless, whereas it was, in any matter of the gardening kind, probably one of the best worth having in the world.

The greatest perfectionist in the horticultural field is probably Mr Lionel Fortescue of Buckland Monachorum. He is one of the rare gardeners who can combine good plantsmanship with a sense of garden design; he is very remarkable for the care he has taken and still takes in the placing of plants so that their colour shall contribute to a pattern and not simply swear at it. He will have a large and very heavy rhododendron wheeled round the garden, in flower, so that he can 'try' it for colour in some chosen places. The ruthlessness with which he uproots fine plants because their blue is not quite true, is startling. If there is a poor plant or an unhealthy plant in his garden, I have never seen it.

VIOLETS

A garden I made in Devonshire was extremely rich in violets: they grow on banks, under shrubs, beside and even in some of the paths, and they were especially fine at the foot of south-facing hedges. Moreover, whereas in Kent, I had only dog violets, which are very charming with their pointed petals and what, if I were not afraid of being called silly, I should identify as their air of naïve astonishment, but scentless, all the Devon violets, planted or wild were very large-flowered specimens of *V. odorata* or of 'Russian' violets in three principal varieties: deep violet flowers; white flowers; and another which I suppose one could call lavender but which, upon fairly close examination, turns out to be variegated, that is the flowers are white, finely marked with violet striations, so that under a glass they appear to be striped. In fact, I have not seen these before; and although they may in fact be commonplace, they may also be a natural but unusual cross which has occurred in this garden. More remarkable than any of these was a deep rose-pink violet. And I myself planted some yellow ones.

Although violets are not difficult to grow anywhere, they are much easier in the south-west: they do best in mild, moist weather and rich loamy soil, and they abhor heat quite as much as they dislike cold. *V. odorata* is very easy to propagate. The simplest method is by runners, like strawberries, which are formed during the growing season and whose cadet plants take root and establish themselves in the same season. All you have to do is to cut the stolon and move the young plant to wherever you want it. But the species is readily propagated from fresh seed; indeed, where it is well established even in a single clump, it will spread itself over a wide area, for the sweet violet is what is called a *myrmecochore* species. I do not know how you pronounce this, but it means 'ant-dispersed'. The seeds contain an oil attractive to ants, who therefore carry them off and scatter them about the garden.

The sweet violet is, among the very numerous species of this genus, what one may call the violet of History. It was this violet which Homer had in mind when he called Aphrodite *iostephanos*, 'violet-crowned'; it was the sweet violet which Plutarch referred to when he said that its 'exhalations greatly assist in removing affections of the head caused by wine'. It was the sweet violet which was given as a reward or prize to the Minnesinger until, in decadent times, the flower became an imitation violet made of gold. It is the sweet violet which attracts the nightingale; for there is reason to think that Milton's observation was sound when he wrote:

'In the violet-embroidered vale
The love-lorn nightingale
Nightly her sad song mourneth well. . . .'

even if he did get the bird's sex wrong. It was this species which Shakespeare thought of when he called violets '. . . dim, But sweeter than the lids of Juno's eyes.'

Nor does the reputation of this exquisite little flower rest only upon its form, colour and scent. Here is Gerarde on the subject:

'Violets have a great prerogative above other, not only because the mind conceiveth a certain pleasure by handling and smelling these odoriferous flowers but also for that very many by these violets receive ornaments and comely grace; for there be made of them garlands for the head, nosegaies, and posies which are delightful to look on and pleasant to smell to, speaking nothing of their appropriate virtues . . .'

What are these virtues? Having added that violets are the

greatest ornament, chiefest beauty and most excellent grace of gardens, Gerarde says that syrup of violets is good against inflammation of the lungs and breast, against pleurisy and cough. Is it true? Pliny would have agreed with Gerarde and would have added to this list quinsy and swellings, while the great Arab doctors would have prescribed an oil of violet seed against the sting of a scorpion. This reputation as a medicine endured until well into the nineteenth century, for syrup of violet petals was used against 'infant disorders' whatever that may mean. The one scientifically established medicinal quality of *V. odorata* is not so pleasant to think of: violine, isolated by a French physician named Boullay rather over a century ago, and once officinal in the French, if not in the British, pharmacopoeia, is a violent emetic with much the same properties as ipecacuanha.

But for all its superlative qualities the sweet violet is not the only one for the garden. However, before leaving it, it will be as well to name some of the varieties which are easily bought from nurseries and can be grown in association with our own wild *V. odorata*. Perhaps the best known is 'Princess of Wales': the flowers have more blue than red in the colour, they are large, stand up well with long stalks, and are strongly scented. Very early flowers can be had by growing this variety in a cold frame on a compost of loam, leaf mould and a little coarse sand. The frame, however, must not be so placed as to receive direct sunlight, or the plants will be overheated and grow weakly and fail to flower. 'Governor Herrick' makes, in my experience, the largest plants and the sturdiest flowers, with strong stalks. 'Red Charm' is almost wine-coloured, but if scented at all the scent is very faint and ephemeral. The 'bluest' violet I know is sold in France by any good nurseryman as '*odorante des quatre saisons*', while Vilmorin-Andrieux's '*odorante des quatre saisons Verrières*' has the same qualities but is a true deep violet. The 'reddest' violet I have seen, but not grown myself, is '*Admiral Avellan*'. This I saw growing under glass and it was as strongly scented as any blue violet. I was told that it will do very well in the open. The same gardener, who was a collector of violet species and varieties, had an extraordinary amethyst-coloured violet in the same frame, equally fragrant, and with very large flowers: I think it may have been the variety listed in the Supplement to the R.H.S. *Dictionary* as 'Tina Whitaker'. I have never seen it elsewhere.

The genus *Viola* includes the pansies, so if I write of a 'yellow violet' I fully expect to be told that I am talking nonsense and that the plant must have been one of the *V. cornuta* varieties which we call violas. Well, no: the plant was a true violet, that is, of the *Nomimium* section of this complex genus, with a rich yellow flower. It was shown to me at Sissinghurst by the late Lady Nicolson and it was growing, as I recall between two flagstones of a path. I have since grown it.

Only once have I seen a really good collection of Parma violets magnificently grown, and that was a few weeks after D-day, at the château of a French nobleman in Normandy, where I had been taken by a friend invited to lunch. The entertainment was as noble as our host's ancient name, and if we did have to endure a complaint which lasted an hour about the conduct of a Resistance Party which had pinched the count's electric power plant, we were consoled by a visit to the greenhouses. There I saw, among other things, half a dozen richly flowering beds of Parma violet varieties—and this in midsummer. It would be disingenuous to pretend that I remember, or that I made a note of, their varietal names. But I have tried since to identify them from memory. There was one kind which had large, perfectly double lavender flowers which were darker at the base of the petals, almost true violet: this was surely 'Duchesse de Parme'. The one I knew and recognized, having grown it as 'Lady Hume Campbell', had dense, glossy clumps of foliage and sweet-scented blue flowers, also perfectly double. This would seem to be the 'Parme de Toulouse' of old French garden books. There was also a double with a white eye: I find one so described in the R.H.S. *Dictionary* Supplement under the name 'Mrs Arthur'. A pinkish-lilac double, very sweet-scented, may have been 'Mrs J. J. Astor'. There was also a white double, which I cannot find anywhere.

SOME GENTIANS

When I went from chalk to peat I had a new range of plants to learn; among them were gentians. I did, in fact, grow a few gentians in Kent; but I was unsuccessful with the allegedly chalk-tolerant species; and for the others I had to make special beds completely isolated from the ordinary garden soil, for which purpose I used old baths buried to the rim. Even so, I did not do very well. And this was disappointing because I had, in the past, had some curious or pleasant encounters with gentians in the wild. On one occasion, when driving over the Maloja Pass from Switzerland into Italy, getting out of the car to look at the magnificent view at an altitude where the ground beside the road seemed from the car to be nothing but barren stone and scree, I discovered that stone to be bright with the pure sky-blue flowers of a small species of gentian growing over several acres.

But almost my oddest acquaintance with any plant also concerns a gentian rarely seen in gardens, although it can be grown as a border plant. During years of crossing Alpine regions of France, Italy and Switzerland, I had observed a massive, burly plant thrusting up through the soil in great numbers in many meadows, in the form of a spearhead of tightly-folded sword-like leaves, or perhaps lanceolate is the proper term. Time after time

I asked people what it was; time after time I was told with a shrug, in French, in Italian, in Basque, and in the extremely peculiar German spoken by the Swiss, that it was a wild flower. The peasants of Europe do not dignify plants they hold to be useless with a name. It so happened that I never crossed a habitat of this plant during its flowering season. At last, only two years ago, and in the Puy de Dome region, I found a man, well-informed enough to answer my question with a surprised '*Mais, m'sieur, c'est de la gentiane!*' To me, gentian had always been a dwarf, creeping plant with blue trumpet flowers. This stately species, however, grows three to four feet tall and carried a fine head of yellow flowers. Time after time I had drunk 'Gentiane' as an aperitif. It had never occurred to me that the name was anything more than a proprietary brand, whereas it now transpired that the stuff was made from the great bulbous root of this same mountain weed. The root is macerated and steeped in white wine. One could make it oneself at home. But the plant has to be an old one and one needs a considerable area devoted to it. The species, by the way, is *G. lutea*, and it may attain a height of six feet.

However, to return to the plants which most of us understand by the word 'gentian': in my experience there are only two which are not difficult to grow and which will usually flower in suitable conditions, although even these are sometimes temperamental and while growing freely will not flower at all: they are *G. acaulis* and *G. septemfida*.

G. acaulis is a European species synonymous with the garden *G. gentianella*, a name not much used now. It spreads itself over rocks, forming a small mat not more than four inches high, and this becomes covered with trumpet flowers of a deep blue. It is an excellent edging plant, flowering in May.

G. septemfida, sometimes called *septemfida gigantea*, is a fast-growing, trailing perennial whose stems turn up and grow erect to nine or ten inches and terminate with a cluster of large trumpet flowers of a duller or rather a less brilliant blue than *acaulis*. It comes from Asia Minor and flowers in late summer.

Next in order of difficulty—I am talking of personal experience and not propounding a general rule—is *G. verna* var. *angulosa*, also known as *G. angulosa*, which comes from the Caucasus and is a plant clinging close to the soil so that its mat may be as low as one inch from the ground and will hardly be more than three inches. Its vivid blue, starry flowers decorate the tiny foliage in May and, like the other two, it makes a very good edging plant. All these like full sunshine, firm planting, plenty of moisture in spring and summer but good winter drainage, for they will not survive water-logging.

A species which seemingly all gardeners want to grow but which presents difficulties is *G. sino-ornata*. It comes from west China or Tibet and it flowers in October, possibly beginning with a few flowers in September, and carrying on with some belated ones into November. The blue of its flowers is exceedingly rich and luminous. They are very regularly shaped trumpets carried about five inches above the ground at the tips of flowering stems which, having run some way over the scree or rocks, turn upwards in a very charming fashion. The difficulty with this species is its extremely calcifuge nature: it will fail to grow and will soon perish if there is even a trace of lime in the soil and its requires, to do well, a soil entirely composed of peat and leafmould, the latter taken from the surface of an acid soil.

Another September-flowering species which—and this is also true of *sino-ornata*—does better in partial shade than in full sun, although I am not sure that it will not do well enough even in full sun, is *G. farreri*. It forms a prostrate mat a foot or so across and, like *sino-ornata*, bears its flowers on upturned tips of shoots so that they are carried five or six inches above the soil level. It is not so intolerant of lime traces as *sino-ornata*. Its trumpet-shaped flowers, one to a stalk, are about two inches long and Cambridge blue.

These are the very few species of a genus that has no fewer than 400, of which I have some small experience. I have also grown the Willow Gentian, *G. asclepiadea*, the name being based on its willow-like, paired ovate-lanceolate leaves and perhaps also on the gracefully arching habit of its rising stems which, in a flourishing specimen, will be between eighteen and twenty-four inches tall, so that this is not an edging gentian; it prefers a wet soil and shade and may even naturalize itself in suitable conditions. It is a European species and it has been grown in England for at least three centuries. The intense blue trumpet flowers (white in the var. *alba*) cluster thick in the leaf axils of the upper part of the curving stems, thus being laid in a heaven-aspiring attitude. *G. lagodechiana*, an East Caucasus species sometimes listed merely as a variety of *septemfida*, looks like the latter but has flowers of a slightly deeper and more luminous blue. It flowers in May. Finally there is a variety, a cross between *G. farreri* and *G. veitchiorum* and called 'Inverleith', which I have seen flowering in a Surrey nursery, and should like to grow. This variety is remarkable for the size of its pure blue trumpet flowers which appear in late August and carry on into September.

I have already explained that I am not an experienced or knowledgeable gentian-grower, but I have discussed the genus with other gardeners and I find that a common experience, even where all the conditions demanded by the plants seem to have been provided, is failure to flower even when growth is satisfactory. Nobody seems to have explained this.

Note: we think of gentians as the bluest of flowers, and the Old World species are predominantly blue, white or, rarely, yellow. Does anyone in Britain, I wonder, now grow the Andean *G. scarlatina* with its scarlet flowers? Many years ago Sir F. Stern flowered it at Highdown near Worthing, but later he lost it; in his garden it opened its flowers only between noon and one o'clock.

CARBON DIOXIDE

One of the gases which compose the atmosphere is carbon dioxide. It is a waste gas of the animal metabolism and is poisonous to animals in sufficient concentrations. It is, however, necessary to plant life. Much of the carbon which, by photosynthesis, plants combine with elements drawn from the soil and with oxygen to make the carbonates of their substance, is drawn from the atmosphere. In a sense, then, they breathe in carbon dioxide although only during daylight.

From the plant's point of view there is a chronic shortage of carbon dioxide in the atmosphere. That is to say that while there is enough for all plants to grow, they would grow faster and better if there were more. This, in fact, is one of the reasons why tropical plant metabolism is faster than temperate zone plant metabolism; one of the products of plant decay or animal decay, i.e. of rotting carrion, more plentiful in the tropics than in our latitudes, is carbon dioxide. In short, there is an optimum condition of atmosphere, an optimum supply of CO_2 which is rarely if ever attained in natural conditions.

These facts have long been well known but it was not easy to make any use of them. It is clearly not possible to generate carbon dioxide for the benefit of the plants in one's garden; it would simply be blown away. But in the greenhouse it is quite another matter. It was always theoretically possible to enrich the atmosphere of a greenhouse with carbon dioxide, raising the CO_2 content to the optimum figure, by burning coal, or mineral oil in some suitable kind of stove or burner. But CO_2 is by no means the only gas given off when such fuels, derived from ancient plant carrion or animal carrion, are burned; among the others is, for instance, sulphur dioxide which is very poisonous to plants; for that matter, pretty poisonous to people as well, but they are obliged to put up with it excepting in smoke-free zones, whereas the plants just fade and die. It is true that methods of generating pure CO_2 were known. But they were too difficult or too expensive to be of practical use to the gardener, even to the market gardener on a large scale.

But now things have changed. It so happens that when you burn the natural gas butane in certain easily achieved conditions, the by-product gas is CO_2 free from SO_2, or at least so nearly free from it that the plants are not affected by the very small volume of it present. Consequently, one of the newest tools which science has put into the hands of the greenhouse plant grower, market gardener or amateur, is a butane-burner which raises the CO_2 content of the greenhouse atmosphere to the optimum figure, resulting in quicker and healthier growth and very considerably greater weight of crop from a given amount of space and a given area of soil.

Just how much use this will be to the amateur gardener is not clear. But the thing works and some of the biggest firms in the market-garden industry have installed the necessary burners and ducting for feeding their plants with CO_2 through the leaves just as they have long fed them with the other elements they need through the roots.

CYCLAMENS

One of the hedge-topped banks which enclosed part of my Devon garden was completely colonized by *Cyclamen neapolitanum*. So generously do these cyclamens seed themselves that every year one can dig up a few dozen small corms and move them to another part of the garden wherever you want this lovely little autumn-flowering cyclamen to naturalize. The bank itself was a typical Devon bank, that is, it had a core of stone and a covering of rather loose, very gritty but fertile soil held in place by grass and weeds. When the corms had to be thinned, I put a sharp spade into the bank, heaved up a great sod of roots, grass and soil, and got my hands right in under the cyclamens. You have to do this in winter, when the leaves are all there at their finest. Some of the corms taken out were as large as a dinner plate, great flat disks of tissue with both leaves and roots rising from the top surface. They move happily at that season, and flower in their new situation the following autumn.

I was reminded to write about cyclamens because while I was moving these Neapolitan ones this year there were other species in flower. The best of the early ones is *C. coum.* When I planted it I had six corms; four never grew again, but two established themselves and are going to spread, although I doubt whether any cyclamen has the remarkable naturalizing power of *neapolitanum.* My form of *coum* is very richly coloured, deep carmine about describes it. The species flowers in February.

Another cyclamen which I planted to naturalize was *C. europaeum.* The leaf has not the beauty of *neapolitanum* which, zoned and richly marked, is almost as decorative as the flowers, but it flowers in March and sometimes also in the autumn, it does not seem able to make up its mind whether it is a spring or autumn flower. In this respect it is like some others of the primula family to which it belongs, but when it does flower in autumn it is not sporadically, like primroses, but generously. But it is usually treated as spring-flowering. Its flowers are either carmine or white; the white variety has scented flowers, but I was not able to keep it for long. On the other hand the white variety of *neapolitanum* is very vigorous indeed, tending to overwhelm the true cyclamen-coloured type.

These three are not the only cyclamens which will naturalize in English gardens. In warm gardens it is possible to establish the white-flushed-pink *C. balearicum* although I have not seen it very flourishing in Britain. *C. graecum*, an autumn-flowering species with carmine flowers, will settle down readily in suitable stations and more or less establish itself, but it rarely naturalizes.

Cyclamen repandum flowers, in English gardens, rather later than any mentioned yet, often in April. This, like *neapolitanum*, has very handsome leaves, although again not as fine as the latter species which has no rival for foliage. The flower-form of the spring-flowering *repandum* is particularly good, the colour some shade of carmine, rather variable.

Although *C. coum* commonly flowers in early February, it is possible to get forms which flower earlier, in January, not long after Christmas. A rather rare species from the Taurus, *C. hiemale*, flowers at the same time. It is, therefore, not very difficult to have cyclamens in flower from the beginning of the year until the end of April. And, again, from September until November. The three which are notably best for naturalizing are *neapolitanum, europaeum* and *repandum*; the others are best treated as rock garden perennials although they will naturalize in ideal conditions. There is another winter or very early spring cyclamen which grows well for some gardeners although it never has for me; this is *C. vernum*, a species with very pretty almost circular, toothed, silver-zoned foliage and flowers which are either carmine, white or, in one rare variety, a true red. This one from North Persia is hardy but difficult to establish.

All these cyclamens seem to like much the same kind of conditions; a fertile but very gritty soil, rather loose, preferably on a bank but in any case with extremely sharp drainage. The three easy naturalizers will stand a certain amount of partial shade, for they can be established at the foot of large trees, and even among shrubs provided they have a clear gap overhead and can, as it were, see the sky. I have found both *neapolitanum* and *europaeum* wild when I have been wandering about Europe:

they are always best on banks with a steep fall. All the others mentioned like stony soil and full sun.

The species from which the giant cyclamens in such an astonishing range of colours, those pot-plants which people give each other as Christmas presents, have been developed, is *C. persicum*. You can get the wild form of this, its flowers are larger than any other and it would be fine if it could be established in the open. But it is tender. I have tried it three times and always lost it. I think it could be established very near to the sea in the extreme south-west. I have on one occasion seen a group (and not even of the wild form but of what had formerly been pot-plants), flowering well in the open, and looking magnificent. This was at the foot of and between two huge root-ridges of an enormous beech-tree. A dozen plants had been set there, in John Innes compost, the tree-roots giving protection from east and west, the trunk itself from north, and the plants exposed to the south. In winter it was quite easy, in cold weather, to lay some protective covering across the two ridges of root. The plants were in their third year out of doors. But the conditions for this sort of special stunt are not commonly met with.

It is easy to raise all cyclamens from seed provided you can get fresh seed; old seed is very slow to germinate. It is worth while taking trouble to sow the seed one by one at a fair distance, allowing each one at least two square inches, and using a deep pan. I suggest this because if you just raise them anyhow, you lose a lot at the pricking out stage. If you allow plenty of space for each one, then a corm the size of a shilling can develop without any need for disturbance. Germination is better, by the way, if the seed is exposed to cold before being brought under glass. But protect the pans against mice which would rather eat cyclamen seed than anything in the garden. It is not wise to plant out the young corms until they are at least as big as a shilling and preferably bigger, so keep the seedlings in their pan for two or three seasons.

LEAF-COLOUR AND FORM

There are two ways in which it is easy to bring out more sharply the beauty of those plants in the garden whose forms and colours are the commoner ones; one is to plant here and there shrubs and herbaceous subjects whose foliage is not green but some other colour; the other is to plant shrubs whose form, whether of individual leaf or of general bearing, is uncommon, or at least uncommon in an English garden.

To deal first with the subject of form: the use of fastigiate shrubs among the spreading, sprawling or bushy forms, is too obvious to call for any discussion; an erect, narrow juniper among spreading shrubs or herbaceous plants which hold themselves like the water of a fountain, is always a striking object drawing attention not only to itself but to the shape, so often unnoticed in detail, of its contrasting neighbours. But there are at least two plants, both of them hardy and not particular about the nature of the soil, which certainly should be more widely planted than they are: I mean the yuccas, and the New Zealand 'flax', *Phormium tenax*. Both give to any plantation in which they are carefully sited a touch of the exotic which favours both themselves and their surroundings. Both have sword-shaped leaves, yet they are very different.

Phormium tenax is a liliaceous plant whose name of New Zealand flax or flax lily derives from the use made of the leaf fibres. It has hitherto been confined to the south-west and Victorian greenhouses, but it is making its way elsewhere, for it is apparently hardier than it was long supposed to be. I know two fine plants of it growing at a high altitude in Surrey where frosts can be sharp; but I do not suppose it is hardy all over the country. It needs a lot of room. The magnificently stout, leathery leaves, beautifully shaped like broadswords, can, in suitably rich loam, attain a height of nine feet although, as a matter of fact, I have not seen any plant with leaves more than six feet long. With age the plant forms a dense, stout clump of these huge leaves rising from a complex crown below which is an enormously thick, tough root. Propagation is by dividing this root, and even with quite a young plant this requires a very sharp tool and a lot of sheer physical strength. One really grows this plant for its leaves, but there is a flower; the stem, rising from among the leaves, ascends to a height of from six to fifteen feet before the flowers open; they are borne in a panicle and are a dull red, rather like hemerocallis. The variety *purpureum* has a much subtler colour than the *purpureum* varieties of green plants usually have. The seedlings of this variety do not germinate purple, or rather, the deep mauve which is the real colour, but green, turning colour later.

Yucca is related to phormium, for it is also liliaceous. The yuccas come from the coastal region of the Southern United States and from Mexico, yet they are extremely hardy, withstanding zero Fahrenheit without suffering any damage. One of the handsomest species, *Y. filamentosa*, does not require a great deal of room, for its head of narrow, sword leaves about thirty inches long rises from a crown, not a real stem. The specific name refers to the filaments, dark, wiry growths from the margins of the leaves which, turning inwards and growing in a series of curves across the faces of the leaves, make the latter look very much as if they had been cut up with a fret-saw to make a jigsaw puzzle, and carefully reassembled. The panicle of flowers on their five- or six-foot stem are creamy bells two inches in diameter and look like Brobdingnagian lilies-of-the-valley. *Y. flaccida* is a smaller plant and, in my opinion, not so handsome, but it is, nevertheless, useful. *Y. glauca* is twice the size and has pale green flowers, but it does not flower regularly. For a regular flowering plant, if you have room, either *Y. gloriosa*, which, having a trunk-like stem which makes it look like a palm-tree, attains eight feet or more; or *Y. recurvifolia*, another tall yucca. There are other species of which I have no experience, and there was, at one time, a considerable number of hybrids produced in Italy but widely planted here; it would be interesting to know if any survive. Hybridization, or even just selection, might give us a truly red-flowered yucca, for at least in *gloriosa* the flowers are frequently tinged with pink*.

For contrasting with and throwing up the beauty of green-leaved plants we can plant those with silver, golden, red or blue foliage. By blue I mean that blue-green described by botanists as *glaucous*. Red-leaved perennials are quite common; among the shrubs the most graceful and manageable are the Japanese maples. However, it is the silver-leaved plants I have a special taste for. A number of these are to be found in the enormous genus *Senecio*, all of them having white, cream or more commonly yellow daisy-flowers of less importance than the foliage. *S. compactus*, not quite hardy north of London, looks almost snow-white when growing among green plants. But its leaves are entire whereas the most beautiful senecios have much divided leaves, some of the finest but, alas, least hardy, looking almost like silver ferns. In the hardy *S. laxifolius* the silvery-white of *compactus* becomes pewtery-grey. The most commonly planted senecio is *elaeagnifolius buchananii*, the plant famous for its indifference to salt spray at the seaside. Other species share this tolerance. Among the most beautiful of the pinnate-leaved varieties are those of *S. leucostachys*, a true silver

* In June 1968 I saw in the Tashkent Botanic Garden the impressive collection of scores of Yucca hybrids bred by Professor Russanov of the Uzbek Acad. of Sciences. As far as I know very few of these magnificent plants have reached the West.

in colour, but not very hardy, though it can be planted in fairly cold districts as a wall shrub.

One of the pleasantest of silver-leaved shrubs, and of very manageable size even in small gardens is a convolvulus from the Mediterranean, *C. cneorum*. Like all the above, it is an evergreen, or, rather, ever-silver. This silvery look is owing to the silky hairs which densely cover all the younger parts of the plant. I have not seen a specimen more than three feet tall and about as much through, and, as a rule, the plants are rather smaller. The flowers are typical convolvulus flowers, white tinged pink, and they are borne in succession throughout the summer so that the shrub is more or less in flower from late spring until early autumn. This convolvulus cannot be planted just anywhere: it is hardy all along the south and west coastal strips, inland in the south and west, near the sea in the east. It is apt to be damaged by hard winters in the Home Counties north-east of London, but even there and in the Midlands it can be planted where there is a really favourable site, with protection from the cold quarters, full exposure to the south, and a dry, sunny bed. I think this plant dislikes cold water rather than just cold.

While on the subject of silver-leaved plants there is one tree which I should like to see widely planted, and which is an object of great beauty: the weeping, silver lime, *Tilia petiolaris*. Growing as a specimen tree, it is one of the most beautiful objects any park or large garden can boast. It attains about eighty feet in time, and perhaps more, although those I have seen are not so large. Its habit is most graceful, the branches pendant in tiers; the silvery look comes from the underside of the leaves when they are stirred by the wind, for they are densely felted with white. The flowers, which appear in July or August are exceptionally fragrant and their nectar is apparently narcotic; at all events, bees get dead drunk on it, and doubtless an infusion of *tilleul* made from this species would be even more soothing than the one commonly served in France.

TWO ITALIAN GARDENS

In her book *Italian Gardens* Georgina Masson distinguishes several different styles and periods of which the two most important to my mind are the Humanist gardens of Tuscany and the great Roman Renaissance gardens. They are very different; and in each of these two classes one garden made a greater impression on me than the rest, although all I have seen, about twenty I suppose, are very beautiful.

When the Tuscans, whose taste was restrained and austere, and the Romans, whose taste was exuberant, the former under the influence of Petrarch, the latter of several artists of genius, began to make gardens they thought they were recreating the classical, hellenistic past. They were surely mistaken about that: nothing seems to me more curious in all the great Italian artistic movement from the fourteenth to the seventeenth century than the difference between what the artists seem to have thought they were doing, and what we can now see them to have been doing. They thought they were reviving Graeco-Latin civilization; in fact they were creating a new one in emulation of the spirit of the old, and particularly in emulation of the moral and intellectual freedom of ancient Greece.

This is true of their garden making as of their other arts. Because they had the letters of the younger Pliny about garden design, and rules laid down by Varro, they thought that they were making Roman gardens. But they were not, they were making something quite new on an old pattern, and the resemblance between Hadrian's Villa and some of the great Renaissance gardens is really rather superficial.

A Tuscan garden which is exquisite in its simplicity and the one which I enjoyed and coveted most, is that of the Villa

Capponi. It is on a hillside, commanding fine views of Florence and is composed of a number of enclosures—rooms without ceilings walled by clipped cypress or box—on different levels connected by stone stairways. The strictest meaning one can give to the words 'Italian Garden' is a garden composed only of a more or less elaborate pattern of clipped box to form a sort of embroidery or *ricarmi* on the ground. The finest I have seen of these is that of the private garden of the Villa Doria Pamphili. The Villa Capponi garden has its *ricarmi* garden, and in it, in the framed spaces provided by the box pattern, stand great terracotta vases planted with old lemon trees; that is called, if I remember rightly, the Lemon Garden. On its walls are climbing roses and its issue into the next enclosure is by way of an imposing griffin-crowned gateway. The stairway to the lower level and another enclosure, or rather two more, is planted with wistaria. One of the lower enclosures exactly demonstrated the simplicity of the Tuscan garden taste; it is an oblong enclosure walled by clipped cypress and containing nothing but a long, narrow pool coped with ancient stone and fed by a small dolphin fountain. The most interesting thing about it is that it was made quite recently by the American owner of the villa; it could not have been done with more perfect aesthetic tact.

These Tuscan gardens of connected garden rooms made of evergreens and decorated with only a few flowering plants and fruit trees, are exactly what a garden-as-living-room ought to be; they are not merely to look at, but to live in. They do not excite, they soothe. They do not emulate or reproduce 'nature', they order and defy her.

The other garden, to me the superlative example of the grand Renaissance style, is that of the Villa d'Este at Tivoli. Georgina Masson says of it:

'. . . it represents the quintessence of the Italian garden of the High Renaissance. Every inch of space within its boundaries was subject to man-made order and symmetry, and although scaled to draw the fullest effect from the vast spaces of the surrounding landscape, it is entirely separated from it. As Luigi Dami pointed out in his classic book on Italian gardens, the Renaissance garden architect treated his terrain as an artist who sets out to plan the composition of a picture with the limits of his canvas. He first reduced the ground to a simple regular figure and inside this everything was arranged in accordance with an overall design. The main perspectives, whose effect was carefully calculated, began and ended at clearly defined fixed points. Usually, as in the Belvedere and Villa d'Este, they crossed the terraces of a hillside garden at right angles. These crossings, and even those of subsidiary paths, were marked by open spaces and all of them were planned in relation to each other like the traffic centres of a city, and accentuated by fountains or stonework of some kind.

'The Villa d'Este might well be cited as the textbook example of a garden of this type, for perhaps nowhere else have the details of such a layout been so carefully worked out and these basic principles of Italian garden design so clearly demonstrated. Unfortunately, we approach the garden today from the wrong end; it was never intended to be viewed from the house but to be entered from the gate on the old Tivoli road at the bottom. From here, even with a much freer type of planting, it still appears as a magnificent series of vistas, rising one above the other and culminating in a grand climax where the great villa stands outlined against the clear blue sky.

'Each pause in the ascent of this hillside garden, whether by the direct perspectives of the paths and steps or by the diagonals of the ramps or *cordonate* that recall Praeneste and the Belvedere, is marked by a new and varied use of water; by fish ponds at the lower level, glittering water staircases as the climb begins, then by great monumental fountains enclosed in garden rooms among the trees. The superb promenade of the "hundred fountains"

. . . provides a breathing space before the steepest part of the journey, but even here, in the thickly planted *bosco*, the terminal and junction points of the ramps are marked by grottoes and fountains. Finally one last silver jet sprays upwards to the sky as the great open terrace before the villa is reached and at last the climber turns to gaze at the vast panorama of the Roman *campagna*.

'Where did Ligorio draw his inspiration for this dramatic and all-pervading use of water? The answer is almost certainly in Hadrian's villa that lies only a few miles away in the plain. In his somewhat muddled description of Hadrian's villa, of which he drew a plan for Ippolito d'Este, Ligorio even employed some of the same terms as were applied to the fountains in Villa d'Este. Thus he described the stretch of water in the Canopus as being made like the Euripus, and he imagined that the semicircular triclinium at the end had some connexion with the Tiburtine Sybil, because it was designed, so he maintained, to echo the whispered (in Italian to whisper is *sibillare*) answers of the Gods. Some of the results of his examination of the Canopus *triclinium*, and his muddled thinking about it, are embodied in the great fountain of the *ovata* in the Villa d'Este, of which Hubert Robert made a bistre wash drawing which is one of the most beautiful and evocative representations of an Italian garden scene in existence. Here a great waterfall flows out from beneath the feet of a statue of the Tiburtine Sybil, beneath which a semicircular loggia is cut into the hill. This contains fountains, niches, and small waterways that were undoubtedly inspired by the similar arrangement, on a larger scale, in the *triclinium* of the Canopus. It is interesting to note that Antonio Del Re, who wrote a commentary upon Ligorio's work at Villa d'Este and Hadrian's villa in 1611 and published part of his descriptions of the latter, refers to both the waterways of the Canopus and the fountain of the *ovata* as being '*a guisa di euripo*'—like an Euripus.'

But whereas the water works in Hadrian's villa are level and calm, the water works of the Villa d'Este compose a great orchestra of gushings and tricklings, and a great picture of moving patterns in water.

There is a garden at Bagnaia, the Villa Lante, which was made for Cardinal Gambara by the architect Vignola which in some measure combines the qualities of the simple Tuscan garden and the grand Roman Renaissance garden; and it is certainly one of the half dozen loveliest gardens I have ever seen. Water is important in this garden, but it is not overwhelming in its effect; immediately inside the gates is a pool with a Pegasus surrounded by water nymphs by Giambologna. (Was this Pegasus the inspiration of the pair at Powerscourt, I wonder?) And central to the whole garden, a sort of backbone, is an extraordinary water-staircase or cascade in which the water falls from a fountain at the top through a stone channel made in the form of an elongated series of *gamberi* (crawfish, a play on the Cardinal's name). The water, at the foot of the stairs passes through a central channel in the great stone outdoor dining table—a device copied from Hadrian's villa—and into a formal square lake centred on a lovely fountain composed of four boys holding up the 'mounts' (little hills) of the armorial coat of a later owner, Cardinal Montalto; and this is surmounted by a star of water. This garden is grand, but, as it were, very quietly grand. And like all Italian gardens of whatever type, age or style, even to the modern attempts at abstract or surrealist gardening, it is a setting for the recreational activities of men, and not for the display of flowers; a lovely frame, not a picture.

VARIEGATA

A clever and successful gardener of my acquaintance insists that foliage is long and flowers short, in the sense that art is long and life is short: we should, he says, pay more attention to foliage and less to flowers when we plant.

In her introduction to the pamphlet which she wrote to describe the gardens at Dartington Hall, Mrs Dorothy Elmhirst begins: 'If the word garden implies a wealth of flowers, then for Dartington it is a misnomer, since flowers in profusion will not be found here.' The design of the garden, she goes on, has been dominated by form. What, in fact, had been achieved there as in other gardens in which the classic and the newer English traditions have been well combined, is the perfect use of flowers as grace-notes. But colour in mass is not wanting, and a thorough examination of this and similar gardens will convince all but the flower-fanatic that mass colour effects are better achieved with foliage than with flowers. Too often if flowers are massed to accomplish a big splash of colour, the result is 'noisy' and furthermore the beauty of the individual flowers is lost. Some of the most shocking blunders in garden design are, for example, produced by the mass planting of Kurume azaleas: their colour shrieks at you across half a parish. It is significant that the Japanese, with their exquisite if austere taste in gardening, often refuse to allow these azaleas to flower at all: they use the plants as clipped evergreens.

It would be quite easy, however, to make the same mistake with leaves as with the mass planting of flowers for large areas of colour. A garden, in my opinion, should be chiefly green; but shrubs with variegated or coloured foliage can be used to vary the background, to lighten it, to give it texture and depth. I do not mean the planting of one here and there; the effect of that is apt to be spotty. Groups of colourful foliage shrubs are better than specimens, although there are obvious exceptions to this general rule. Reverting to Dartington, for an example, a great bank of the purple-leaved rhus (*R. cotinus foliis purpureis* 'Notcutt's variety') is immensely effective.

There are, however, some variegated shrubs with the most subtle and beautiful colouring and although they are not the hardiest of their kind more use might be made of them in many gardens. There is, in particular, one colour scheme of which I am especially fond and which is to be found, with variations of great interest, in at least three different genera and probably in more of which I know nothing. This colour scheme is at its best in *Pittosporum tenuifolium* 'Barretii'. I have no idea how hardy or rather tender this exquisite plant may be; at one time there was an idea that pittosporum of all species must be confined to the south-west; then it was found that some would grow and survive the winter along the south coast. And some even survive in inland gardens where they can be sheltered by the house or by garden walls and other shrubs and trees. I do not pretend that they are hardy. As for *P. tenuifolium* 'Barretii', it is a rare plant and very likely tender. It is hard to describe: the base colour of the leaves is a silvery-gilt but they have a narrow margin of burgundy red and this has, as it were, 'run' into the silvery-gilt and in running lost some density, so that the surface of the leaves is shot with pink. The stalks of the leaves are a darker version of this same purplish-red.

The other two shrubs which I have grown which have a similar combination of colours are *Drimys colorata* and *Cornus alternifolia variegata*. In the latter case there may be another adjective missing from the name, for this shrub or small tree is described in the reference books as silver-variegated. But, as I saw it, the variegation was not really silver, but silver-gilt, and the leaves were splashed, dotted, striped and blotched with a soft purple, the colour being dense and concentrated and continuous in the margins. For neatness and delicacy the drimys lies between the other two; again we have silver-gilt, and several shades of the same purplish-red, sometimes dense, sometimes watered down to pink. Though neither the drimys nor the pittosporum are hardy, the cornus, as far as I know is. But for the really cold garden I believe that the finest variegated shrubs, whether the variegation be silver or gold, are our own variegated hollies, and I have occasionally seen in silver hollies a touch of the same pink as in the species named above.

Here are two other fine variegated shrubs which are hardy anywhere in Britain: *Elaeagnus pungens aureo-variegata* and *Elaeagnus ebbingei*. The first has large leaves for the genus, with deep green margins and deep yellow centres, and is extremely effective. Its greatest charm, however, is in the young growth; the young leaves open neither green nor yellow, but exactly the colour of gold-dust. This shrub needs watching: from time to time it produces strong growths with plain leaves; these, having an ample supply of chlorophyll are more efficient than the variegated foliage, and unless they are promptly cut or broken off at the junction with the main branch they spring from, the whole shrub, will, in a surprisingly short time, become a plain green one. Such growths should be removed every season. The other elaeagnus is silvery-green, rather like a good *Pittosporum tenuifolium*.

If you can grow that pittosporum, by the way, you can probably grow its very beautiful variety 'Silver Queen'. The leaves of this are in two shades of silver, dark in the centre and lighter on the margins. But the variety, one of the most beautiful of all silver trees, is not quite as hardy as the type and it should have some shelter. As, in any case, it is best planted against a background of ordinary evergreens, they can also shield it from the east and north. Even more lovely than this one is a pittosporum which really is only for mild parts and the frost-free (or almost frost-free) coastal strip: *P. eugenioides* 'Argentea Variegata'. The leaves of this one while they have the same pretty waviness as *tenuifolium*, are much larger, especially longer. Here again we have the silver of the middle part of the leaves darker than the silver of the margins, but an extra beauty is that there is, in this variety, a trace of the pink flushing of the silver which makes *P.* 'Barretii' such a beauty.

Red leaved shrubs, like the rhus mentioned above, are not strictly in place under this heading; so I will pass over the range of maples which are the best plants for that colour. A silver variegated shrub which delighted me when I saw it but which is by no means easy to obtain, is *Osmanthus ilicifolius argentea.* It looks like a dwarf, very bushy, and very fine-leaved holly and the silver variegation is snow white without, in the specimens I have been able to examine closely, any tinge of colour at all.

If you are propagating variegated shrubs by making cuttings, there is one point of importance to remember: do not use shoots in which the leaves are almost silver, pale gold or white; they are so short of chlorophyll that they will not survive separation from the parent plant. You must use shoots with some green or near green.

CLEMATIS

Clematis are grouped according to their specific origins, and the groups are numerous, but for the gardener's purposes, e.g. of pruning, they can be reduced to three: (i) *montana* and *alpina* varieties; (ii) *patens* and *florida* varieties, and the *lanuginosa* group; (iii) the *texensis* group, the *jackmanii* hybrids and the *viticella* groups—there are two of these, large-flowered and small-flowered.

The *alpina* clematis have many small, often bell-shaped flowers, and they do not seem to be much grown, which is a pity. The variety *sibirica* is white, and flowers in May. The nearly-related *sibirica* 'Ruby' has rose-pink flowers which open in April. Of the *montana* group, the best known and most commonly seen is *grandiflora*, which produces a dense mass of small white flowers, and, where it does well, so dense that the flowers completely hide the foliage and the supporting structure or tree. *Montana rubens* has pink instead of white flowers, and there are several strains, one of them scented and the best being much nearer red than the type. All these, and others in the *alpina* and *montana* groups, should be pruned to form a permanent framework of main branches properly set out and tied in by cutting to within a foot of the ground a year after planting, say in February; and, again, to within five or six feet a year later. Thereafter the main branches can be allowed to grow to the length required to cover the space available, and then kept pruned back at the tips. As to all other growth, it is what fruit-growers would call 'spur' pruned. After flowering, say in the first two weeks of August, all side-shoots are cut back to within an inch or two of the main branch. The short spurs left then make flower buds for next year, and a close, neat pattern of flower will result, instead of a tangled mess. However, this method really only relates to wall plants or clematis on trellis. Where it is being left to ramble over old trees, hardly any pruning can be done.

A very good violet-flowered clematis of the *patens* group is 'Barbara Dibley', which flowers in early June. In this group, the deepest, almost purple, blue that I know is called 'Lasurstern'. Included with *patens* here, simply because it needs the same kind of pruning, is the only *florida* I know (although there are others), and it is, in my opinion by far the most striking of all the clematis, which is saying a great deal. This is *florida bicolor*, and it is not particularly easy to buy a plant: I saw it first in the beautiful garden of Great Dixter, in Sussex; and later at Bodnant. The flowers have cream sepals (clematis flowers have no petals; the things that look like petals are, in fact sepals), then a rosette of very deep purple petaloid stamens—which are like small petals, so that they are suggestive of passion flowers.

Patens and *florida* clematis all flower on new shoots from the previous year's wood. They cannot, therefore, be rigorously pruned at all, or you will get no flowers. The plants are bound to get slowly larger and larger. Tangling can only be avoided if the main branches are carefully set out and fixed in place. After flowering, remove the dead flowers or fruits just above a good bud on the flowering stalk, for that stalk will send out the shoots which carry *next* year's flowers, and so on *ad infinitum*, or at least until the plant dies in the mysterious and distressing manner of its kind.

Of the *jackmanii* group, with their large flowers, the best known and commonest, and very good it is, is *jackmanii* itself. 'Gypsy Queen' is dark purple, 'Perle d'Azur' light blue. All this group flower in July and into August. The only *lanuginosa* I know personally is 'Miriam Markham', with lavender flowers; there are better ones, notably 'Mrs Cholmondeley', which is a purer colour and flowers more freely over a longer season, beginning in May. I had one *texensis*, 'Gravetye Beauty', which flowered in September and is quite a good red.

These, and all the others in their groups, and in the *viticella* groups, are pruned either by cutting back everything to the base at the main branch or to just above the first node from the base. Or they are even cut right back to the ground, as they often throw vigorous new growth, which will flower, from the root.

If you can persuade it to clamber over some not-very-distinguished shrub or small tree, there is a great deal to be said for a Chinese clematis, *C. tangutica*, which has small, brilliant yellow flowers shaped like little lampshades, but with the sepals pointed. The Gravetye variety of this species is an improvement on the type. It produces, after flowering, the same kind of silky seed-heads as our native *vitalba*, but instead of being silver, they are gold. I confess, however, that, for whatever reason, I cannot get it to survive in my garden.

Not many gardeners know that there is a winter-flowering clematis, *C. calycina*; it is an evergreen: it cannot be planted just anywhere, for it is not perfectly hardy, but it seems to be happy on walls in the south-west and would probably be worth trying anywhere in the southern half of England, where it can be given a protected site. The foliage turns from green to bronze in winter; the flowers, which may be produced from November to February but apparently are most plentiful late in January, are broken white with reddish speckles and about one and a half inches in diameter when open. A synonym for this species is *C. balearica*, its habitat is South Europe, presumably including the Balearics, and that will give some idea of the kind of climate it requires.

The prettiest clematis I know is *C. macropetala*; the very numerous flowers are as nearly blue as any clematis, and shaped like little bells. I have found this an easy and good-tempered plant in a wide range of soils; I have grown it in chalk; I have had it doing very well with its roots mixed up with those of a flourishing young camellia, that is in acid peat. I hardly pruned it at all, but found it necessary to bring down the main stems from time to time and tie them in horizontally, otherwise all the growth occurs at the top and these stems become bare.

The evergreen clematis are rare in our gardens, and there is no need for this. *Clematis armandii* could be much more commonly planted: it has deep green, glossy evergreen leaves of three narrow leaflets, a stout woody stem, and racemes of pure white, rather waxy-looking, flowers about two inches in diameter; the plant is a great beauty of the very highest class. At Dartington Hall, where it has been cleverly used to decorate the balustrade of a stone staircase in the garden, they have had a curious difficulty with this clematis: the bark of the stems seems to be relished by wood-lice which do it great damage. The worst enemy of the woodlouse is, it seems, lizards, if only you can establish them permanently in your garden. *C. armandii* will climb to about twenty feet, but it is better used as a scrambler; as to its hardiness, it is safe in the south and west, elsewhere it needs, and would ordinarily in any case get, a wall.

An evergreen clematis which is unfortunately tender is one of the most beautiful, *C. indivisa.* It comes from New Zealand, where it is common in the wild. The very many pendant flowers are on long stalks, they are greenish-white, about an inch in diameter, cup-shaped, and with most decorative stamens, for their stalks are yellow but their anthers pink. The species is dioecious, and the male plant has the larger flowers. *C. indivisa* grows well at Bodnant, although temperatures can be quite low there, but even in such a climate it needs a very protected site. In Cornwall it is very much at home.

THE CLIMBING FIG

Although it may once have been not uncommon on the walls of conservatories and may indeed still survive in some old green-houses, *Ficus stipulata* is a rare shrub out of doors in this country. It is referred to by W. J. Bean as growing on the wall of St Matthew's Church, Chelston, 'near' Torquay. Chelston is, in fact, more or less in Torquay, or at least connected with it by residential streets. I was pleased to find that the plant is still flourishing; obviously, it must have survived the savage winters of 1947 and 1962/3, which is encouraging since it is regarded as very doubtfully hardy, even in the milder counties: but I have more to say about that.

This fig is a woody shrub at the base, with the very smooth, elephant-grey bark characteristic of the genus, a genus which has, incidentally, no fewer than 600 species including such interesting ones as the india-rubber tree, *F. elastica*, the Bo-tree, *F. religiosa*, and the Banyan. But the branches and lateral shoots which grow densely from the trunk are self-clinging to walls or trees; a careful examination shows that this is one of the all too rare plants which cling really tight and close, like ivy or *Hydrangea petiolaris*. It is a most attractive shrub: the leaves, elongated heart-shaped, or rather like those of a small-leaved camellia, are a bright, clean, glossy green, and being evergreen, they are like that all winter. I did not actually measure the Chelston plant, but I should say that it had covered about ten feet laterally and was rather more than seven feet tall. Quite possibly it has been bigger and has been cut down by hard weather and recovered. Or it may be fairly slow-growing. I have not been able to find this fig in any nursery catalogue, only a variety or cultivar of it, of which more later.

Does it bear fruit? As far as I can discover, it has done so occasionally in the past in conservatories. Whether it has ever borne any at Chelston, I do not know. The fruit as described by Bean must be spectacular if not edible, another thing I do not know. Here is Bean's description:

'Fruit of the ordinary fig shape although more tapered at the end than in the common fig; 2½ inches long and 1½ inches wide at the terminal part, tapering thence to a stalk which is half an inch long; in colour it is at first green, then bright orange, ultimately tinged with reddish purple and decorative.'

These fruits are not borne on the lower part of the shrub, the part I have described. This part is what botanists call the 'juvenile state' of the plant. But after the fig has grown to a certain height (Bean says after it has reached ten or twelve feet and over-topped its support), it starts to produce growth of quite a different kind: stout shoots which are more or less at right-angles to the direction of growth which is erect, appear, and the leaves which they bear differ from those of the juvenile state: these adult leaves are described (I have not seen them) as being ovate, leathery and at least twice the size of the juvenile leaves. It is among these bigger, thicker leaves that the fruit is borne.

On the subject of hardiness, Bean has this to say:

'. . . I did not realise how hardy it really is until the late Mr W. Robinson of Gravetye told me that he had seen it growing on the walls of Knapp Castle near Horsham, covering up much of the front to forty feet high. It has been growing there for over thirty years.'

Now, this means that the plant had survived, at a place where the winters can be severe although less so than in the Midlands and the North, no fewer than five, and probably more, really hard winters. On a wall, then, the species is not so tender.

I mentioned that the only *F. stipulata* I can find in the catalogues is a variety, not the type. Messrs Hillier of Winchester, the nursery with by far the widest range of species and especially of rare plants in their stock, have *F. stipulata minima*. Of this they say, in the rather terse and business-like style which distinguishes their extraordinary list:

'This pleasing miniature creeper will cling like a limpet to the flat surface of a rock or wall. In a sheltered position it has survived twenty-five years out of doors at Winchester.'

F. stipulata is the only climbing fig which Bean includes as hardy in favoured parts of the country, but it is not the only one in the genus and it might be worth trying to discover whether one or two of the others are as tender as they are supposed, and by their habitat ought to be. There is a Malayan species, *F. villosa*, occasionally met with as a hothouse creeper which has the same climbing habits as *F. stipulata*, which, by the way, is more commonly and for all I know correctly known as *F. pumila*. And there is *F. radicans*, apparently a ground-covering evergreen trailer of unknown provenance.

DIOECIOUS

The majority of flowering plants either have hermaphrodite flowers or they bear the flowers of both sexes on the same plant; in relatively few cases the male flowers are borne on one individual, the female on another. As a general rule this is of no great importance to the gardener but there are two kinds of cases when it is: sometimes the flowers of one sex are better than those of the other; and, in the second case, where a plant is being grown for its ornamental or edible fruits, then it is important to have individuals of both sexes.

There are a few cases in which whereas the wild plants are dioecious—that is have the male flowers on one individual, the female on another—the cultivars of the same species have hermaphrodite flowers: the outstanding case of this change is that of *Vitis vinifera*, the wine-grape of History and the desert fruit vine on which we depend for table grapes. In the wild there are vines with male flowers, vines with female flowers; and a very

very small number of vines with hermaphrodite flowers. How is it, then, that almost all cultivated grape-vines have hermaphrodite flowers? Simply because when, thousands of years ago, vines were first being taken into cultivation from the wild, those which bore the most fruit were, generation after generation, selected for propagation as the best in the plantation. Now a plant with hermaphrodite flowers will obviously set more fruit, as a rule, than a vine with female flowers only, since such a one depends on pollen being carried to it from a male-flowering plant. The males would have been eliminated from a plantation of vines brought in from the wild, since they were, of course, unfruitful. This would have left the females in the plantation without a source of pollen, so they too would have become unfruitful, or much less fruitful, (they would have received some pollen from the hermaphrodite members of the plantation). Thus the hermaphrodite vines would have been the ones retained, and by vegetative propagation would have come to dominate the vineyards until they were the only kind grown.

But that is an exceptional case.

In a few flowering shrubs it is worth knowing that the genus is dioecious because male and female flowers differ. Two cases which come to mind are the tender *Clematis indivisa*, in which the male plant has the larger flowers; and *Garrya elliptica* in which whereas the catkins of the male plant are from six to twelve inches long depending on the local climate, those of the female are only about two inches long.

The two most striking cases of dioecious berrying plants which occur to me are *Skimmia japonica* and *Ilex aquifolium*, the common holly. Skimmia, for those who do not know it, is a low, bushy, handsome evergreen remarkable for its tolerance of shade and for its decorative merit in fruit. But as the male flowers are very rarely to be found on the same plant as the female, it is necessary to plant about one male to every half dozen females in order to get a good display of berries. The same is true of hollies but here the matter of choosing the right ones is complicated by variegation.

You may want your silver or golden hollies to bear berries, like the green ones. But the particular variegation you prefer will usually be found confined to one sex, and if it happens to be male then, of course, you will get no berries. It happens like that because named variegated cultivars are clones, that is all individuals of the kind derive by vegetative propagation from a single mutant plant, and are virtually identical with it. So it is important when buying hollies to study the nurseryman's list of varieties very carefully and be sure of the sex of your plants. And do not judge by name alone; for example, 'Golden Queen' is a male and so bears no berries, while 'Golden King' is a berrying female.

PERIWINKLES

> Through primrose tufts, in that green bower,
> The periwinkle trailed its wreaths,
> And 'tis my faith that every flower
> Enjoys the air it breathes.

Thus Wordsworth; and thus, for that matter, the facts, at least as to the first two lines: for there are half a dozen places in any old, neglected garden where periwinkles trail their wreaths among primrose tufts, and indeed among every other kind of plants. No genus is easier to naturalize in damp and shady places, on banks and at the foot of hedges and I fancy that it is because such are the places where it is usually planted that flowering in Britain is apt to be rather sparse. I should not have known this, and would have taken the rather spotty blooming of this plant for its natural habit, had I not seen it in Portugal and in the Canary Islands blooming with such abandoned freedom that hedges and grass plots were dyed blue for hundreds of yards. I noted that in such cases of generous flowering, the plants, all of them *Vinca major*, had raised themselves into the sun by clambering up a support. In Britain, one's impression of this plant is of an evergreen, its green sparingly relieved by a few trumpet-shaped flowers of heavenly blue. In Portugal it has no such modesty, but is a tangle of closely-packed blue flowers relieved by a touch of green leaves. No doubt the periwinkle likes to have its roots and those barren repent stems which enable it to spread and re-root itself, in the shady damp; but I believe that its erect flowering stems should be given a chance to see the sun.

The name *Vinca* has been derived from *vincio*, I bind; and certainly the plant binds everything within its reach. But one of Pliny's names for it is *pervinca*, and it must have been the commoner one or we should call the plant winkle rather than periwinkle.

Is this genus, in the two species *V. major* and *V. minor*, a native? Modern authorities say, of its habitat, 'Europe, including Britain,' but Sowerby, albeit usually ready to confer British nationality in doubtful cases, says of it, 'Doubtless planted, though perfectly naturalized.' At all events, it has been here for a very long time: I have a note in my ill-kept garden diary, again culled from Sowerby, of a single line in an unidentified border ballad: 'A garlande of pervenke set on his head.' Periwinkle was evidently used as a chaplet to crown heroes, like bay. Chaucer has this plant as *pervinke*, which is the link between the Latin and our own name for it. Sowerby drily accounts for its rarity in 'modern' poets by reference to the difficulty of bringing in its unmanageable name.

Periwinkle is said to flower in April and May: I have seen it in full flower in south Europe by mid-February. Probably, in this country, its full flush of blossom is in late April, but *V. major* has a valuable and charming habit which the books ignore: that of producing a few flowers almost throughout the winter months. Wherever in my Devon garden, a trailer of *V. major* managed to get an erect shoot up into full daylight and the wintry sunshine, there were half a dozen of its caerulean flowers, quite undamaged by even very rough weather. It may be that this habit is confined to the warmer counties or to favourable sites, but I have seen periwinkle flowers in Kentish hedge bottoms in December, and the habit is well worth noting.

V. major has larger leaves, larger flowers, longer trailers, which are tip-rooting, than *V. minor* which re-roots at shorter intervals. This habit of tip-rooting makes the propagation of both species very easy: you just cut a trailer, lift it, and replant elsewhere. I would choose *V. minor* for ground cover: it is excellent for that purpose for where it is well suited by the soil and situation it smothers almost everything else. For covering banks or clambering through hedges, *V. major* is preferable.

It is a pity that one so rarely sees either the excellent varieties of these two species, or still more rarely the exotic species. The pink flowered *V. rosea* is a tropical plant needing a stove house; but what of the autumn-flowering *V. difformis* with its elegant habit of carrying the flowers in the upper leaf-axils of erect shoots, to form a natural bouquet? I can find it in only one of the catalogues I keep by me. I saw, near Malaga, a variety of this species, presumably *bicolor* with blue and white flowers, and the variety *dubia* has flowers of a very deep true blue. Both *V. major* and *minor* have white varieties, but of all my nurseryman's lists only Jackman's, Ingwersen's and Notcutt's seem to carry any stock of these: 'Miss Jekyll's White', is recommended for its very repent habit as an ideal over-carpet for dwarf bulbs; *minor alba* has smaller flowers. Jackman's and Ingwersen's but none of the others whose lists I have, also carry double-flowering varieties, *flore pleno*, with double blue rosetted flowers; and *multiplex*, with double purple rosetted flowers. Ingwersen alone stocks *difformis*. *V. minor* has more varieties than *major*. It has double white (*alboplena*), several different kinds of variegated varieties, one of them silver, a variety with coppery red flowers, *cuprea*, which is very hard indeed to obtain. There are a number of purple varieties and *V. minor* var. 'La Grave' has very big lavender-coloured flowers, but the only garden where I have seen it is the Vilmorin-Andrieux nursery in France: Ingwersen lists it, but as 'deep blue'. The same nursery's 'Burgundy' is wine red.

A species which I do not know personally, which appears in none of my lists, but which, from its botanical description, sounds interesting, is *V. herbacea*, not, like the others, a sub-shrub, but an herbaceous, hardy perennial. This plant has no barren shoots, all its stems bear flowers; and it sounds as if it would make a border plant, for its habit is relatively compact.

V. minor nana variegata (what fun taxonomists must have), looks like a miniature of *V. minor argenteo-variegata*, that is to say it has the same silvery variegated foliage, and very pale periwinkle flowers, but it is in every way a much smaller plant. Its leaves do not exceed half an inch in length, and its flowers are about the size of a shilling, or smaller. It makes a very charming rock-garden subject and it is as easy to propagate as any other.

It is probable that wherever the ordinary *vinca* species will grow, all these varieties will do just as well, so that unless you have a passion for pure blue your carpeting with vincas can be done in quite a wide range of colours.

SHRUBBY POTENTILLAS

Among the least troublesome and most rewarding of small shrubs are the potentillas. Rock gardeners are as a rule enthusiasts for the herbaceous perennials of this genus, but the shrubby species and their hybrids are less frequently planted than they might be. I have a number of them both doing very well in the garden and I propose to plant more, for among other good qualities they are in flower from early in June, or even late in May, well into September; and between the middle of July and the end of August, they are completely covered with flowers.

The species involved are *Potentilla fruticosa*, which has a very wide range and is native to Britain as well as so many other places; and *P. glabra*, from Central China. Each has its varieties, and there are several hybrids between them. This, naturally, means that there is some variation in the habit, size and bearing of the plants, and in flower colours; but, broadly speaking, they are all rather dense, twiggy shrubs which do not much exceed four feet tall even when quite old, but some of which may sprawl over six feet of ground or more, making useful medium-height ground cover. The colour of foliage varies between a good bright green to a dull silvery-green, the leaves being 'stipulate', 'palmate' or 'pinnate'.

The flowers range in colour from pure white, through cream and lemon yellow, to deep chrome yellow, and in size from one to one and a half inches in diameter, being shaped like strawberry flowers.

P. fruticosa arbuscula, perhaps the commonest garden species, comes from the Far East. It does not grow above four feet in height, but in time will cover six feet in both horizontal directions, and perhaps more. This makes it very useful as a base for a pyramid-shaped *massif* of shrubs planted about a tall-growing tree, whereas in a mixed border it is apt to become too demanding of space. The dense shade under it, for it is very close in texture unless pruned, is discouraging to weeds, and nothing but the most perennial weeds such as couch-grass, which ought not to be there anyway can really grow under this potentilla. Its flowers, with which it is extremely generous over a period of four months, are pale yellow. The flowers of its near relation *P. fruticosa farreri* are a brighter yellow and it has extremely fine, delicate foliage with tiny leaflets. It is a better border plant in that, being about as tall as *arbuscula*, it rarely sprawls or spreads beyond three or four feet.

'Jackman's Variety' has three good points: it is a strain of our native *Potentilla fruticosa*, the flowers are a very bright yellow and slightly cup-shaped, and it confines itself to about a yard square of the border, growing to a yard tall. However, unless you have a very large garden, or a mania for potentillas, *one* of the above three is really enough.

The kind usually listed as *P. fruticosa mandshurica* is actually a variety of the Manchurian (also Japanese and Chinese) species *P. glabra*, introduced only about forty years ago to our gardens. Its white leaf pubescence gives it a silvery grey look, its flowers, too, are ghostly, a pale cream, and its habit of growth is exceptionally graceful, the branches being arched instead of straight and rigid. This potentilla is a dwarf for the front of the border or the foot of a larger congener, for although it may in time cover four square feet of ground, its height does not exceed eighteen inches. There are other grey or silvery foliaged potentillas: the dwarfish *P. fruticosa tenuifolia*, and a white-flowered *P. glabra*, neither of which I can get. And, going from the dwarfs to the giants, *P. f. sulphurascens* var. *vilmoriniana*, usually listed as *P. fruticosa vilmoriniana*, which may attain six feet and which has white or pale ivory flowers coming into their main flush of bloom in August and continuing into October. A white-flowered variety of, I think, *fruticosa*, but with green foliage, is 'Mount Everest' which begins to flower in June.

These are the ones I know, but there are others. The dwarf varieties require no care at all, excepting for ordinary cultivating round them. But those which grow to four feet or more should occasionally receive some attention: if they are to be kept growing to a satisfactory shape and flowering well, the old branches should be pruned out in March, whereupon there will be new growth from low down. One experienced nurseryman recommends, for those who wish to keep their shrub potentillas small and bushy and never allow them to sprawl, that they be pruned to the ground every spring, so that the season's growth is always new. At all events, they are highly adaptable plants and quite willing to take whatever shape and to some extent to assume whatever size is convenient to the gardener.

Fresh stock can be propagated by digging down beside the old plant and cutting away one or two twigs of the 'crown'—it is not really a crown—with some root to them. Potentillas will also grow from cuttings, layers and finally from seeds, coming true or nearly so. Incidentally all the shrubby potentillas intercross readily, so that if you have a number of varieties growing closely together, and collect seed, you may get something new and interesting among the seedlings, although that is not perhaps very likely.

ANEMONES

By far the most striking of true anemones, that is excluding pulsatillas and hepaticas, which I have ever seen growing wild, were in Sicily. These were *A. coronaria*, better known by the name of a race of cultivars derived from the species, 'St Brigid'. I found them flowering everywhere and in great profusion very early in the year, February if I remember rightly, and that despite the fact that it was horribly cold, for I was there in that infamous winter/spring which slew orange trees and injured olive trees well south of Naples. I found these anemones in the grass of ditches and banks, but more plentifully on ploughed land, as a weed of cultivation, and looking like poppies among the young corn. This seems to me curious when one considers that the tubers must have been constantly disturbed by plough and harrow. It may be, however, that the tubers go deep and that Sicilian cultivation, being rather primitive, is shallow. I could not see that the cultivated 'St Brigid' anemones were in any way superior to the species, excepting for variety of colour: in the wild, the red were predominant.

Another handsome race of florists' anemones derives from cultivars of *A. pavonina*. These, the 'St Bavo' anemones, I have seen wild in Italy, and again they compare well with the garden strain. I have never been very successful with either of these races in the garden.

The year of my encounter with *A. coronaria* in Sicily was a good 'ranunculous' year, to coin an adjective, for it was while crossing the Col de Tribes on the way home that I found—never to identify and never to see again at least until now—by far the most magnificent pulsatilla I have ever seen. Its strong, stout stems held the flowers waist high, and the flowers were great burgundy red cups in a hairy ruff of silvery green.

Many years ago I saw in a Cornish garden to which I was introduced by the owner's son, and which has since, like so much of that outraged county, been covered with bungalows, a single perfect clump of *A. glauciifolia*, perhaps the most beautiful species of the whole family, and certainly the most lovely of the genus. The gardener had brought the seeds home with him from,

I believe, South China. The flowering stems stood about thirty inches tall and the big, satiny, mauve flowers were carried in groups of two or three, forming umbel-like heads. I promised myself to grow this distinguished anemone, only to discover that it will not grow in the eastern counties and is extremely rarely successful in the west. The books describe the plant as tap-rooted, so that presumably it requires a deep soil.

For naturalizing in open woodland or near the skirts of shrubberies, the best species are *A. nemorosa*, our own wood anemone; *A. apennina*, which has small, frilly, pale-blue flowers, and *A. blanda*, whose flowers are much darker blue. If you plant *A. nemorosa* an effort should be made to get the best varieties, for this is a very variable species; *grandiflora* or *alba major* has much larger and more substantial flowers than the type; *robinsoniana* has lavender-blue flowers, so have *allenii* and *cornubiense*. There are likewise some more or less pink forms, but I find the colour poor, even in the variety *rubra*, which starts white and turns pink as it opens. The finest display of these wood anemones, including the *apennina* and *blanda*, which I have yet seen was in the backs of one, or perhaps several, Cambridge colleges; I think *blanda* was the principal species. But they were also very fine indeed in one part of the late Lady Nicolson's Sissinghurst garden, and I hope still are. A short, sloping path in my own garden, which is in deep shade and gets only a glimpse of sun for a couple of hours a day, was edged with anemones . . . mostly *apennina*, and they were in flower and looking very charming even during bitter weather in early March.

A. fulgens is a spectacular colour . . . pillar-box red and formed rather like a very formal daisy, the shape which a child would draw if you said 'Draw a flower'. These too can be naturalized with luck but they must be planted in quantity from the start for, at least in my experience of them, they do not increase much, if at all.

Despite opinions to the contrary, none of these is really particular about soil. *Pulsatilla vulgaris* is often said to like chalk; it will certainly grow happily in chalky soils, but I have it doing well within two feet of *Gentiana sino-ornata*, which is also flourishing, and as the latter is supposed to curl up and die at the smell of chalk I presume the Pasque Flower is growing in a definitely acid soil. My *apenninas* are also in acid soil but flourish equally well in chalk. Texture is more important, then, than the *p*H; and that should be light and open; even so, I must say that I have seen these anemones doing well in quite dense clays.

More difficult to establish, in my experience but not perhaps everyone's, are the hepaticas; these, like pulsatillas, are no longer included by botanists under anemone, but we need not bother about that. There are only three species of these and only one commonly grown. Like wood anemones, they can be naturalized in semi-shady woodland, that is, in the skirts of woods where they do receive some daylight. *Hepatica triloba* is as variable as our own wind flower, coming in white, pink and blue varieties; the blue, at its best, is deeper and richer than that of any other anemone. The varieties *coerulea* and *marmorata* are both blue, the former true to its name being a heavenly colour; the white form is, of course, called *alba*, and the *rubra*, an ugly red-ink pink, should be avoided. Double hepaticas are, on the whole, better formed than double anemones. There is a Central European species called *H. transsilvanica* which I have seen once, and which seemed to have no special merit unless you count size as such; it was larger than the common hepatica. I have never seen the American *H. acutiloba* and as far as I know it is not a garden plant in this country.

HARDY ORCHIDS

Some years ago I achieved a garden ambition by flowering *Cypripedium reginae*, one of the most attractive of the North American hardy ground orchids, in the open. Two consignments of these plants reached me: one from the United States and another, together with some *C. parviflorum*, from Canada. The first planted and first to flower were the American ones.

As regards the soil and general conditions we were able to follow, more or less, the advice of the Professor of Botany at a famous American University, which was obtained for me by an American correspondent. That is, we were able to give the plants a top layer of slightly acid soil above a neutral subsoil, and at least in some cases to keep the top of the soil covered with live sphagnum moss. As to the site, we had enough of the plants to try five different ones, which has enabled me to reach the following tentative conclusion: that they like neither full sun nor deep shade, but broken shade with full shade during the heat of the day. One or two other things were noted: the Canadian plants seemed to be somewhat sturdier than the American ones, probably pure coincidence; and these orchids will not stand a dry soil. Where watering of the cypripediums was neglected during a dry spell, they obviously suffered badly. The height at flowering was between twelve and fourteen inches, very inferior to their height in the wild; for, two years after establishing these orchids in the garden I saw them in the wild, in New England and later in Virginia. My friend Mr George Elbert, an expert in the flora of the eastern United States, tells me that he has commonly found *Cypripedium reginae* up to two feet and even two and a half feet tall, always in swampy open woodland.

Although a hardy plant this orchid looks very exotic, for the flowers are large and the colour of the pouch very rich. *Cypripedium parviflorum* is much less impressive, with its yellow wings and brown pouch, but it is also easier to establish in gardens.

I received from another correspondent a quantity of newly gathered seed of *C. reginae,* taken from Canadian plants in the wild. Knowing that nobody had ever succeeded in germinating the seeds of this orchid, I sent the seed to one of the most famous firms of orchid growers in the world and asked them to try, at my expense, to germinate them in the manner used for tropical orchids, on a nutrient jelly in sterilized flasks. They agreed to do this. The experiment was a complete failure, not a single seedling was obtained. Until a way of germinating the seed and raising the seedlings is found, this very beautiful and ruggedly hardy orchid will remain a wild flower very rare in gardens.

SNOWDROPS

There are some flowers which, partly because their beauty is an expression of perfect simplicity and partly because of their season, are moving, almost touching in the impression they make on us. The superlative example is that little Iberian daffodil whose vernacular name is 'Angel's Tears'. But snowdrops have this quality in a greater measure than the other flowers of our native early spring. I never really succeeded with them in Kent; but in Devonshire I had snowdrops galore. They came up not only everywhere in the garden, but on many of the roadside banks, although whether as true wild plants or as garden escapes

I do not know enough about the species to say. I prized this most distinguished of bulbous flowers so greatly that certain garden operations such as the removal of worthless old shrubs were often postponed or abandoned entirely where it meant seriously disturbing one of the better groups of snowdrops. At some time in the past there is no doubt that several of the species, and not just the Common Snowdrop, were planted there, but to distinguish them was difficult for anyone but a professional botanist and it would not surprise me to learn that there were a number of crosses in the garden. Certainly I did not find it possible to name them all with any degree of assurance by, for example, the size and shape and position of the green markings on the flowers.

There are fourteen or fifteen species and they do not all like the same kind of treatment, some preferring a warm and sunny corner and others flourishing in the shade of bushes and trees. One thing I did discover when trying to establish snowdrops in Kent, instead of wading ankle-deep through them in Devon, is that where there is difficulty about this it really is not much use even trying with bulbs which have been dried and stored in the ordinary way of commerce; the only way is to arrange to have bulbs which are lifted as soon as the flowers have withered and when they still have green foliage in good condition, and to plant them at once. In that case they may establish themselves and in time increase. The same is true, by the way, of that other valuable winter-flowering genus, the Winter Aconites. Dried corms fail where corms lifted just after flowering and with plenty of leaves, succeed.

The Common Snowdrop is *Galanthus nivalis*; it is native to all mainland Europe, but not, as far as I know, to England, although it is certainly naturalized here. It would be impossible without devoting several pages to this species to deal with all its varieties, for it is the most variable species in the genus. I had at least six different ones in Devon, including the *flore pleno*, that is the double-flowered kind, which I do not much like, the grace of the flower is spoilt by doubling. The earliest of this species flower in February or even in late January, and the latest in late March. It is not very often that nurserymen offer *G. nivalis* in named varieties, but if you can get either *imperati* or *rachelae*, they are finer and larger than the type, with wider leaves and bigger flowers.

Galanthus elwesii begins to flower in January; I had two forms of it, one of which had a much rounder flower than the type, and sometimes bore more than one flower from the spathe; it was probably variety *globosus*. This species is tall, often nine inches, but it comes from Asia Minor and it enjoys direct sunshine. I do not think it should be grown, like *nivalis*, in grass under trees. It is a plant for cultivated soil, but should nevertheless be where it can increase into clumps without interference; and where it gets all the sun there is.

A species which looks like *G. nivalis* and which, certainly, the ordinary gardener could not tell from that common species at a glance, is *G. plicatus*. It comes from the Crimea, however, and it flowers later than *G. nivalis*, so that a planting of it with the latter species will mean a longer season of snowdrops. Distinguishing one from the other is made even more difficult—not that it matters—where both are present, by the fact that they readily interbreed, and you will soon have seedlings which are hybrids between these two species. Some of these seedlings will have larger flowers than either parent; where these are noticed, it is worth while to mark them, move them to a suitable place of their own, and let them increase until you have a particularly good home-grown strain. *G. plicatus*, and perhaps some of its hybrid seedlings, will flower well into April.

Another species which will flower into April and which is like *G. nivalis* in size, though distinguished from it in some details of the flower markings, leaf colour and morphology, is *G. ikariae*.

Late last November I saw a group of snowdrops about seven inches tall and with glaucous foliage, in full flower; they were in a garden on the far side of Dartmoor and there was nobody at home when I went to enquire about them, for I immediately wanted this species or variety for my own garden. However, after looking up all the books which mention snowdrops at all, I think that these flowers must have been *G. byzantinus*. This species, which is another from Asia Minor, is at its best in December, but as it always begins to flower in November, it is another of those which help to lengthen the snowdrop season. Another species which begins in November is the Caucasian *G. cilicicus*. Thus, if some of all the above species be planted in your garden, and this should not be done unless the Common Snowdrop has shown itself to be happy there, it is possible to have snowdrops in flower no less than six months of the year.

Good bulb nurseries make a special price for snowdrops in large quantities for naturalizing, and if you have the kind of garden where the genus is really at home, this offers a way of getting the right snowdrop effect, drifts under trees, within a short time. If you are going to plant for that effect, then do not be afraid to plant the bulbs close together. The sort of soil they seem to prefer has a considerable amount of leaf mould in it, and that is about all one can say, for I have seen them doing very well indeed in heavy soil districts as well as in light sandy gardens. It seems, however, that some account of the texture of the soil should be taken when considering planting depth: six inches in sandy soils and four inches in clay soils. I quote this advice from a specialist, but it does not, I must say, accord with my own observation. Some of the snowdrops which flourished in my Devon garden were, indeed, deep in the soil; but there were a number of groups so near to the surface that one could see the tops of the bulbs; yet these did quite as well as the others.

DEEP SHADE

A major problem in any great woodland garden and in many lesser gardens, is that of finding plants which will grow in the shade of trees and shrubs. It is better, from the maintenance point of view, to have the ground under such plants covered or partly covered by an under-storey of green but the problem of accomplishing this is not really easy to solve. Such places entail difficulty for the gardener, because although there are a great many plants which will survive in deep shade, there are few which will flourish and flower in it. The plants which succeed in shade are those whose leaf-structure is such that atmospheric carbon dioxide can permeate it only very slowly. As plants need light for photosynthesis only in proportion to the rate at which their leaves can take in CO_2, those which are slow in doing this are as well off in shade as in sun; indeed, rather better off. But I have gone into the reasons for this on page 139. A majority of herbaceous subjects like full sun; the best shrubby subjects enjoy half shade; light shade or broken shade; or full sun. Many of the best bulbous plants do well with their roots in cool shade, but like to have their heads in the sun. Quite a lot of plants simply die in deep shade.

It is important to be clear as to what we mean by shade. There are parts of any garden, say on the north side of the house or of a stand of trees, which do not receive direct sunshine but do receive the full light of the northern sky, the light which painters prefer. A very large number of plants of all kinds will do well in those conditions; camellias and other shrubs which produce their flowers very early in the year, are better planted so, for the damage which is said to be done by frost to their flowers is often done, in fact, not by the initial freezing but by the subsequent quick thaw where such plants are exposed to morning sun. But a north exposure is not shade. By deep shade I mean the conditions under a canopy of trees which interpose between the ground and the sky, not merely the ground and the sun.

If you consult the kind of nurseryman's catalogue which gives some instruction in gardening as well as a price list of plants, you will usually see that certain kinds of berberis, and also *Mahonia bealei* and other mahonias, are given as suitable shrubs for shade. And it is true that they will grow in shade. But I found by experience that to plant mahonia in shade under trees is a mistake: one never, in that case, sees this fine plant at its best. In shade it grows slowly, is unshapely and leggy, and flowers rather poorly. Only in almost full sun, and certainly with full sun part of the day, will this shrub grow into the well-clothed handsome object it wants to be and produce its long racemes of yellow flowers. Some large-leaved rhododendrons need a lot of shade, and I believe that some of those in the *sinogrande* section with enormous leaves do need full shade, but these are not for the ordinary garden.

The plants I found to do well enough in shade are as follows: nearly all kinds of ferns, including *Osmunda regalis.* Far more use should be made of them. Aucuba (the spotted laurel of the London suburbs) does well in deep shade. But I would not plant the spotted kinds; much handsomer are the plain green varieties with serrated leaves. Of the other laurels, cherry laurel is not really a handsome plant, or, if it is, I have a blind spot about it; and Portugal laurel, very handsome and with fragrant flowers, prefers light to shade.

As for flowering plants, I have found that not only primroses, both the pale cream natives and the pink and blue exotics, do quite well even in deep shade and commonly seed themselves and flourish well away from the light, but the fine hybrid polyanthus also do well under a tree canopy. And so do violets, and lilies-of-the-valley. All three kinds can be planted and then safely allowed to look after themselves for years; they can compete with any weeds which occur in deep shade excepting dog's mercury. That must be kept down or it will smother everything. A pleasant little native which also does well in deep shade is sweet woodruff (*Asperula odorata*). There are two other genera of flowering plants which are tolerant of these conditions: hellebore and hosta.

The green-flowered *Helleborus foetidus* is always found in deep shade; I had some rose-pink flowered hellebores, possibly *abchasicus*, which grew enormous in deep shade, but which flowered sparsely. *H. niger*, the Christmas rose, behaves in the same way. These and other hellebores do well enough in deep shade to be worth planting under a tree canopy, but in my experience, for what it is worth, are only at their floriferous best if they receive some direct sunshine during part of the day.

Hostas, again, the erstwhile *Funkia*, or plantain lilies, while they will grow and even flower in quite deep shade, really flower better in half-shade. I do not know this genus at all well, but the species *fortunei*, with its glaucous leaves and pale lilac flowers, is attractive, and still better, under trees, is *undulata variegata*, which has a white edge to the green leaves and a taller spike of lilac flowers. I believe that there are some new hostas worth enquiring about, with flowers of a much deeper, richer colour. Whether they need sun, or will tolerate shade, I don't know. A strikingly fine one which I saw in someone else's garden was among other herbaceous subjects in full sun all day long.

Finally, and especially among ferns, why not Solomon's Seal? *Polygonatum multiflorum*, with its gracefully curved stems, handsome pinnate leaves and creamy little bell-flowers, deserves restoring to favour. And it really does like unmitigated deep shade, flourishing away year after year in conditions which would reduce most plants to pale and etiolated invalids and finally kill them.

Among shrubs, *Aucuba japonica*, preferably in the plain green form, *Skimmia japonica* with its scarlet fruits, and *Paeonia delavayi* do very well in deep shade.

Unless I have quite forgotten the little Greek mythology I ever knew, Danaë was the daughter of Acrisius king of Argos, and the mother of Perseus, first of the knights-errant. Her relations with the god Zeus were those of a starlet with her sugar-daddy, for the god descended on the girl with dishonourable intentions in a shower of gold, thereby confirming one's suspicions that the Olympian gods were a vulgar lot. It is by no means obvious why the name of this princess should have been given to so modest a plant as the Alexandrian Laurel, *Danaë racemosa*; and yet, come to think of it, the poor young woman was not really to blame for any of the things which happened to her: she was the victim of masculine terror and lust, for her father had shut her up in a brass tower because an oracle had foretold that her son would be the death of him; and if she nevertheless had a son, and what a son, well, few girls of her age and upbringing can resist showers of gold. Perhaps after all she was modest, and fit to be the eponymous heroine for so humble and shade-loving a plant as Danaë.

The plant is allied to our own native Butcher's Broom and can be planted with it in shade under trees; I find both will even grow under conifers. But whereas Butcher's Broom is very dark, matt green, Danaë is a bright and cheerful colour. Neither of these plants has proper leaves; in both the apparent leaves, the organs which, indeed, fulfil all the functions of leaves, are flattened stems. But this is less obvious in Danaë than in Butcher's Broom; its 'leaves' are tapered, lanceolate, up to three, even four inches long. They are grown on erect green stems which rise from the ground in a slowly but steadily spreading evergreen cover where hardly any other plants but ivy will grow at all. As in Butcher's Broom, the flowers are insignificant, being minute and green. But the red berries which follow are quite large and would be decorative if more freely borne. But this plant comes from Persia and it does not bear fruit very well in our climate, so that it is rare to see a Danaë with a really good show of berries. One purpose which it does serve, once well established, is that of providing stiff but very attractive evergreen foliage to be used with flowers in the house, and it does this for twelve months of the year. It is, by the way, extremely hardy.

A plant which, labelled Danaë, I bought for my garden turned out to be not Danaë at all but something much better. I did not spot this myself so that I cannot blame the nurseryman for making this mistake in identification; it was a visiting friend, with an unsystematic but wide-ranging knowledge of botany, who put me right. The plant I had set in numbers in the deep shade of evergreen trees, was *Sarcococca humilis. Danaë,* like *Ruscus* (Butcher's Broom), is liliaceous; *Sarcococca* is a member of the *Buxaceae.*

Sarcococca humilis comes from West China and the plant collector Wilson sent it to Veitch (now of Exeter) half a century ago. It is a low, spreading evergreen. Like Danaë, it has a neat, tufty habit, sending up stems from below the ground to form an ever-widening colony. These may reach a height of two feet but as a matter of fact as a rule they don't, and one can almost count on this particular species remaining very short, not much more than a foot. The narrowly oval, pointed leaves are a good bright green, shiny on the upper surface, pale and matt below. Some time between November and March, often in mid-winter, this *Sarcococca* flowers; the season is most variable; the flowers are not spectacular, but coming, as they may do, in January or February, they are very welcome. They are small, but many go to each raceme; and they are sweetly fragrant.

There is a fine collection of Sarcococcas under the trees of the woodland parts of the great Dartington Hall garden, including other species as well as *humilis*. All multiply themselves by dropping their seed which germinates well. *Sarcococca hookeriana* is described by botanists as a shrub to six feet. But there have been two separate introductions of this plant; late in the nineteenth century it was introduced to Kew from, probably, Afghanistan; it survived there but could not, according to Bean, be called really hardy excepting farther south and west. The one which is much planted at Dartington does not seem to grow more than three or four feet tall and on this ground I expect it is the West Chinese variety introduced by Wilson in 1908; this is called variety *digyna* and it is important to get this one because it is perfectly hardy anywhere in Britain. Quite likely it has displaced the earlier and less hardy type, for in good catalogues I see it described as attaining only four feet. Like its congeners, it is a suckering shrub, forming widening clumps as it grows, so that it will, if left to itself, form thickets. It bears its light green lanceolate leaves very gracefully, is tolerant of deep shade, and it flowers well. The flowers are white, very small, and borne in the axils of the leaves; and like those of *humilis*, they are borne in winter and are very sweet scented. They are followed by black berries.

Another species in cultivation is *S. ruscifolia*, also evergreen, but this time from Central China so that it is extremely hardy. Although it is capable of growing to four feet it is usually much shorter and consequently is admirable for planting beneath trees or taller shrubs to form a permanent green cover. It thrives very well in shade and it makes a pleasant contrast with its congeners for it has very dark, shining leaves. Whereas both *hookeriana* and *humilis* sometimes flower in autumn or in spring, rather than winter, this species invariably flowers in winter, usually in January. The flowers, in small clusters carried in the axils of the leaves near the top of the shoots, are, again, white and, again, fragrant.

To sum up then: a permanently green, sightly and interesting planting under the shade of trees and shrubs, even under deep shade, can be made with *Ruscus aculeatus*, Butcher's Broom, some care being taken to get plants of both sexes or you will have none of the handsome scarlet berries; *Danaë racemosa*, the 'Alexandrian Laurel', with not dissimilar foliage of a very much lighter and brighter shade of green; *Sarcococca hookeriana* var. *digyna*, planted as a background to the planting since it is apt to be taller than the other two. In front of it, *S. ruscifolia*, shorter, with darker green foliage and winter flowers. And, finally, *S. humilis* for the front of the mass. Planted close and once well established, this evergreen mass will exclude ivy, and the few shade-loving weeds, but it is possible to get periwinkles growing among it and producing a few blue or white flowers as 'incidents' in contrast with the red or black berries, which remain long on the shrubs.

THREE UNCOMMON HYDRANGEAS

The climbing plants which will hold on to any surface by means of aerial roots or suckers are very few and very useful. Ivy, of course, is the best known; and *Hydrangea petiolaris* the most uncommon and yet one of the most useful.

This climbing hydrangea makes a number of thin, woody stems from the root and these climb and clothe vertical surfaces, such as tree trunks, walls or stumps, exactly like ivy. Their leaves are much more freshly and brightly green than those of ivy. On the other hand, they are deciduous. The species is said to climb as high as eighty feet. The highest I have seen in one or two old gardens in Britain were about fifty feet and, in full leaf, very handsome. The flowers, or rather inflorescences, are of the lacecap type, that is there are many fertile flowers very insignificant in appearance, surrounded by a fringe of showy, sterile flowers. These are white, or perhaps rather cream than white, and they are held out from the foliage on horizontal shoots. This hydrangea deserves to be much more widely planted than it is.

Although ordinary hydrangeas of the *Hortensia* type and the 'Lacecaps' will grow in any soil, they are only at their best in peaty loams and very moist climates. But the Japanese *Hydrangea paniculata* does as well in limestone and chalky soils as in any other, is very hardy, and an excellent garden plant anywhere in Britain. Here is a note I wrote on this plant some years ago and one which has been thoroughly confirmed by further experience.

'*H. paniculata;* in its third year from a cutting, planted in a gritty loam and top-dressed with leaf mould, comes to my chin; the panicles are really too big and heavy, and after rain it is weighed down. However, the stems are strong and once it has dried off, the flowers stand up again. The flowers open greenish white, become pure white, then mature to a rich cream, and finally, as they age, turn a kind of creamy-pink which is most delicate and charming. In my opinion this is one of the finest garden plants we have, ruggedly hardy, tolerant of all kinds of soil provided it is not too shallow, and intolerant only of severe root competition.'

The biggest species of the genus, suitable only for large gardens of the woodland kind, is *H. sargentiana.* I recall being put off by the word 'gaunt' applied to this by Bean; but it is, in fact, a most handsome plant. Not only does it need shade, even some quite deep shade, but also protection from wind. It is perfectly hardy, but its leaves, enormous, heart-shaped, with a deep, velvety pile, are very easily damaged by wind, and after a brisk wind, let alone a gale, they have brown patches and tears which deform them. The plant consists of a number of stems from ground level, often ten or twelve feet tall, very few if any branches, these great leaves, and lace-cap inflorescences in which the fertile florets are blue or lavender, the ray florets white. The inflorescences may be a foot in diameter. Propagation is by suckers, you simply dig one up, they come up often a yard from the crown of the plant; or by seed which is freely set.

WHY SOME PLANTS PREFER SHADE

All green plants need sunlight in order to grow: it is the energy they use in transforming the carbon taken from atmospheric carbon dioxide into sugars. But whereas many plants will grow only if fully exposed to light, others prefer a measure of shade, that is they do better in a light of lower intensity. What is the difference between these two classes?

Leaves take in CO_2 through numerous pores in their skin called stomata and which may number as many as quarter of a million to the square inch. From genus to genus and even from species to species there are differences not only in the number of stomata but in the internal construction of the leaves. In some the internal structure is such that the gas CO_2 taken in through the stomata can rapidly pervade the whole interior of the leaf, so that there is an ample supply for the sunlight to make use of. But in other cases the internal structure is such that the CO_2 can be diffused only slowly throughout the leaf and consequently not all the light shining on the leaves can be used. In full sunlight energy is wasted for want of raw material to work on. This would seem to mean that although a shaded situation with lower light intensity would suit such plants as well as an exposed situation with high light intensity, it would not actually be any better because it would simply mean that the plant would waste as much of the light as it could not use.

But there is more to it than that. Bright sunlight destroys chlorophyll, the green stuff which the plant uses to turn sunlight into the kind of chemical energy it needs to make food. So some of the plant's energy has to be used all the time in making fresh supplies of chlorophyll. Thus the kind of plant which can use light only slowly because it can absorb CO_2 only slowly, is actually worse off in bright sunlight than in partial shade. And there is still another way in which such slow CO_2 absorbers are set back by too much light intensity: plants in bright sunlight naturally get hotter than plants in shade; they therefore transpire more water, whereupon energy has to be used in taking up water from the soil to replace the loss. In dry conditions they may not be able to do so and will then flag. So unless a plant can, by reason of its rapid absorption of carbon dioxide, use all the light shining on it, it is much better off with a lower light intensity, i.e. in shade.

And still that is not the whole story; here is a passage quoted from Sir John Salisbury's *The Living Garden* (Bell, London, 1935):

'If we go into any wood in which the undergrowth has not been coppiced for some years we shall probably notice such plants as the Yellow Dead Nettle and the Bugle growing freely and spreading rapidly by their runners, but almost entirely non-flowering. After the wood has been cut we find these same plants flowering profusely. The change is due to the increase of light. . . . The fact that many plants grow well in shade, even though they do not flower, shows that the light is sufficiently bright for them to make the necessary food for growth, but a greater amount of illumination is necessary for the production of their flowers than for the production of their leafy shoots.'

In all the above what counts is the intensity of light and not the amount of time during which light is shining on the plants. But many plants are affected in an important way not only by the degree of light irradiating them but by the time during which they are daily exposed to light.

There are a number of plants which cannot be given too long exposure to light provided the light be of the intensity they like, high or low. But a great many plants which come from low latitudes or latitudes lower than ours, but which are growing in our gardens, are adversely affected by exposure to light for a time longer than they are used to. The commonest effect of too long exposure to daylight of what are called short-day plants is the delaying of flowering, or total failure to flower. This is not always a disadvantage in gardening: for example, the reason why chrysanthemums and dahlias do not bloom in our latitude until very late in the summer or early in the autumn is that they cannot make flowerbud until the days grow shorter—as short as they would be earlier in the year in their native latitudes. As it happens, their late flowering is a quality which we value.

At one time I was growing about a hundred different kinds of strawberries in my garden in an attempt to find and introduce one or two of the better autumn-fruiting varieties, the so-called *remontant* or ever-bearer strawberries. Some which were satisfactory in the places I brought them from would not flower at all, or hardly at all, in my garden, but produced a prodigious quantity of stolons and cadet plants; others, however, flowered and fruited too abundantly and produced no stolons at all. And this was because strawberry plants are very sensitive to length of day and therefore to latitude. In parts of North America where the production of autumn strawberries is on a large scale, plants satisfactory for fruit production at a given latitude will produce no stolons; so propagation farms have to be established in another latitude where stolons will be produced at the expense of flower bud. Some strawberries which in England flower only in June, become ever-bearers in, for example, the Maritime Alps where the day is shorter.

One of the plants which can use light all the time and is a very long-day plant indeed is the greenhouse cucumber. If, in addition to daylight it is irradiated all night by artificial light, it will grow faster and produce more fruit. But the light must be of low intensity, that is the greenhouse must be shaded. If the cucumber is given bright daylight, it will grow perfectly well but it will then produce such a preponderance of male flowers and so few female flowers as to be wellnigh fruitless.

It is, of course, this sensitive reaction to various qualities and durations of light which has made possible such tricks of commercial horticulture as the production of chrysanthemum flowers all the year round. By giving plants periods of darkness artificially their behaviour can be controlled and the date of their flowering almost exactly planned for.

PLANTS UNDER ARTIFICIAL LIGHT

If plants which require either higher light intensities than they can get in, for example, our living rooms or offices or if they can be made to behave in a way more profitable to us by being given light for longer than the length of a mid-winter day, the obvious thing is to irradiate them with artificial light. But to do so effectively is not quite as easy as it sounds.

The human eye is at its most efficient when dealing with that part of the spectrum of sunlight which we call yellow. It is much less efficient in red or blue light. Chlorophyll, on the other hand, the green stuff used by plants to trasnform light into another kind of energy, the kind it needs for its own use in growing, is more efficient under red and blue light, less efficient in yellow light. As a matter of fact one might almost have guessed this from the fact that leaves are mostly green: they are reflecting the green and yellow light, therefore they are not absorbing it and therefore they are not using it. They are absorbing the red and blue for use, and therefore not reflecting red and blue, and so do not look red or blue. There are, of course, red-leaved plants, but the redness is due to the presence of pigmentation which only masks the chlorophyll.

As far as we know yet, it is the blue light which provides most of the energy for photosynthesis. As to the red light, green leaves contain a blue pigment called phytochrome and it exists in two forms; both of them work as enzymes but in opposition to each other. One reacts to the red light causing maximum growth of the plant; the other reacts to a light rather higher in the spectrum (and which is called 'far red') by checking growth. When there is a satisfactory balance between them the plant grows at the speed proper to it and takes on the shape proper to it and the correct habit. If these processes are unbalanced, then the plant will be misshapen—drawn and spindly should the 'far red' effect be too small, stunted if the ordinary red effect be too small.

All this and more information gathered by scientific experiment gives us some idea of the kind of light which plants need. But what it does not do easily is to enable us to reproduce sunlight intensities at an economic price and in a practicable form.

If you use even the most powerful incandescent lamps to irradiate plants, to be effective they still have to be so near to them that the heat from the lamps scorches and otherwise incommodes and damages the leaves and flowers. Moreover although incandescent electric light bulbs are strong in the red region of the spectrum, they are weak in the blue which is the wavelength providing most of the energy for photosynthesis. Fluorescent tube lights are strong in the blue and weak in the red; a combination of the two kinds of lights provides something nearer to the right spectrum but there is less of a problem in getting them near enough to the plants to make them effective in maintaining growth.

'Daylight' (white fluorescent) tubes are more nearly correct as to the spectrum they provide and they have a light output so much greater than that of incandescent lights that they can be placed further away from the plants. On the other hand they are also so much cooler that they can be brought much closer to the plants if necessary.

There are now properly designed 'growth' lamps of the fluorescent type, strong in the blue and red regions of the spectrum. Their principal use is in germinating seeds and raising seedlings in nurseries, but they can be used with advantage by the house-plant amateur to irradiate the plants he grows indoors. These commercial horticulture tubes have a peculiar mauvish-pink light which ruins leaf and flower colours, but there is a newer 'wide-spectrum' type of tube which looks yellow (i.e. suits our eyes) but from the plants' point of view isn't.

Some of the above statements are worth examining in a little more detail. Take the matter of comparative intensities of light. If we say that the value of unclouded sunlight at a given time of day and for a given latitude is 10,000 foot-candles we shall have a roughly valid average figure for the temperate zones. No plant can absorb CO_2 fast enough to use more than 1,200 foot-candles. So no plant actually needs the full intensity of unclouded sunlight or anything like it. But it happens to be very difficult to give plants 1,200 foot-candles by artificial means. It is a question of projection and travel of light. As Mr George Elbert has pointed out:

'The top of the tallest free standing tree and its lower leaves receive practically the same amount of sunlight. Not so the top and base of a plant under fluorescent light. The reduction is drastic and swift. . . . If a plant a foot high is just below the lights it will receive a foot-candle illumination of, say, 650. A four-inch plant on the same shelf may well receive less than 250 foot-candles. The lower plant will be starved for light and the taller one is likely to lose its lower leaves and have poor offshoot growth.'*

There are other difficulties: and one of them is the deterioration of the value of light from the tubes. The loss of light valuable in promoting plant growth is much swifter than the loss of the light apparent to our eyes, so that we are not warned of what is happening. Mr Elbert says that within 200 hours of installation there is a drop of over 10 per cent; in short, for the most of the life of a tube it is working at well below its rated output of light.

Something, then, can be done to provide a substitute for sunlight in growing plants: but we have still a lot to learn about the light requirements of plants and our lighting techniques and devices are very imperfect.

BRIGHT LEAVES

In certain rather dark corners of many gardens it is quite possible to depend upon leaves to provide light, colour and contrasts, regarding any flowers which may be produced as a bonus; or

* *Houseplants*. Nelson Gardener's Library. London.

even, if the shrubs and perennials in question have to be dead-headed, as a nuisance. In the one country where gardening was always regarded as one of the fine arts and reached a degree of sophistication it has never yet attained in Europe, Japan, foliage has long been more important than flower. It was not always so: Japanese gardening really began to be important in the seventh century of our era and during its first phase flowering shrubs and herbaceous plants were cultivated in, instead of outside, the garden. But with the rise of the warrior caste with its austere tastes, of the equally austere Zen sect of Buddhism, and under the influence of a Chinese school of painting, the Sung black-and-white, Japanese garden designers banished flower colour from the garden, depending upon foliage for a range of contrasting shades and forms; in the extreme case, of course, they banished plants altogether, making their gardens, very rich in symbolism, with nothing but raked sand and a few carefully chosen and very carefully sited rocks. We are not likely to go so far, however greatly some garden-designers may be influenced by abstract painting. But there is something to be said for the foliage garden and, come to think of it, the great landscape gardens of the eighteenth century were never flower gardens.

The size of most modern gardens makes it difficult to use large trees, and we are obliged to rely on small ones and on shrubs. A number of these have the habit of burgeoning in some shade of red instead of green and of these the two which seem to me the best are *Photinia serrulata* and *Pieris formosa forrestii* 'Wakehurst'.

The photinia is either a small tree of a large shrub. It is related to our hawthorns, and will in time produce flowers not unlike those of the hawthorn, but it has large laurel-like leaves which are a good mid-green in their maturity; but in infancy and youth they are the rich red of new copper, and on a well-grown specimen with many growing tips, this makes a most striking but never gaudy spectacle.

The pieris, which like all its kind will grow only in an acid soil, looks not unlike a narrow-leaved rhododendron bush; but its flowers are racemes of white bells. This plant has the habit of producing its flower buds in autumn, holding them through the winter to flower in spring; consequently they are very often destroyed during cold spells and the pieris may never flower for you: this does not matter in the least; it should be planted for its young foliage which burgeons an astonishingly rich shade of salmon-pink. I have found it a mistake to plant it in a position exposed to sun: the young leaves can stand it while they are red, but as they fade in colour to pale yellow before turning the rich green of their maturity, they are very tender to sunburn, and are always badly scorched: it could be that the habit of burgeoning in red instead of green, is, in fact, a protection against sunburn. At all events, plant this pieris in shade.

As a source of sheer brightness some of the oleasters are ideal, two in particular being outstanding. *Elaeagnus pungens* var. *aureo-variegata* is a dense, spreading well-clad bush of medium height: I suppose it has flowers but I have never seen them; in any case what matters is the leaves, which are bright green so richly variegated with golden yellow that the bush radiates light. The markings are not simply marginal, but very diverse, and the stout, stiff leaves, up to four inches long, are sometimes all green on one side of the midrib, all gold on the other. It will grow in shade or exposed; the young foliage of this shrub, on burgeoning, is remarkably beautiful, being covered with tiny golden scales and looking for all the world as if it had been carefully covered with gold-dust.

My other oleaster, unlike that one, is deciduous and its special colouring is silvery instead of gold. This is *E. umbellatus*, the young foliage being covered with silvery scales in infancy, but maturing to a bright and very silvery green. The plant is a small, full, often more or less fastigiate, tree. The flowers, small bells, are silver and very fragrant. (This is presumably the *E. umbellata* of Bean, and that may be the right name.)

There is no need to say much about the copper-leaved beeches, rhuses, barberries; they are very well known, but I recently came across another small tree of that colouring which I had not met with before, *Pittosporum tenuifolium* with leaves of a remarkably dark copper-red, so dark that the whole plant, about six feet tall, looked almost black. The advantage over other shrubs and trees with copper leaves is in the extreme glossiness, and the leaf-undulation typical of the species, also the small size of the leaves, these attributes combining to give a different and interesting texture to the foliage.

Some of the most pleasing foliage effects are obtained with conifers: some of the broad-headed (as distinct from conical) pines were, I think, the most important plants in the great Japanese landscape gardens. After very considerable difficulty in getting them I planted three kinds of silver-blue conifers as being the best I have seen, during years of looking and admiring in other gardens or in pinetums. *Cupressus arizonica fastigiata* is a very fastigiate tree, growing rather slowly, to perhaps thirty feet and not much broader than the Italian cypress. The foliage is very light and delicate and in colour the most lovely silver-blue, more silver in Italy where, indeed, it may be almost white. I recently talked to an experienced Gloucestershire gardener who has had this tree for many years and finds it remarkably hardy, much hardier than *C. sempervirens*. The two other species are firs: *Abies concolor candicans* or, as the Italians who grow it best call it, *argentea*; and *Picea pungens kosteriana forma speckii*. A specimen of the fir in Mount Usher (Co. Wicklow) is the most whitey-blue tree I know. The picea, too, is remarkable for the silver-blue of its leaf colour.

For formal beauty of shape and texture, to contrast with these silver firs and cypresses, I think that *Libocedrus decurrens* is one of the most beautiful trees you can plant. In outline when mature, and even when quite young, it is broadly and regularly columnar with a bluntly tapered or rather rounded top, that is, it is not a narrowly pointed tree. The foliage is borne in fans and these fans are set round the tree in an ascending spiral; I do not know any other conifer which has this very beautiful form and a group of three, or even a single specimen, makes a most striking feature either alone, or mingled with the silver firs and cypresses.

For what one may perhaps call a 'Japanese' effect, *Pinus radiata*, with its flat, spreading head and often leaning trunk, can hardly be bettered in this country: the leaves are so dark as often to look black. But *Pinus montezumae*, with its very long and slender needles, its lovely silver-blue glaucous colouring (but this varies from form to form) and its perfectly rounded dome when well grown, is probably the most beautiful conifer we can grow (in the warmer parts) in Britain.

CLIMBING ANNUALS

There are several plants for covering low trees and shrubs, which, although perennials and therefore capable of surviving over the winter in very mild districts, or if given some sort of protection, are only half-hardy and can be treated as annuals. That is, if they fail to survive the winter, they can be grown again from seed every spring. Here are three well worth trying.

Tropaeolum speciosum is a sort of gigantic 'nasturtium'. Its flowers, though smaller, are similar in form and colours, at their best a vivid flame-red. But it will ramify and climb very fast to a height of over twenty feet. And although it will be cut down by frost, it is possible to keep the roots alive by covering them, in which case the plant will sprout again in the spring. Such a plant, allowed to fulfil its perennial nature, will be larger and grow faster than a seedling. Nevertheless, it is possible to re-cover your tree or shrub with seedling tropaeolum every year.

Eccremocarpus scaber is hardier than the above, but still not perfectly hardy. It survived several years with me in Kent, in a warm corner, and for all I know still does. This, again, can be grown from seed every year. It is a very fast-growing plant, making hundreds of thin, fragile, climbing branches with very delicate tendrils and finely divided foliage. The narrow funnel flowers are very numerous, and either orange or red.

Another and better climber which can be treated in this same way, as a half-hardy annual with a chance of survival to become a perennial if you are both lucky and careful, is *Cobaea scandens.* It is a widely ramifying clamberer with glabrous foliage and its hanging flowers are green and violet if analysed, but give a general impression of blueness. As a rule this plant is grown in a cool-house, but it is perfectly possible to treat it as a half-hardy annual and so grow it over a tree or shrub out of doors. This *Cobaea* does remarkably well in London gardens and I have seen huge plants of it on the walls of houses in Chelsea and Kensington.

This is by no means an exhaustive list, of course. I happened to have a distinguished academic horticulturist staying with me while I was writing this, and we thought of numerous other possibilities. In the course of the discussion I mentioned, tentatively, polygonum—*P. baldschuanicum.* My friend's answer just about sums up my own opinion of this all-smothering plant: he said, 'By all means, if any of your readers have a disused brewery in the garden to cover.'

DAPHNES

Daphnes are difficult; some will deny this and point to the fact that certain daphnes are to be found flourishing like the wicked in old cottage gardens. This is true, however, of certain other temperamental plants, for example madonna lilies and cardinal lobelias. There seem to be certain plants which either find their commodity by chance or not at all, so that the greatest skill and care are not of much use in getting them to grow well. Daphnes belong, in my opinion, to this heterogeneous category of incalculable plants.

Not all the daphnes which have been brought at some time into cultivation, are easy to get. But most of the better nurseries have six or eight species. A difficulty of planting many species in one garden should, in theory, be that whereas some daphnes are native on lime-stone, others are very definitely not. Yet, having observed them wherever I have come across them for many years, it seems to me doubtful whether any species is either altogether chalk-hating, or altogether addicted to lime. That, in short, a generally neutral soil, with special minor adaptations for each species, should suit them. Another difficulty in forming a massed collection of species is that whereas some are certainly sun-worshippers, others are quite as certainly retiring plants with a taste for damp shade. But this, in a garden where there are trees, and where other shrubs are being planted, is not impossible to allow for.

Among the taller daphnes, *D. burkwoodii* is outstanding. Where it is happy it attains more than four feet, growing into a dense, dome-shaped evergreen bush as great in diameter as in height. Its foliage is pale green, the leaves being about half as broad as they are long and snub-pointed. The flowers are quite large, with a long tube, a tender pink in colour, very fragrant, and borne in dense terminal clusters during May and June. It is a hybrid plant, the parents being the tall *D. caucasica* (not worth growing for its own sake) and the very dwarf *D. cneorum*.

A species which I had seen only once in flower and that was in Italy before I grew it myself, is the rare Chinese daphne, *aurantiaca*. This is an evergreen which, in the Italian specimen I saw, cannot have been much under six feet tall and as much, or nearly as much through. It seemed to like the climate of the Dolomites, and the priest in whose garden I saw it said that it had been grown from seed in his lifetime. Its flowers are shaped like the individual florets of a lilac inflorescence, but are larger, a bright golden-orange in colour, and very sweetly scented.

Another fine but very difficult Chinese daphne is *D. genkwa*, a deciduous species which grows about four feet tall, and bears its lilac-coloured flowers on the naked wood in May.

Among the taller ones there is, of course, *D. mezereum*; it is too well known to need describing, and it very often fails or, after a few years, dies suddenly. This may simply be the nature of the plant, but it may also be that it rarely gets the conditions it likes: by the best accounts, these are *damp and shade*, whereas more often than not you see the shrub set in full sun.

The only really attractive thing about *D. laureola* is its name, which would hardly earn it a place in the garden. But it is very tolerant of shade and has its uses in woodland gardens. *D. odora*, on the other hand, is what American writers call 'mandatory'. It can quite easily attain six feet, so that it is, I suppose, the tallest of the daphnes; it is evergreen, the foliage being dark and shiny against the black wood of the branches, and the deep-red, or white and red, flowers are exquisitely fragrant. Flowering begins in January and continues for months. The species is from China, again, and it is not perfectly hardy in the south-east, nor, presumably, in the east and north. It is, however, happy enough in the south and west and perhaps anywhere really close to the sea.

Daphnes of middle stature are numerous: *D. retusa* rarely attains more than two feet and is usually smaller. Its leathery leaves are sparse towards the base, dense towards the end of the twig, and the flowers appear in very dense terminal clusters, each flower being purple on the outside and silvery-white striped with purple on the inside. Fragrance is strong. *D. neapolitana* grows to about three feet, usually less I think: it is evergreen, hardy, erect in habit but appearing very densely clad in leaves by reason of its elaborate branching. The flowers begin in March and continue for three months, well set among the leaves, pale rose, and sweet-scented. This species, of confused origin, is said to like lime in the soil and is grown successfully on chalk. Another middle-stature evergreen which is not, however, perfectly hardy, is *D. collina* from the near east; there are several other good species in this height class.

There is a good range of very dwarf species for the front of the plantation or, of course, for the rock garden where they are usually planted. Perhaps the most charming of all is the minute *D. petraea* of the Tyrolean mountains: it is a miniature woody evergreen, rarely exceeding six inches and bearing luminous pink, fragrant flowers in June; it likes full sun and is found on limestones, growing in crevices. *D. blagayana* is evergreen, a foot tall at maturity, bearing its white and fragrant flowers in March or April. *D. cneorum*, another one-footer, with a tendency to wander and sprawl, bears its pink and sweetly-scented flowers in May. I have never seen *D. striata*, which is also very dwarf and sprawling in habit, whereas *D. alpina*, from the Alps, although rarely attaining fifteen inches in height, is an erect and compact little deciduous shrub, but not by any means one of the best.

PROSTRATE

A plant which has long been a favourite with me which is very useful in rock gardens and which makes a very good front to a shrubbery, is *Rhododendron forrestii repens.* It is evergreen, of course, with rounded oval leaves of a pleasant medium green, about an inch long. There is a lower tier of branches which creep along the ground. There is a second tier of branches, so that the whole plant is about six or eight inches tall in older specimens. The flowers are crimson and quite large for the size of the plant, about an inch and a half across the mouth. They open in April. The growth habit of this plant is so close and dense where it is well grown that there is no question of weeds under it; they do not get a chance. There is, by the way, a rhododendron which is not only prostrate but is so-called *R. prostratum*, but it must be rare in gardens, at all events I have never so much as seen a specimen. It is described as a prostrate and trailing plant in stony, Alpine conditions, but I know nothing about it. There are, of course, other very small rhododendrons, such as *impeditum* and *radicans*; but of these only *radicans* has the ground-hugging habit I have in mind here.

Singularly rare in gardens, excepting among the rock-garden specialists, are the shrubby penstemons; they deserve more attention. *P. scouleri*, though small, is not prostrate; *P. menziesii*, although its purple flowers are borne on erect stems, is often, though apparently not always, a ground-clinging trailer. The one which has taken my fancy however is *P. roezlii.* It is not described in the books as prostrate; but as it seems to remain less than six inches tall, while growing out sideways and much more than that, it is to all intents and purposes a plant of prostrate habit. Its flowers, typical of the genus, are borne in clusters of a few at the tips of the shoots, and they are a very pleasing, soft red. The plant has a fault; this is a sort of die-back which may kill only one ramification, or may kill the whole plant. It is said to be caused by a fungus, but I doubt it because, seeing two plants suddenly turn greyish and look like dying, I nipped off their tip growth and put the pieces into the propagator, whereupon they perked up at once and were soon rooted. The flaw, then, is either in the root, or the main stems. But faulty or no, this is a plant very well worth growing.

In an Irish garden some years ago I saw a remarkably fine very prostrate cotoneaster with broader leaves than one associates with *C. dammeri.* I was allowed to take cuttings, and these were struck when I came home; even in the pots, to which they were transferred after rooting, they grew out sideways, forming flat tiers without the least tendency to become erect. Apparently this plant is *dammeri,* though perhaps a good form of it rather than the type. There is no plant more useful for covering banks, stones or old tree stumps, though it is best where it can follow its normal practice of rooting itself as it grows, to form a dense, flat mat. It flowers in June and its berries are large and a fine coral in colour.

A plant which I saw recently for the first time and made a note of for future ground cover is a blackberry, *Rubus nutans.* It is an evergreen, it is completely prostrate, it bears quite large pure white flowers and its purple fruits are edible, it seems. I don't know where to get it: it does not even appear in Hillier's astonishingly rich centenary catalogue. However, that catalogue does list some other prostrate brambles, notably the charming *R. fockeanus* which I have grown. This has mallow-shaped leaves which are 'bullate', that is the surface bulges, as it were, between the veins in a way which is decorative. These two, and also the Chinese *R. tricolor*, are not only completely prostrate and self-rooting so that they make fine ground cover, but they all grow in the shade. Another group of shrubs which have the same qualities (that is, are evergreen, completely prostrate and shade-loving), is that composed of *Euonymus fortunei* (formerly *radicans*): the best of these ground-huggers are *E. f. colorata*, whose leaves in winter take on an under-tinge of bloody purple; 'Silver Queen', a variegated form which brightens the shade where it grows; and *minima*, a miniature one with tiny leaves which should only be used where the area to be covered is small. One of the virtues of the euonymus is its tolerance of very poor soils and its ability to compete with tree roots.

But a prostrate shrub which is ideal on limestones is *Dryas octopetala*, the Mountain Aven. My best plant of this was raised from seed and collected on the mountains of Clare, and although the soil of my garden was far from being limey, it flourished on the top of a low retaining wall which enclosed the little terrace where I had a rose-garden and lily pool. This plant, in its third year, had formed a mat thirty inches by twenty-five, of bright green crinkled ('crenate') elliptical leaves which was most pleasing in texture and form; the flowers, like single white roses, are borne on erect stems all over the plant.

One of the best prostrate shrubs I have grown is *Potentilla fruticosa mandshurica*. This forms a low broad dome; the lower branches, as they grow out along the soil, take root and so form a mat, and also provide an easy means of increase; the leaves are silvery and the flowers, copiously borne for months, are white. Incidentally, I am inclined to regard the relatively new, orange-flowered *Potentilla fruticosa* 'Tangerine' as being prostrate. It is true that it sends a few branches up semi-erect, but for the most part it grows horizontally and its lower branches take root quite readily if notched. It is too open in habit to form a real mat, though maybe it would do so if pruned to check tip-growth. It combines very well with *mandshurica*, by the way, its coppery-yellow flowers being in fine contrast with the silver and white of that shrub.

Finally, I would mention the Creeping Dogwood, not, it seems, really a shrub but a perennial, though hitherto called *Cornus canadensis* and listed as shrubby. It forms, in suitable soil, mats of cornus-like leaves in rosettes on short upright stems, and these bear the cornus-like white flowers, also on short erect stems, starring the whole mat very prettily; the flowers are followed by bright red fruits. The plant is still fairly rare in gardens; I first saw it at Malahide Castle, I think; it is very fine at Crarae, good at Knightshayes; I had a small piece of it which spread fast even in a rather unsuitably heavy bit of soil.

CRANESBILLS

Among the plants which, either by introduction or in the course of nature, are native to Britain in general, are some of the finest of the geraniums. The two which I have in mind are the Great Meadow Cranesbill and the Bloody Cranesbill. As a rule they only appear on limestone soils, but like most lime-loving plants, these two beautiful geraniums will, if planted, do very well in almost any soil, even in peat. And where they are cultivated as garden plants, given room, full sun, and watering in drought, they respond with a more spectacular display than is usual in the wild.

The Bloody Cranesbill, *Geranium sanguineum*, is where I have seen it in the wild, a prostrate and repent perennial on limestone rocks and other poor soils, its handsome and deeply-divided foliage decorated with not too many one-inch flowers varying in colour with the soil, but generally speaking a sort of purplish crimson. Planted in the paving of my garden the species varied its behaviour according to the degree of exposure: plants in full sun made beautifully rounded, flattened domes which become completely covered with flowers rather larger than in the wild; in partial shade, on the other side of the terrace, they were less shrubby in habit, more scandent or repent, sending out trailers lying close on the stone, and bearing fewer but often even larger flowers of a richer colour, much nearer to the blood-red of the specific and vernacular names.

Cultivated in an ordinary border, with richer soil and less restriction of the roots, this plant can make a dense ground cover, very freely flowering. Finally, the geranium is good if roots of it be set between the edging stones of a border, to grow half on the bed, half out on to the gravel or stone path. In those conditions it seems to bear its fruits on longer stems. This cranesbill, and other, allied geraniums, seed themselves freely, and it is hardly worth while to gather seed for you can usually find a seedling or two beside an old plant, often sheltered half under it.

The Great Meadow Cranesbill, *G. pratense*, is a very different matter. Planted in a border where it has room to expand, it can become a terrible nuisance, forming very rapidly huge clumps and overwhelming everything in the immediate neighbourhood; I have seen it kill even rose bushes. I have grown it in two ways: in soil which is already or soon will be grassed-down, at the point where a line of *Thuja plicata* trees lay their lowest foliage so elegantly on the ground; and, again, in cracks between paving stones. In the former case what I got was a line of vivid blue sharply defining the point of meeting between ground and thuja foliage; in the second case, clumps of elegant, upstanding stems bearing very attractive foliage, about two to three feet tall, and topped by hundreds of the one and a half to two-inch flowers which were a quite deep blue veined with reddish-purple, in my opinion one of the most beautiful perennials we have.

Some other geraniums proved very good in my garden and above all I like *G. reynardii*, a most curious plant very good in stone edges or rocky banks or walls, but best in full sun. It comes from the Caucasus, and its leaves are very reminiscent of those of its tropical or subtropical relatives, the pelargoniums; they have five rounded lobes, and they are softly felty, a beautiful grey-green in colour. The base colour of the relatively large flowers is white, or greyish-white, but each petal has a pretty pattern of vein-like purple markings. This geranium increases to form a large clump and can be propagated by division. I should have said the same of *G. pratense*, but added that *G. sanguineum* often layers itself so that rooted pieces can be removed to other situations.

A remarkably distinguished native, or at all events thoroughly naturalized, cranesbill, rare in the wild but which should be more often seen in gardens, is the Mourning Widow, *G. phaeum*. It has the great merit shared by some other cranesbills, of doing quite well in shade as well as in sun. The thick, deeply-toothed leaves look a little like those of creeping buttercup, but the purple spot at the base of each lobe serves to distinguish it if there is any doubt . . . there isn't really, of course. The flowers, something under an inch in diameter, are so dark purple as to be nearly black; they are, in fact, the colour of concentrated blackcurrant juice; this handsome sombreness is relieved by the white spot at the base of each petal, these spots uniting to give the flower a heart of white. The tallest stems of this plant are described as reaching two feet; I have never seen one exceed eighteen inches.

Once when I was on leave during the war I was walking in Devonshire and came upon a whole bank, in a lane, covered with *G. striatum*, a European cranesbill naturalized in Britain, which has pale rose-pink flowers veined darker pink, I noted the place and after the war went back for seeds; not a plant to be found. However, better for the garden is the rose-pink *G. endressii*. It has the same striped flowers but the stripes are paler. This species, and *striatum*, flower quite late, in late summer and into the autumn. If both these species are planted not far apart in the same garden, then chance seedlings found between them will often be hybrids, but it is not easy to distinguish them from each other or either parent at a glance.

ANOTHER CHILEAN

A sub-shrub which is difficult to establish, rare in gardens, but much hardier than is generally conceded, and which is a wonderful plant to cover a big stone, a tree-stump, or a mound of soil, in shade or semi-shade, is the lovely *Philesia magellanica*, or *P. buxifolia*, whichever is correct. This plant is allied to that curious group of liliaceous subjects which includes *Lapageria rosea*, Smilax, and Butcher's Broom. The finest plant of it that I have ever seen, and it is probably the best in Europe, is in the famous Glenarn garden of Mr and Mrs A. Gibson. I believe that I am right in saying that it covers about fourteen feet by six at least, closely clinging to a big rock and penetrating the crevices and cracks as it spreads. It does not exceed about twelve inches in height from the ground, and is perhaps less than that; it forms a close mat of stiff, hard, dark green leaves about an inch to an inch and a half long and not more than a quarter wide. The leaves look much more like, say, yew, than the box of the specific name, because they are not only narrow anyway, but they are reflexed at the margins. The flowers are long, tubular bells with exactly the same waxy look as those of lapageria.* They are borne terminally, are very numerous on a well-grown plant, and are a rich rose-crimson in colour. The plants likes a peaty loam, or a peaty-leafy-gritty soil.

The trouble I have found with it is this: starting with a small rooted cutting, it will not begin to grow until you have found the right place for it; I think that constant moisture is important. It will simply sit there, not dying, even flowering, but not growing at all. Then, suddenly, one year, it starts to grow and after that it will spread quite quickly. Mr Gibson told me that once you have the right place for it, on no account move it. There it must stay. I confess that the two I planted grew about two inches in two years; but I lived in hope. And it would be nice if more gardeners tried this plant, for when it does find a place it likes, it is a gem of great beauty.

HYDRANGEAS DWARF AND GIANT

Until I had seen it grown in woodland shade I did not like this genus: that dislike was based upon seeing it grown in full sun so that the plants were solid lumps of colour. In shade and woodland, all its species are quite transformed.

First, something about propagation; no genus is easier once you know exactly what to do, and that is to take tip cuttings only and while they are still soft or at least not really hardened. I

* To which *Philesia* is so closely akin that they can be cross-bred. Incidentally, *Lapageria rosea* grows and flowers very well in my London flat.

have found that if you take longer cuttings they do not root, unless they happened to be planted so deep that the inch or two of stem immediately below the unfolding tip bud is under the ground; in that case they root right at the tip; so there is no point at all in taking cuttings more than, say, two inches long; such cuttings root in a matter of days if put into a close case and a compost of mixed coarse grit and peat; or simply pure grit. That is true for *H. villosa*; *H. macrophylla* (the ordinary florists' lace-cap hydrangeas); *H. acuminata*; in short, all kinds of hydrangeas excepting *paniculata*, *sargentiana* and *petiolaris. H. paniculata,* which hardens its thin, wiry wood as fast as it grows, is not quite so easy, but I have succeeded with tip cuttings of that one too; easier are small sideshoots pulled off with a heel. Also not quite so easy as the rest, but it can be done in the same way, is *H. quercifolia*, the handsome and curious oak-leaved hydrangea. This has paniculate flowers like, but smaller than, those of the *Hydrangea paniculata.*

The *H. quercifolia* has no great floral merit; it is worth planting a clump of it for its handsome leaves, especially for the matt gold of the young growth, but where space is limited you can leave this one out.

The hydrangea which, for charm and flower, should be planted far more often than it is, is the one I call *acuminata* although I should it seems, call it *H. serrata* 'Acuminata'. It does not exceed three feet in height and the flowers are of a flat, lace-cap kind; the tiny fertile florets of the centre are blue, and as far as I have been able to see, they are blue in any kind of soil; the big, surrounding sterile florets are porcelain blue in acid soils, white in limey soils, and a lovely shade of mauve in many other (neutral?) soils. In the variety 'Grayswood' of this species the ray florets start white, turn pink, and finally turn crimson, while the fertile flowers are blue. I would emphasize that not only are these *serrata* hydrangeas much more subtly beautiful shrubs than the ordinary *hortensis* ones; they are, by their smallness, very suitable for the small garden, which the others certainly are not.

As for 'ordinary' hydrangeas, there are only two points I should like to make. First, never mind what the experts say, grow them in shade, even quite deep shade. Will they not, then, grow tall and straggly? Yes, what of it, they are far more agreeable shapes so grown than the solid blobs one sees in the sun. And will they not, in shade, be reduced to relatively few flower heads? Again, yes, they will, and so much the better, for in sun they are overwhelming and coarse. Best of all is that kind of shade which, morning and evening, is shot through with long shafts of sunshine filtered through the heads of trees; not only will this give the plants a helpful ration of sunshine; but it will make with them such patterns of light and shade, in both the foliage and the flowers, as will hold you entranced. There is no finer woodland under-storey plant than this, in variety. The other point I should like to make is that if you want blue, not pink, and your soil is such that hydrangeas tend to be pink, then variety is almost as important as soil. In soils where most hydrangeas flower pink or mauve, even when much peat and rotten dung is used, as they should be, by way of top-dressing, the *Générale Vicomtesse de Vibraye* is most likely to give you blue flowers. This is not from books; it is from personal trials. The famous 'Blue Wave', by the way, is only blue in really very acid soils or where it is blued with aluminium sulphate. In nearly all soils, even where rhododendrons flourish, it is pink.

Now for the big ones: two big shrubs for half shade are *H. villosa* and *H. aspera macrophylla.* The latter flowers in June and July, the former July and August. Both reach nine feet or a little less, forming a big, full plant, with woody trunk and branches, long, pointed, velvety leaves, pale on the underside, and the most graceful and lovely lace-cap type flowers, on the blue side of lavender in acid soils, and on the pink side of lavender in neutral and alkaline soils, but in any case a very soft and delicate colour, with no sign of that trying, screaming pink which can spoil some cultivars of this genus. Cuttings of these two should be taken much earlier than cuttings of other hydrangeas; tips, again, but early in July or even late in June. Growth is slowish for two years, but then quite fast. These hydrangeas are hardy.

A very interesting conclusion to my experience with *Hortensis* hydrangeas in Devonshire: by 1965 scores of plants which, at their first and second flowering in 1963 and 1964, were pink, flowered blue; while plants which had flowered pale blue had flowers of a much deeper shade. What had happened? Either it had taken several years for my heavy dressings of peat to acidify the soil and so change the flower colour; or this change demonstrated the truth of a theory which the late Mr J. Johnson, garden superintendent at Dartington Hall, once expounded to me about this genus which he grew so well. He believed that very young hydrangeas always have pink flowers, whatever the soil (unless it had been chemically treated); and that, in soils on the acid side of neutral, the colour of the flowers would turn to blue as the plants aged, probably because they accumulate acidity in themselves. Certainly it is true that in my garden all young plants flower pink, and in their third year, change to blue; it is also true that one often sees large, old plants on which some of the flowers are pink, some blue, which suggests to me chemical differences localized in parts of the plant.

THE QUALITY OF IRISH GARDENS

William Robinson of Gravetye fame, an Irishman who spent most of his working gardening life in England, had more than any other great gardener to do with the creation of the modern, romantic, woodland, 'paradise' garden, represented in England by a score of such diverse manifestations of the style as Bodnant, Dartington Hall, Caerhays, Knightshayes, Nymans *et al.* So it is fitting that a number of the finest examples of the style to be seen anywhere in the world are in the Irish Republic and Northern Ireland.

Mount Usher, thirty miles south of Dublin, in County Wicklow and the village of Ashford, is in many ways the most remarkable garden of this Robinsonian style which I know. Based on a river and covering many acres, its makers, five generations of the Walpole family, have accomplished a rare feat in it, since they have reconciled plant collecting with good design and the creation of an integral work of art. The collection of exotic trees alone would distinguish this garden; or the river-bank gardening which is flawless. As a rule where a really vast range of exotics are grown the individual plants dominate to such an extent that there is little or no design, but at Mount Usher they are simply the material with which the general design is executed, which is just as it should be. A picture is no less valid as a work of art for being painted with a very rich palette.

In the art of landscape gardening large boskages of ever-greens have an important place: at Mount Usher they are no less correctly placed for being made not of holly or yew or laurel, but of, for example, *Crinodendron hookerianum* and *Eucryphia* in several species. And one of the most remarkable things about this garden is the flourishing state of its Chilean and Australian shrubs and trees: both the two mentioned above reach a height, bulk and floriferousness most unusual in our latitudes. In walking about this great garden one's attention is now on the effects achieved by the whole, on general vistas, along glades or walks, or the river; and now, again, on some single detail, the quality of a Callistemon or some other rare exotic, or the beauty of a single tree such as the mighty specimen of *Pinus montezumae*.

Less rich in exotic species but richer in the mass plantings of the finest Chinese rhododendrons, camellias, embothriums and evergreen trees, Annes Grove in County Cork is the most romantic garden I know. In part this is due to the shape and fall of land which has made possible the creation of narrow, steeply sloping plantations like miniature gorges whose sides are crammed with the most glorious flowering shrubs of Yunnan, Szechuam, the Himalayas and the Chilean Andes. This garden also has its formal part, its walled enclosure of rectangular borders where herbaceous perennials are perfectly grown in very great variety. The water garden, allowed to run almost wild, is full of oriental primulas in incredible quantity, meconopsis in all its species, and numerous other genera. It was in this garden that I first realized what magnificent shrubs the big hydrangeas, e.g. *H. villosa*, can be when the soil and climate suit them well.

Ilnacullin, on the island of Garinish in Glengariff Bay, is an extraordinary mixture of romantic English and classical Italian gardening. The island was at one time a more or less barren rock used for some purpose by the Royal Navy. Bryce, who bought it, his garden architect Harold Peto and Bryce's son Annan Bryce, made it from the rock up, even importing soil. It is difficult to believe this when you see the garden now. It is the property of the Irish Republic and perfectly maintained and gardened. Its nucleus, with formal pool in marble, and marble pavilions, is English-Italianate, a style in which Peto was a great adept; the rest of it is a rich garden of winding and hilly walks planted on both sides with beautifully planned borders, coppices and plantations of exotic trees, shrubs and perennials. It is a garden to spend a week in. The surroundings are as remarkable and as beautiful as the island garden itself, sea and mountainscape, a sort of Chinese print of mixed water and land which one can gaze at with pleasure for hours.

Of the three greatest gardens in Northern Ireland, Mount Stewart, Rowallane and Castlewellan, my favourite is Castlewellan. Favoured, like Annes Grove, by the shape and fall of the land, it differs greatly from the other Annesley garden, Annes Grove, in that the formal and informal parts are better married together. The broad walks between borders leading to *ronds points* centred on stone fountains form the skeleton on which the woodland garden of magnificent trees, scores of them rare exotics, is built. Like so many Irish gardens this one has splendid views beyond the garden, which are drawn into the garden by clever planting of trees.

The gardens created by the Earl and Countess of Rosse about Birr Castle in County Offaly are another very fine example of Anglo-Irish romantic mixed with formal French and Italianate styles. As well as the woodland gardens and river bank gardens, there are more formal enclosed gardens, and notably one of clipped box parterres and old-fashioned roses which is one of the most successful and accomplished works of the kind I have ever seen. Box, incidentally, attains an astonishing height in that garden and there are two ancient box hedges which must be at least twenty-five feet tall and still in very good condition.

I do not want to rewrite here my own book on Irish gardens but to try to convey something of the quality which they all, however different from each other, share. It is a kind of green opulence and an opulence of flower which these gardens owe to the mildness of the climate and its humidity, and the richness of the peaty soils. Only in the wetter parts of maritime Portugal have I seen anything to compare with it. But in Ireland it is incomparable, really, because of the quality of the light, the swift change from misty rain to bright sunshine, the washed look of foliage and the sheer exuberance of growth.

So extraordinary are Ireland's advantages of soil and climate for gardens that it is to be hoped that the making of new great gardens of exotics will not be left to such private gardeners as Mr Ambrose Congreve of Mount Congreve who is lavishly replanting his ancestors' grand garden in County Waterford, but will in some way be promoted by the Government; for it would be in the Republic's interest to create more and more of what is among other things, a wonderful tourist attraction.

GIANT RHODODENDRONS

I do not like the hardy hybrid rhododendrons with their dull, laurel-like foliage and great heads of garishly coloured flowers. But in this enormous genus there are very many other classes to choose from, and the miniatures, the Chinese rhododendrons, many of the Himalayan species and a few choice hybrids are very beautiful. In some ways the most interesting group are the primitive giants from China and the Himalayas.

They are to be seen at their best, in Europe, only in the gardens of south-west Scotland, notably Glenarn, Rhu; in some Cornish gardens; and some Irish gardens. I planted a number of them, for posterity so to speak, and in doing so got to know a little about them, having first made their impressive acquaintance in other people's gardens.

Rhododendron sinogrande was discovered by George Forrest in 1912 and by him introduced to Britain. It comes from Yunnan, N.E. Burma and S.E. Tibet and it is one of the most imposing plants in the world's flora: an evergreen tree to about thirty or forty feet, its young shoots are about an inch thick. The leaves are up to thirty inches long and a foot wide, beautiful great ovals of deep green, leathery in texture. The new buds in spring are splendid objects, four or five inches long or even more, upright and pointed. As the young leaves unfold from them they are a striking whitey-silvery-grey and show up brilliantly from far across the garden. This is due to a covering of down which they shed as they grow. The leaves are set round the massive stalks in huge rosettes which may be as much as five feet across. The flowers are borne in grand racemose trusses of up to thirty; they are bell-shaped, fleshy, cream or pale yellow and with maroon markings at the base.

There is an enormous plant of *R. falconeri* at Glenarn, more than a century old. This species was introduced in about 1850, and the Glenarn tree is probably from the first batch of seed which Hooker sent home. The specimen in question is about thirty feet tall and more through its grand head. The oval leaves are about nine inches to a foot long and up to six inches wide. On the upper face they are very dark green; but the lower face is covered with a dense red or ruddy felt, giving the foliage a most attractive bi-colour quality. The creamy, bell-shaped flowers, blotched purple and stained mauve, are two inches across and borne in tightly packed clusters or trusses of about twenty. They are faintly fragrant. There must have been several thousand of these flower-heads on the Glenarn specimen when I saw it in May. The old tree is very scrupulously cared for; every flower-head is picked off when the flowers go over, to prevent the formation of seed; and an annual mulch feeds the huge root system.

The flowers of *R. macabeanum*, another giant but this time from Assam, are very similar in form, colour and size. The leaves of young plants of this species are almost as large as those of *sinogrande*, and in plants of a hybrid *R. sinogrande* × *R. macabeanum*, quite as large. There is a big-leaved form of *R. fictolacteum* which Kingdon-Ward discovered in West China which has leaves up to a foot long and so dark green that, in the sort of shaded site this genus prefers, they appear to be black and as if thoroughly polished: that is another species with the underside of the leaves very handsome, a clear silvery-pewter.

The commonest tree rhododendron in Britain is probably *R. arboreum*. There are forty-foot specimens in many west country gardens and as far east as Kent, although this species is not very hardy. It was introduced in 1815, bears crimson flowers in late winter or very early spring, and can easily be recognized by the fact that the underside of the leaves is silvery, although there are forms with red felt instead of silver scales. *R. arboreum* was the first red-flowered rhododendron to be seen in the West; to it we owe all the older red-flowered hybrids, first of which was the mid-winter flowering *R. nobleanum*. But *R. arboreum* is not, like the giant-leaved kinds, a primitive plant.

The greatest of the rhododendron giants, and another of the primitives, is *R. giganteum* which was discovered by George Forrest at an altitude of ten thousand feet in Yunnan, in the year 1919. Forrest found a whole forest of these trees; the oldest were eighty feet tall with a trunk girth of over seven feet at five feet from the ground. The leaves are up to eighteen inches long and six inches wide, and the underside is covered with red down. Its flowers I have never seen but Forest described them as 'deep rose-crimson without markings but with a slight blotch of deep crimson at the base'. Bean has an amusing note on this tree: '. . . worth planting in the south-west as a noble evergreen, and the best place evidently would be the base of a bluff from the top of which one may be able to appreciate the blossom. It would be difficult to do that with even the noblest rhododendron truss if it were poised 40 to 80 ft in the air.'

There are other species in this series of gigantic rhododendrons which are primitives in the sense that, having evolved to the present habit many millions of years ago, perhaps fifty million, they have not since made any changes, being perfectly adapted as they are to their natural environment, one which must have been quite exceptionally and massively stable. In our great woodland gardens these superb rhododendrons have a very special quality; they are not only exotic, they look it, no plants more so, and they were just the material needed by the late nineteenth- and early twentieth-century gardeners to give expression to the feeling for romantic, paradise gardens which had developed out of the cult of wild gardening started by William Robinson.

FIGS IN ENGLISH GARDENS

There is no particular difficulty in getting crops of good figs in English gardens. Although the fig-tree is, of course, a Mediterranean plant, it does well here if the right variety be planted; it is not even confined to the south of Britain. The late Justin Brooke got good crops from his fig-orchard in Suffolk, and I have seen abundance of ripe figs on old and handsome fig-trees as far north as Yorkshire. Fig-trees have, in fact, been in Britain for about seven centuries at least; for Matthew Paris refers to the severe frost which killed many fig trees in the year 1257. Moreover, English gardeners seem to have taken a lot of trouble with figs and to have made almost a cult of them. At all events, by 1894 when the United States Department of Agriculture sent to Europe to buy as many varieties of figs as possible, for trials in California, it was at the Royal Horticultural Society's gardens in Chiswick, and not in Spain, Italy or the south of France, that they found the most, over sixty varieties.

This apparent advantage got the Americans into difficulties, for a number of the varieties which they took back to California needed either some special kind of hand pollination or the attentions of the fig-wasp *Blastophaega psenes*. This little wasp is the only known pollinator of those fig trees which need one (not all varieties do, fortunately), the only creature which can make its way into the fig, along the very small tube whose mouth is masked by the 'eye' of the fruitlet, to reach the flower which is borne, uniquely, *inside*. The figs planted in California failed to bear fruit and it was not until later, when the Americans applied for advice to Italian peasants, that they heard of the fig-wasp, an answer to the sneer that peasants are not observant. This insect was introduced to California, throve there, and made possible the great Californian fig industry.

But the varieties commonly grown in England do not need the attention of the fig-wasp. The flowers are hermaphrodite; or the varieties are parthenocarpic.

In Kent I grew five varieties of figs out of doors. They were planted in brick-earth clay in a raised bed enclosed in brickwork, so that drainage was very good. They were fully exposed to the south and shielded from the north and east by the walls of some sheds. They were never adversely affected by cold. Their growth was short and stubby with many nodes, so that figlets were produced in great quantity. Most of these dropped off but a sufficient number survived to maturity. The two best varieties were 'Brunswick' which has very large fruit of good quality; and 'Brown Turkey' which has smaller fruit of excellent quality. 'Brunswick' figs are often as large and much the same shape as, a large 'Conference' pear. The varieties producing the smaller, round and flat figs, such as the two 'Marseilles' and some others, were not nearly so fruitful and I do not really recommend them for cultivation in this country out of doors.

Propagation of figs is very easy; you can use some of the numerous suckers which grow from the roots; or you can use hardwood cuttings. It is easy to dig round and separate suckers with a little root on them. No special advice is called for, the thing is so easy it is impossible to fail either way. As for pruning, the chief object should be to stop the growth of tall and vigorous shoots so as to make them branch freely; to remove thin and wiry shoots which never carry any fruit; and to keep the tree short, open and stubby all over. Long, stout water shoots should be cut out from the base.

It is frequently pointed out that if the roots of a fig tree can be restrained or restricted in some way, the tree will bear more fruit; this is true, but then it is true of all fruit trees. You can, if you like, make a concrete box sunk in the ground and about eight cubic feet in volume, and plant into that. Any roots which, in due course, make their way over the top edge of this box can be cut off. Probably the best way is to plant in extremely poor soil, full of stone and close above rock, but few English gardens can provide that. Alternatively, it is possible to plant in dense clay or over unbroken chalk which act as a severe restraint on the roots.

The word fig provides us, curiously enough, with the word sycophant: its first syllable is said to be from the Greek for fig, *sukos*, and its second from the Greek for an informer. It seems that after the defeat of Athens in the Peloponesian War the Athenians, whose country had so long been famous for good figs, fell into factions and produced a swarm of delators. Their enemies named them fig-informers—fig for Athens; that is sycophants. It was a sad come-down for the very close association of figs with Athens had, in the past, led to a use of figs which did honour instead of dishonour to the city; for it is said that King Xerxes used to keep a dish of figs on his table to remind him that the Athenians were the only people in the known world who had defeated and who still defied him.

SOME CONIFERS AND THEIR CONES

The great parks and woodland gardens of many English, Irish and some Italian and American gardens are embellished by plantings of conifers. The Forestry Commission's plantations of certain conifers as crop plants have, by their ugliness, brought the conifer in general into bad odour; but it is a fact that many of them are among the most beautiful and interesting trees in the world. By the way, it is grossly unfair to abuse the Commission for planting the only kinds of trees which will give them a fairly quick profit when we, the nation, insist that the Commission must pay its way.

Pinus aristata, the Bristle-cone Pine, is interesting as being probably the longest living creature in the whole creation. Although it forms a tree to forty feet or thereabouts, it is often a shrubby plant not exceeding twenty feet, especially in those barren and exposed situations where it grows very slowly and lives very long indeed, to an age, in fact, which is almost incredible. It is one of the pines whose leaves are borne in tufts of five, green but speckled all over with spots of white resin. The three-inch cones have a bristle to each scale, which serves to distinguish this species.

There are some very ancient plants of *Pinus aristata*, stunted and mis-shapen but still very much alive in the high mountains of Southern California. Ring counts made by taking microscopically small bores with a hollow drill, a technique developed by American dendrologists, show that some of these trees are as much as 4,700 years old. They were, it seems, very ancient trees at the time of the Crucifixion; they were multi-centenarians before the rise of the Greek City states and already old when

Egypt was the greatest power on earth; when Moses was leading the Israelites out of the land of Egypt and the house of bondage, these trees were 1,000 years old.

Very much younger, only three centuries old at the time of the Norman Conquest of England, are the oldest of the Californian *Sequoias*, the 'Redwoods'. Ring counts show that trees exceeding 300 feet in height and having a girth of between sixty and seventy feet above the trunk buttresses, are about 1,200 years old. There are some trees as much as 360 feet tall and they are, of course, still growing. Sequoias were introduced to Britain in 1848 and there are a few English grown trees exceeding 130 feet, a good height for a young tree of only a century or so. These huge conifers have small cones, hardly an inch long, but bark which is often a foot thick. Not quite so large in their own country, the Wellingtonias, Californian 'Big Trees', have, curiously enough, attained greater heights in Britain, trees of just over a century being as much as 160 feet tall. There is a beautiful form of Wellingtonia (*Sequoiadendron giganteum*), 'Pendula' whose branches point downwards at such an acute angle to the trunk that the whole tree is like an eaved spire.

Pinus parviflora, the Japanese 'White Pine' is a tree to sixty feet in Japan but in Britain it is often shrubby. The name comes from its silvery stomata which mark its short leaves. The three-inch cones are as broad as they are long. But the distinction of this pine is that it is beyond question the most frequently and widely illustrated in the world, for it is the pine of the Willow Pattern china.

The largest cones in the whole realm of the conifers are borne by *Pinus coulteri*, a 'three-leaved', very glaucous pine to seventy feet. Its cones are a foot tall and six inches through and weigh up to four pounds apiece. There is, however, a very beautiful fir, *Abies nobilis*, which runs this close. In the right soil and climate this will attain the great height of 200 feet, and it is noble indeed, one of the grandest of evergreens. In good forms the leaves are very blue. The abundant cones are ten inches long by three thick and a bright purplish-brown.

For beauty of the cones the *Abies* are superior to other conifers, if we discount mere size. My own favourite is *Abies koreana*, a smallish fir of very regular conical shape and handsome foliage which bears an enormous number of erect, stout, bright violet cones. In *Abies forrestii*, a lovely fir to forty feet with vividly whitey-blue stomata rows on the underside of the short, stout leaves, the cones are bright blue. In *Abies concolor*, whose rare and difficult variety 'Candicans' is the silvery-whitest tree I have ever seen, the shape of the tree, broadly conical, is pleasingly regular and the cones a rich plum-purple.

Araucaria araucana, the 'Monkey Puzzle' tree was introduced into Britain in 1795; the cones are, again, impressive by their size. This splendid tree is very much finer grown in rich and moist soils in country gardens than in the poor soils of London suburban gardens.

Archibald Menzies, a member of the company of Vancouver's survey ship, was dining with the Viceroy of Chile when Vancouver was there in 1795. Some unfamiliar nuts were served by way of dessert and Menzies put a few in his pocket. He does not seem to have known that they were *Araucaria* seeds. Back aboard ship, Menzies sowed the seeds in pots, cared for the seedlings during the rest of the voyage, and arrived back in England with the first five *A. araucana* to reach this country.

The best place to see this tree well grown and bearing quantities of cones is in the valley walk which leads from the formal Powerscourt garden in Ireland, to the waterfall which is one of the sights. The cones are globular, burly objects up to seven inches in diameter.

JAPANESE GARDENS

The art of gardening in Japan began in a ritualism and ended in a sophistication both unknown in European gardening. In his *Japanese Gardens* (The Studio, London) Mr Jiro Harada tells how, about half way through the thirteen centuries of the history of this art, in the middle of our own fifteenth century:

'The Shogun Yoshimasa (1436–90) was deeply fond of *ikebana* (flower arrangement) and gardens, and it was he who is generally believed to have brought 'auspicious' ideas into interior decorations and gardens. What was then known as an auspicious garden was a type of Horai landscape, centred on a rock composition representing the crane and the tortoise, symbols of long life, considered man's greatest happiness, the crane being traditionally believed to live one thousand, the tortoise ten thousand, years.'

Horai was a mythical island shaped like a tortoise somewhere in the ocean; and it was 'auspicious' because it was believed to be, or to have been, inhabited by tortoises, cranes and Immortals. The myth belongs originally to Chinese Taoism and seems to have reached Japan in the first century of our era. In gardening, Horai was an artificial island or group of islands in the pond or lake or, in the later, abstract, version, area of raked sand, which is the nucleus of all truly Japanese gardens of whichever style and epoch.

Water seems to have been important in all schools of garden art, eastern or western: in classical Italy, formal pools, in Renaissance Italy and France fountains and formal lakes; in Arab gardens fountains and elaborate water works; in Toltec and Aztec Mexico, pools and streams; in China 'landscaped' lakes;

in Japan the sheet of water becomes a sheet of raked sand; in England it becomes a close-mown lawn.

As well as a lake which perhaps stands for the ocean, with its Horai island, the Japanese garden has a mountain; it may be a single rock of suitable shape; it may be a composition of rocks. This is the mountain Shumisen. As Horai came from China, so Shumisen came from India. It belonged originally to the Hindu mythology and represented the central mountain of every world, which was of fabulous height and brightness. On the summit was Indra's haven, and about it eight circles of mountains enclosing eight seas: thus nine mountains and eight seas constitute the universe. The Buddhists borrowed this myth from the Hindus and in due course carried it to Japan; and the garden designers of Japan represented it in their gardens.

What, before we go any further, is self-evident, from the Western point of view, in this and much of what follows? It is, surely, that from a relatively early date Japanese gardening was one of the fine arts, and not simply a craft or applied art. It was one of the means of giving expression to the feelings, ideas and spirit of the Japanese culture which, like all the most vigorous cultures, borrowed terms and techniques from older cultures but made them very much its own. The early and even some later Japanese gardeners made gardens as a landscape artist paints pictures; and not as an architect builds a house.

We have written only of rocks and water, or sand as a substitute for water, and said nothing about plants. Perhaps in the earliest epochs, in the seventh and eighth centuries, Japanese gardens were sometimes flower gardens. But later, flowers were grown outside the garden proper and quite banished from the garden. There are a few exceptions but the plants used had to be propitious; in the Edo Period (from about 1603) gardens were made with three propitious plants, pine, bamboo and plum (*Sho-chiku-bai*). And these became another element in the Japanese garden.

Here is another passage from Harada:

'With Taoism came the theory of *in* and *yo* which maintained that the universe was produced by the interaction of the male or positive (*yo*) and female or negative (*in*) principles. The association with the theory of numbers is that seven is unchangeable and appropriate to *yo*, five is a combination of *in* and *yo*, and three signifies heaven, earth and man. This theory is still applied to various forms of Japanese art including the garden. For instance, in planning artificial hills, if one is made rugged and precipitous and dynamic in mood, another will be smooth, and serene, and static. If one waterfall gives the impression of masculine power, another should suggest feminine grace. If there is a peninsula projecting into the lake, there should be a bay to counterbalance it. In laying out stepping stones, if a concave-shaped stone is used, it should be followed by one with a projection. Beside a large rock standing erect, there should generally be a low reclining one. The principle of positive and negative is applied to the layout, to the selection of materials, and also to the details of construction.

'Christianity, first brought to Japan by St Francis Xavier in 1549 and prohibited in 1589, has also left its mark on Japanese gardens, especially with the stone lantern of Oribe type. Oribe was a convert to Christianity and Rikyu's disciple in the tea ceremony. He originated the design of a stone lantern with a pillar suggesting a cross and a carving of the Virgin Mary further down. When Christianity was placed under the government this was replaced by Jizo, a Buddhist deity. The Oribe type of stone lantern is still widely used in Japanese gardens.'

A score of Buddhist myths, symbols, legends and ideas are likewise represented in the Japanese gardens. It is doubtful whether, indeed, there is, in a true and uncorrupted* Japanese

* *i.e. by alien gardening styles, not by alien myths.*

work of garden art, a single stone, a single course or sheet of water, a single plant or tree, a single path, which has not at least one and often several superimposed symbolic meanings. But if the great masters of the art had been strictly confined to the use of symbolic material, they would have produced a sort of outdoor temples rather than works of art. How did they escape this, escape from the primitive phase? To quote Harada once again:

'One thing must be noted in this connection, that it does not seem that priests in general regarded these rocks as images of deities; rather they tried to express aesthetic principles by means of Buddhistic doctrines with which the people were more or less familiar.

'Nevertheless designers of Japanese gardens try to infuse the spirit of nature into the creations. They still strive to suggest a sylvan solitude or seaside tranquillity, the grandeur of a tremendous gorge or the sublimity of a mighty river, the rhythmic contour of undulating hills or the peaceful expanse of a plain or a vast stretch of water. In short they try to make a garden a place in which men may commune with nature.'

Which is to say that like other artists in all cultures, these men used the terms and symbols allowed them and proper to their culture, to give expression to feelings of general validity. A very interesting rule of the Japanese garden art is that to make a statement outright is bad taste; one makes a suggestion, gives a hint and it is for those beholding the garden to discover what statement is being made.

'Beautiful objects should be so concealed that only those who seek diligently may find them and thus be thrilled with unexpected joy, even as men should do kind deeds to others in secret, to be found out by accident if at all.' (Harada)

I find one manifestation of this spirit of particular interest. The garden designer decides to place a group of rocks of a certain shape in a certain position. You might think that he would need to bury below the surface only so much of each rock as would hold the visible part stable. In fact, however, good garden makers invariably choose a rock whose top third was the right shape; but they also gave attention to the shape of the whole rock, and then buried it to two-thirds of its depth. And the Japanese believe that it is because they do this that the rocks placed by an artist of talent and sensibility carry so much weight in a garden. As Harada puts it, '. . . the suggestion of latent strength under ground invested them with their dominating power. It is a sort of moral force deriving its strength from sacrifice made in silence.' Nothing in my reading about Japanese gardening has struck me more than this. For I know that it is true. And any good maker of an English rock garden knows the same, even though his aim is purely aesthetic and has no spiritual ulteriorities. The Japanese gardeners went much further than this, however:

'Following this line of thought let me recount what the great tea-master Rikyu did more than 260 years ago in order to give his garden a deep spiritual significance. When his new tea-room and garden were completed at Sakai he invited a few of his friends to a tea ceremony for the house-warming. Knowing the greatness of Rikyu, the guests who accepted the invitation naturally expected to find some ingenious design for his garden which would make the best use of the view of the sea, the house being on the slope of a hill. But when they arrived they were amazed to find that a number of large evergreen trees had been planted on one side of the garden, evidently to obstruct the view of the sea. They were at a loss to understand the meaning of this. Later when the time came for the guests to enter the tea-room, they proceeded one by one over the stepping-stones in the garden to the stone water-basin to rinse their mouths and wash their hands, a gesture of symbolic cleansing, physically and mentally, before entering the tea-room. Then it was found that when a guest stopped to scoop out a dipperful of water from the water-basin, only in that humble posture was he suddenly able to get a glimpse of the shimmering sea in the distance by way of an opening through the trees, thus making him realize the relationship between the dipperful of water in his hand and the great ocean beyond, and also enabling him to recognize his own position in the universe; he was thus brought into a correct relationship with the Infinite.'

The long art of Japanese gardening is divided into eight major epochs of Japanese history in each of which a different style was dominant but in each of which the same sets of symbols were employed, although the emphasis changed with fashions.

The primitive epoch extends from about A.D. 77 to 1183 and historians call it Pre-Kamakura. It is subdivided: there is first the pre-Buddhist period, dominated by Horai but in which gardens were miniatures of nature; landscape gardens, then, from the very first. The Asuka Period, A.D. 552–644, saw the introduction of the Shumisen theme by Korean immigrant artists. Between A.D. 645 and 782, and with the introduction of the pine-bamboo-plumtree theme, the gardens became much larger, landscape gardens centred on lakes and were enjoyed from boats, and they incorporated all the earlier styles. In the subsequent Heian Period, ending 1183 or thereabouts, great landscape gardens became fashionable with the aristocracy (and not merely with the clergy). The garden became less a shrine and more a work of art and there was probably a certain amount of secularization of symbols and relaxation of styles: the primitive phase was over.

The founder of the Kamakura régime whose name was Minamoto-no Yoritomo happened to be a garden enthusiast. Since the greatest man in the land was a gardener, grand gardens were made and some of the principal artists of this period, such as the poet and calligrapher Gokyogoku Yoshitune turned to making gardens. This poet, like Petrarch in Italy at almost the same time, and Pope in England centuries later, wrote on garden making; for he is believed to have been the author of *Sakuteiki* (Book on Making Gardens).

In some respects the Golden Age of gardening and garden making, of the art as a whole, was the Muromachi (1394–1572). Garden talk and garden visiting became fashionable, the habit of garden parties with music and poetry reciting became general among the rich and well-bred. Ladies' fashions in clothes were influenced by the garden seasons: there was a correct style of dressing to admire plum-blossom, a different style suitable for admiring the willows in young leaf. So great by that time had the Japanese reputation for gardens become, that in 1402 the first party of garden-visiting tourists arrived from Ming China, and in the following years others followed. Garden-loving noblemen and plutocrats demolished old gardens to get the materials they wanted for new ones; it became customary to present one's friends with a tree or a fine rock for their garden. Harada, in this connection, says:

'Take, for instance the rock named Fujito-saki now in the Sanbo-in garden. It was first in the garden of the Hosokawa mansion, but was taken to the Nijo castle when the garden was made. From there it was removed to Hidiyoshi's Juraku villa, and finally brought to its present site.'

That was in the later Momoyama epoch in which the importance and mania for gardening continued. The principal development of these periods was the evolution of a garden meant to be viewed from a fixed point and not from a boat on the lake. This led to a higher level or stylization and simplification—a step towards the 'dry-landscape' garden which had already been conceived and is mentioned in the *Sakuteiki*. Still more interesting from the English point of view, since it is paralleled by something which happened to English gardening not many years later, Japanese garden designers came very much under the influence of black-and-white Sung painting and Japanese landscape gardeners began to make their gardens in the spirit of Sung Chinese *paysageistes.*

'Thus instead of being drawn with ink and brush, the picture came to be drawn on the ground with trees and rocks, a great step forward in the progress of painting and also in the development of the garden.'

Precisely the same can be said of such English landscape gardens as Stourhead.

Other changes in Japanese gardening were experienced in the following centuries. With the accession to power of the Tokugawa Shoguns there followed popularization, new styles, such as the Path Gardens designed to be seen in the course of a walk, every point of which had some significance. Later there was a period of austere gardening coinciding with a financial squeeze following some kind of economic decline. Moreover, the newly dominant warrior caste favoured austerity in the arts. But my object has been to give some idea of the spirit of Japanese gardening and not to attempt a potted history. And that spirit is epitomized in the extreme case, the 'dry landscape' or, as I prefer to call it, abstract garden.

Probably as good a case in point as any is the Ryoan-ji garden, Kyoto. Enclosed by a wall there is a rectangular plot of 360 square yards. It is perfectly flat and the material is white sand which is raked in various patterns. In it stand fifteen rocks of various shapes and sizes. Nothing else; no trees, no plants; just space, sand and rock. Yet in it the Japanese adept can see stylized every major symbol used in Japanese gardening and the sensitive Japanese visitor experiences the soothing and sobering effect which the maker of this garden intended. Endowed by Tokugawa Iyeyasu and by Tokugawa Itemitsu, this garden was made in 1488 and restored in 1797. Does any European or American experience what the Japanese experience when they contemplate Ryoan-ji? I have met those who said that they did; others that they did not.

Do the symbols expressed by art refined to the ultimate simplicity of one culture ever really touch the members of an alien one? I do not know; but to most English gardeners Ryoan-ji is simply not a garden at all. The fact is that our gardeners have never carried the art, as the Japanese have, to the point of abstraction.

GROTESQUES

It is probably wrong to describe any plant as grotesque; the most one should say is that there are some whose appearance is so unlike what we think of as the proper look of a plant that it shocks our sense of fitness into laughter or surprise. Few of these strange looking plants are native to temperate zones. But there are some which will grow in an English garden; and one can imagine a gifted amateur using some of them to make a surrealist garden or even a comic garden; for, if a garden is a work of art there is no real reason why it should not be a work of comic art; and the only reason why comedy is rare in all the arts is that it is by far the most difficult mood to succeed in. What sort of material would such a comic artist use? I can think of one or two plants to start with.

There are two species of *Colletia* which one would use in such a scheme. *Colletia cruciata* was introduced from Uruguay in 1824 and is quite hardy. It is a shrub to ten feet composed entirely and absurdly of huge spines. A plant may bear a very few small leaves but as a rule there are none at all, the chlorophyll being exposed in the body of the plant which is therefore a dull green all over. Young plants are made up of spines of two different kinds; one kind is triangular, flat, over an inch long at the base; the others are like stout needles, although also flattened at the base, and about an inch and a half long. In adult plants all the spines are of the flat, triangular kind. These spines are modified branches or twigs of the plant and they are closely set in pairs, each pair at right angles to the next pair. So formidable is the armament of this shrub that it cannot be handled at all with bare hands. In appearance it is like a modern work of sculpture in metal, a complex of angles and points. Nor is the impression it makes softened when the shrub flowers, which it does in our autumn. The flowers are very small, produced in pairs or fours or sixes at the base of the spines, they have no petals, only a calyx, stamens and stigma. Appearing thus on what looks like a metal construction designed to express everything that is rebarbative, they look more absurd than natural.

Colletia armata would be another for any planting of grotesques. It is a shrub to eight or nine feet consisting entirely of a complex of stout, dull green spines of circular section, about an inch long, as hard as iron and with very sharp points. Like its congener this is far too well armed to handle with bare hands. Its flowers, borne in early winter as a rule, are white and very fragrant, but it is not advisable to approach the nose too closely to this ferociously armed plant. The flowers on this one, too, look quite out of place. This plant is like a manifestation of cruelty; and since laughter is said to be a modified snarl, it is also a manifestation of the comic spirit.

Grotesqueness of a different kind is provided by a native plant, *Corylus avellana* var. *contorta*. It is a hazel, an ordinary cobnut tree but most astonishingly contorted or twisted in all its parts. Every single twig on a bush of this variety is screwed or twisted into a corkscrew shape, and the whole plant seems to writhe in some kind of dreadful fit. It was, by one account, found in a hedgerow at Frocester, Gloucestershire, in 1863 and thereafter propagated by cuttings to perpetuate its grotesque habit of growth. I have wondered however if that account of its origin can really be correct.

The only satisfactory explanation for the contortions which I have ever heard is that the first bush of its kind was a graft-hybrid or chimaera. Such hybrids can occur when instead of the rootstock remaining confined below the scion and simply feeding that scion, its substance grows with and becomes involved with that of the scion so that the wood above the graft point is a more or less intimate mixture of stock and scion tissues. If we suppose two kinds of *Corylus* to have become united in this way, with one providing half the cross section of every twig, the other completing the cross section; and if we further suppose one to be slightly faster growing by nature than the other, then exactly the corkscrew growth of *C. avellana* var. *contorta* would be produced. It is, however, very difficult to see how such a union could have been produced by some accident in the wild, although I have seen trees and shrubs in woods and hedges grown together and joined by accident. It seems to me more likely that this corkscrew hazel is the outcome of a deliberate act of grafting by a gardener; on the other hand the finding at Frocester is apparently well established as a fact.

A familiar example of a grotesque plant produced by graft hybridization is that of *Laburnocytisus adamii.* Jean Louis Adam, a French nurserymen of Vitry, near Paris, grafted *Cytisus purpurea*, the purple broom, on to common laburnum. In 1825 his grafted plant produced a branch which bore flowers of a curious shade of brown, intermediate between the yellow of laburnum and the purple of the broom. This was propagated by cuttings and put into commerce and named *Laburnum adamii.* Some trees of this chimaera were producing branches bearing pure yellow laburnum flowers and others bearing pure purple broom flowers, as well as others with the flowers of intermediate type.

The mixture of tissues which occurs in these chimaeras is not so intimate as to be, so to speak, chemical. A section of the wood under a microscope will reveal a layer of tissue of one plant, another layer from the other. The union is close and intimate, but it is not a combination or compound. *Crataegomespilus,* the hawthorn/medlar chimaera is another case in point. And since it is possible for a very skilful gardener to make a chimaera deliberately—the thing has been done several times—it might be better for the comic gardener to rely on skill rather than nature to produce his plant material. Still, I don't suppose he could devise anything more grotesque than the *Colletias.*

COLD NORTH—WARM SOUTH

'It will survive in the south, but is not hardy enough for northern gardens . . .' There are few gardeners who have not heard that said more than once in their gardening lifetime. How much justification is there for it? The answer is, very little; the statement is misconceived, and the winter climate of England is simply not arranged like that at all.

The coldest month of the year is January. There are exceptional years, of course, but in order to generalize one has to use averages. So if a plant is hardy enough to survive the month of January, it will survive all the rest. There is a weather statistic known as the January Mean Minimum; it is an average or mean of minimum temperatures taken at a great many weather centres and other places where temperature records are kept over a number of years, not less than ten. If you take a map of Britain and on it draw lines connecting all the places with the same January Mean Minimum, you get a set of isotherms for the January Mean Minima which divide the map into temperature zones.

This has been done on the map printed on page 190; and by far the most striking thing about the resulting diagram is that the isotherms run more north and south than they run east and west. So that, roughly speaking, it would be truer to say of a doubtfully hardy plant that it would grow in the west but not in the east, than that it would grow in the south but not in the north.

The coldest (winter only, a summer map would reverse the picture) area of England is enclosed by the isotherm of 38°F. (3.3°C) and the east coast of the Midlands, from as far south as Essex to as far north as York and beyond and inland to Sheffield, Derby and Coventry. Compare the extreme south-east about London but down to the Kentish coast, with the extreme north-west not only of England but of Scotland. Even the most northerly region of Scotland is warmer in January than the most south-easterly region of Kent.

The most favoured regions of Britain and Ireland from the point of view of tender exotic plants—all the Australasian and Chilean flowering shrubs and trees for example—are those west of the isotherm 42°F (5.5°C). That is, all the south and west of Ireland; the Scilly Isles; Cornwall and much of Devon; and the three Welsh peninsulas.

If that were all there was to it, the problem of the gardener wishing to plant shrubs, trees and herbaceous perennials of doubtful or marginal hardiness, would be very simple: he would know from his geographical position either that he could or couldn't. But the picture is complicated by the matter of micro-climates. A garden at sea level in the south-east is warmer in

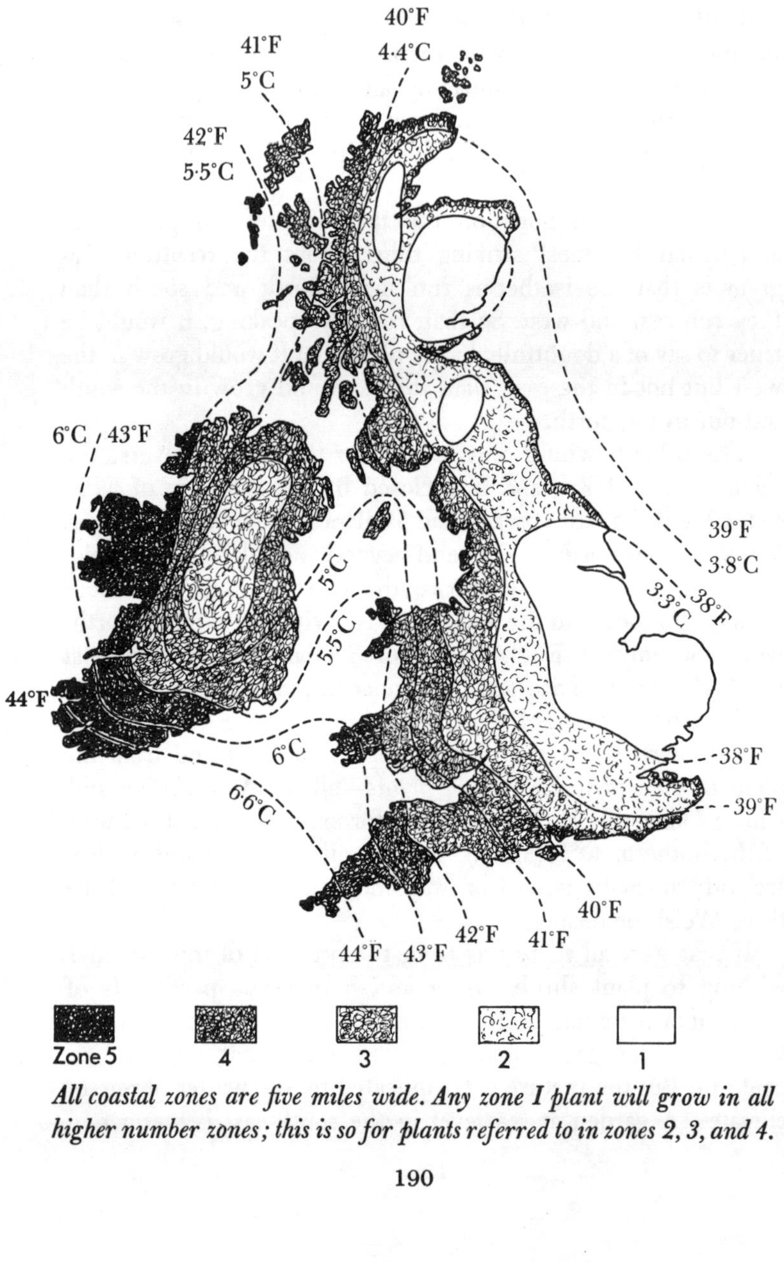

All coastal zones are five miles wide. Any zone I plant will grow in all higher number zones; this is so for plants referred to in zones 2, 3, and 4.

January than a garden in the north-west sited at 1,000 feet on the eastern slope of a mountain. Another very obvious case in point is that of our coastal strip. For approximately five miles inland from the sea the climate of the land is affected by the massive stability of the sea's temperature; both extreme cold and extreme heat are mitigated by this influence. On the map the coastal strip from Scarborough nearly to Dundee, for example, has been sketched by the artist as for the 39–40° region: it is an approximation only, but that strip has an advantage of 1° (average) at least over the country further inland. In practical confirmation of this, there are near seaside gardens all down that narrow strip of England where you can see surviving plants which would not live through the winters a few miles further inland.

Apart from the major area of greatest January cold already mentioned, there are three others. They are the white circles or ovals, all in Scotland; but note that they are arranged north to south, not east to west, and to the east rather than the north of the country. Gardens in the extreme north are better off than those in even the most southerly of those circles when it comes to winter temperature and the cultivation of less than absolutely hardy plants.

DRAGON TREES

A handsome and vaguely palm-like plant which you can easily grow from seed to stock a greenhouse or decorate a room is *Dracaena draco*. It is becoming quite popular as a large house-plant. For the Guanches the Dragon Tree was something much more than that. The Guanches were the ancient people of Cro-Magnon stock who once populated the Canary Islands until, killed or married off first by the Norman conquerors of the Islands under De Bethancourt and thereafter by the Spaniards, they became extinct. For them *Dracaena draco* was a holy object, perhaps one of the trees which have been gods, a sort of Guanche Yggdrasil. To the gardener who has seen this odd plant only as a single trunk to four or five feet with its tuft of sword leaves resembling those of yucca, this may seem surprising: there is nothing awe-inspiring in such a plant. But if you consider the Dragon Tree of Oratava, or the even more remarkable Dragon Tree of Icod which was destroyed in a gale a hundred years ago when, according to local tradition, it was about seven thousand years old, the case is different. I have seen the Dragon Tree of Oratava and it is the strangest vegetable I ever set eyes on and one of the most imposing.

As Dracaena is not a tree at all, nor a palm, but a member of the *Liliaceae* related to *Yucca* and to *Cordyline*, there is no means of telling the age of a specimen. The Icod plant is in fact very unlikely to have been 7,000 years old although (see below), this species of Dracaena does live to a very great age. What is certain is that the specimen at Icod was so huge that the inside of its hollow trunk was used by the Guanches as a chapel or shrine; that after the Spanish conquest it was purified and was consecrated by the Church as a Catholic chapel; and that eight people could hear mass inside it, ten including the priest and server. There are several descriptions of this colossal vegetable extant, but I shall not quote them but confine myself to the younger but still enormous Dragon Tree of Oratava as seen by myself. And there are some other very large specimens on the Islands.

The Royal Horticultural Society's *Dictionary of Gardening* describes this plant, rather cautiously, as 'one of the oldest of known trees'. When I was there I was told 'probably about 3,000 years', but I do not know how this was arrived at. I suppose it might be estimated by the amount of ramification, since its rate of growth has perhaps been closely observed and often described and figured for some centuries. It consists of an immensely stout, buttressed and misshapen trunk of an elephant-grey spongy material which is not quite wood and is yet described as wood since there is no other word for it. This is topped by an elaborate ramification, the main branches being themselves further ramified, of this same spongy grey stuff. At the tip of every branch there is a crowded tuft of twenty-four-inch sword leaves of dull green. The whole thing looks like a nightmare tree or something put into a landscape by a child, a very primitive or a very modern painter. Or, from the gardener's point of view, it looks like a colossal and complex yucca whose woody and green parts are out of all proportion. I have not its latest measurements but the latest I do have give the height at seventy feet and the diameter of the trunk as fifteen feet, which gives us a circumference of roughly fifty feet.

When I saw this Dragon Tree its flowering for that year was long since over and it was covered with enormous racemes of date-like ripening fruits which were beginning to fall so that there were seeds all over the ground under the tree. I brought some home and they were germinated at Wye College. The surviving seedling in the hothouses there is now a fine, large young Dragon Tree. It is ten years old but it has not yet begun to ramify.

In 1594 in Seville there was published a book by Father Alonso de Espinosa who had gone hastily from Central America to Tenerife upon receiving news of a holy image which had miraculously appeared among the heathen there, in the leafy head of a pine tree. At that time the Guanches were still a considerable, although a declining and miserable community. Espinosa's book is called *Del Origen Y Milagros de la Santa Imagen de Nuestra Senora de Candelaria Que Aparecio en la Isla de Tenerife, con la Descripcion de esta Isla.* An English translation by Sir

Clements Markham was published by the Hakluyt Society in 1907. The Father has this to say of the great Dragon Tree:

'There is another tree called "draco" which is large but with few branches. At the ends of the branches there are only 5 or 6 leaves, little thicker or larger than cones. It has no heart within. The wood is very spongy and light, so that it serves for the covering of hives and to make shields. The gum which this tree exudes is called dragon's blood, and that which the tree sweats out without cutting is the best, and is called "blood by the drop". It is very good for medicine, for sealing letters, and for making the teeth red.'

He does not say why anyone should want to make their teeth red; perhaps it was a Guanche fashion. Other chroniclers and historians of the islands have something to say about these extraordinary tree-like plants. For they could hardly fail to take into account the most extraordinary objects in an archipelago which is rich in strange, beautiful and wonderful things.

FLOWERING AND DYING

Plants which flower once and then die are called monocarpic: all annuals and biennials are cases in point; having within one cycle of seasons or two produced seed to continue the species, they die. Much more curious are some very long-lived plants which die also after flowering. A number of the bamboo genera come into this class of monocarpic ancients.

Sasa tessellata, formerly an *Arundinaria*, is a bamboo whose canes attain a height of six feet. The canes are very fine, only about an eighth of an inch in diameter, but the dark green leaves are eighteen inches long and four inches wide. It is a fast spreading species and in gardens can be planted only where it will not interfere with neighbouring plants. This bamboo was introduced into Britain in 1845, that is to say 123 years ago; no plant of it has yet flowered. What will happen when this *Sasa* does flower? The answer is to be found in the case of another bamboo, *Pleioblastus chino*.

This is a five-foot bamboo with six-inch leaves which are dark green mottled yellow. In the year 189*3 every known plant* in cultivation in this country flowered and then died, so that the species was wiped out in Britain and had to be reintroduced. It seems likely that *Sasa tessellata* will go the same way. What happens in nature? There is presumably a pause while the seeds germinate, and then a new generation arises which will perhaps not flower for twenty-five years, fifty years, even for more than a century.

In *Arundinaria anceps*, a bamboo which has handsome purplish-green or bronze canes to a height of fifteen feet, flowering is apt to be at intervals of twenty-five years, and again the plants die after flowering. But this habit of dying after flowering does not mean the death of the whole plant in the case of all bamboos because it occurs only in those species which flower on all the canes at once. In others only some of the canes flower and die, leaving others to flower and die another year, by which time young canes are growing from the root. In such cases a plant may live for centuries.

The 'Century Plant' of popular legend is not, however, a bamboo but *Agave americana*, or perhaps some other species of *Agave*. As is so often the case, popular legend has no truth in it. It is untrue that *any* agave species flowers only once in a century; but it is true that the rosette of leaves which produces the flower spike dies after flowering; in those species which produce offsets, this does not mean the death of the plant, but in some species or perhaps only in individuals of certain species, there are no offsets and thus the whole plant dies after flowering. The small species of *Agave* flower in eight years from seed, the largest in forty years. This does not compare with the bamboo *Sasa tessellata*, but half a lifetime would be a long time to wait for flowers if this were a genus grown for its flowers; but of course it is not. Yet the flowers, when they do come, are spectacular if only for their great height: in *A. ferox*, the Mexican agave which, with *A. horrida*, was used by Emiliano Zapata as a means of execution (see below), the stem which carries the large and spectacular flowers is up to thirty feet tall.

The famous Mexican politician's way of using *Agave* plants to execute his prisoners is curious and horrible. At the centre of *Agave* plants is a tightly packed cylinder of young leaves yet to open, topped by an iron hard group of spines ending in a sharp point. In *A. horrida* this tip spine has the shape of a corkscrew. And the margins of the leaves are armed with ferocious hooked spines as hard as steel hooks. Zapata, a bandit-like revolutionary who finally won to office by conquest, and who was appropriately called by one of his biographers, the Crimson Jester, used to have those of his prisoners and political enemies who were condemned to death, tied down over the growing point of an *Agave* so that he was slowly, but not too slowly, impaled and pierced by the fast-growing tip. As far as I know, and if we disregard the use of trees as gibbets or their fruits as poison, this is the only case of living plants being used to kill men.

Thus the 'Century Plant', while it does not, in fact, take a century to flower, has an even more singular distinction.

GROWING MISTLETOE

Why is it that whereas in the North and near North of France mistletoe is so common that almost every apple tree in the orchards, every poplar tree in sight, carries from one to fifty plants, in Britain this parasite, if not actually rare, is certainly not nearly so common? I do not know the answer to this question. Perhaps our orchard trees are better cared for; on the other hand I have heard that Norman farmers get more money from their orchards by letting the trees carry mistletoe which they cut and sell to the English at Christmas time, than for their apples and cider. It is quite certain that if one had, for example, a coppice of poplars, one of the favourite host plants of the parasite, and could cultivate mistletoe on the trees, it would be a valuable crop during the last weeks of December.

Viscum is not quite so simple a genus as it looks. A German botanist, Tubeuf, whose *Monographie der Mistel* is a standard work, discovered that while all the European *Viscum album* mistletoes look alike, there are three races, one which will grow only on conifers, a thing one never sees in Britain but often in Switzerland; one which is even more specific since it is confined to the genus *Abies*, the fir-trees; and one which will grow only on broad-leaved trees. He discovered, moreover, that this third race, the one we have in Britain, is sudivided into 'sub-races' each with its own preference in the matter of the host to be battened on.

These facts would be very important for any would-be cultivator of mistletoe for market. For example, if the trees he proposed to plant with mistletoe were poplars, it would be worth his while to go round France and gather berries from mistletoe plants growing on poplar; for although it is not absolutely demonstrated that the sub-races of Tubeuf's race number three are as specific as the three main races of *Viscum album*, it is clear that one would have a better chance on poplar with seed taken from poplar, on hawthorn with seeds taken from hawthorn, on apple with seeds taken from apple, and so forth.

To gather ripe berries one would have to go to the chosen country in the middle of May when the berries are ripe—the Pas de Calais would be a good place, or the country round Boulogne, or parts of Picardie. The finest mistletoe plants, perfect spheres a yard in diameter, are always out of reach, which doubtless explains their quality, but that would not matter if it were seed you wanted.

As for the method of planting once you have the seed, that is very easy. You press the ripe berries on to the lower side of healthy branches of the host trees, so that the single seed in each fruit is held in place by a little sticky mess. This, composed of a viscid pulp, quickly hardens, holding the seed in place. On germination the radicle penetrates the bark of the tree and in due course the root grows in the cambium layer, robbing the tree of part of its food, but not killing it.

Unfortunately the mistletoe is dioecious or almost always so. There are plants with flowers of both sexes, but as a rule the sexes are borne on separate plants, and it is necessary to get some of both, preferably on the same host, but at least in the near neighbourhood of each other. If enough seeds are planted, the chances are that you will get males as well as females among the seedlings.

I am not recommending mistletoe cultivation to the man who wants a quick return. It would be several and perhaps many years before any cutting could be done, for growth is slow. I do not even know that the thing could be done at all; but it is an intriguing idea and perhaps one day someone will try it.

AGAINST COLD WINDS

I have already shown that though the east of Britain has a colder winter climate than the west, the north is not colder than the south. But in those parts of the north and north-east where it is an observed fact that plants do not grow as well as they do in the south and west, and are more often killed in winter, the enemy is not cold alone, it is cold wind. A large piece of England stands as shelter from north-east winds between the south-west and the source of those winds, but the north-east has no such protection. Wind is in any case the gardener's worst enemy. Tender plants which will survive surprisingly low temperatures in perfectly still air, are killed outright by a few days of icy north-easters, as I was able to see for myself in Devon and Cornwall in the atrocious winter of 1962/3. So for gardeners in the north-east, special techniques are necessary in gardening.

What does cold wind actually do to plants, especially to evergreens? Almost exactly what drought does, causes transpiration from the leaves at a speed which cannot be matched by the plant's power to take up water which may, in such conditions, be frozen in the soil anyway. As well, it may cause defoliation, and it may even shake the plants loose in the ground.

The worst thing to put between your plants and the wind is a wall. According to Mr Kenneth Lemmon (*Gardening in the North*, Pan Piper), there is a turbulence set up by wind on the lee side of a three foot wall at between nine and twenty-four feet from the wall, which does more damage than the wind itself, while at sixty feet the wind speed is back to normal. A permeable barrier is much better. The wind speed is reduced by it without creating any turbulence. Mr Lemmon says that for practical purposes the gardener may consider that one foot of barrier height will give him ten feet of protection. But what is a permeable barrier? He suggests one inch laths at one inch intervals. I suggest hedges, but I will come to that in a moment.

It is an interesting fact that it was from the work of horticultural specialists doing research on wind-breaks that the engineers who planned the cross-Channel bridge which was at one time being considered as an alternative to the Channel-tunnel, got a hint which led them to the same conclusion about permeable barriers. What they had to allow for was gales of up to one hundred mph sweeping the bridge and simply blowing cars and trucks over. If a low parapet was used, the bridge would have to be closed in gale conditions. But a very high parapet would have meant enormously increased stress from the wind itself: it would have been like a sail with a surface area of nearly eighty acres. It was found in wind-tunnel experiments that a lattice work of steel, leaving the sides of the bridge open to the light and view, would so reduce even very high winds that they would cease to be a danger and yet not offer such resistance to the wind as to put the bridge itself in hazard. This confirmed what horticultural experiments in wind-breaks had demonstrated.

If you are going to do the job properly the best way is to put up a temporary fence of open laths as cheaply as possible and in the lee of it plant the Leyland Cypress, × *Cupressocyparis leylandii*. It is the fastest growing conifer we have, it stands up to wind, and it tolerates even salt spray in seaside situations. Other trees recommended by some writers are *Quercus ilex*, the evergreen oak, and *Pinus radiata*. Neither are good enough, in my opinion: I have had the evergreen oak badly defoliated even in Devonshire by persistent frost winds from the north-east; and *Pinus radiata* when mature is frequently blown clean out of the ground; the great wind-break belt of it planted on Tresco to protect the garden there from Atlantic winds, I mean the famous Abbey Gardens, has been a serious problem for that reason. *Pinus muricata* has all the qualities of *P. radiata* and a stronger root-hold.

Trees are the first line of defence against wind because being tall they have a much longer 'wind-shadow' or lee. The deeper the belt of trees, the better. It is impractical to recommend to the ordinary gardener such plantings as exceed his whole garden area, but it is an interesting fact that in the lee of a forty-foot belt of Leyland Cypress, even a gale is felt only as a zephyr. In the lee of the trees it is best to plant a hedge of one of the plants which have been proved to be wind resistant: among them are escallonias, and several of the olearias. The olearias can, in fact, be planted as a first line of defence, and then the trees, for they are astonishingly indifferent to wind and even salt-spray. The best are *O. traversii* and *O. haastii*, both from the South Pacific and used to ferocious gales. A native shrub which has the same qualities is the pretty, grey-leaved *Hippophae rhamnoides*, Sea Buckthorn. Plant both sexes, as this is dioecious and the orange berries are most attractive.

By carefully thought-out planting under the guidance of a good nurseryman, it is possible to create, even in the bleak north-east, an enclave of almost still air in all but gale conditions, and in that enclave which is to be your garden, to manage the planting in such a way that the less robust plants are protected by the tough ones. You may have succeeded in bouncing most of the wind right over your garden, or so filtering it that it does very little harm, but the fact remains that the long-sustained easterly wind will be drying the air so persistently that some plants will suffer. Evergreen flowering shrubs, like camellias and some of the daphnes and the less hardy rhododendrons will still suffer, but much less if they are in the lee and under the shade of hardier shrubs which although deciduous mitigate the severity of the weather with their network of twigs and branchlets.

It was Cobbett of 'Rural Rides' fame who first remarked that it is always warmer in a wood, albeit a leafless wood, than outside it. The ground is never so cold under a lacing of branches if only because loss by radiation from the surface of the soil is reduced. Gardeners who have never seen for themselves how even a cover of anti-bird netting will protect a strawberry plantation in flower against spring radiation frost, always find this hard to believe. But it is true; and the phenomenon can be used by the clever gardener to grow relatively tender plants beyond the geographical/climatic limits normally assigned to them.

CAMELLIAS

Why are not camellias more commonly planted in Britain? It may be that their completely undeserved reputation for tenderness has something to do with it. My point here is that as evergreens—never mind the flowers for a moment—they are far more attractive and quite as hardy as many which are commonly planted. Now add to that some of the most attractive flowers in the world's flora, and you have a shrub which should be in every garden not in a chalk or limestone region.

The season is a long one. It begins with the winter-flowering camellias. They are forms or derivatives of *Camellia sasanqua*, not, it is true, as ruggedly hardy as the spring-flowering *C. japonica* and its derivatives, from which other winter-flowering camellias derive, but hardy enough for much of Britain. It has dark green lustrous leaves and is so good as an evergreen that I have seen it clipped to shape in parts of Italy. The flowers open from November throughout the winter and in the type plant they are white. But there are some good cultivars: 'Narumi-Gata' has white flowers tinged with rose-pink and fragrant from November to January; the semi-double carmine flowers of 'Hiryu' are also fragrant and there is a lovely pure white semi-double, 'Mine-no-Yuki'. In 'Shishigashira' the double pink flowers are three inches across. The deepest pink is called 'Papaver'. There is a *C. reticulata* x *C. saluenensis* hybrid called 'Inspiration' which flowers in winter.

In very early spring *Camellia reticulata* comes into flower. It is a shrubby small tree to thirty feet and not hardy enough for the east side of Britain, perfectly happy in the west if sheltered from north and east. The species contains the most magnificent of all camellia flowers in the cultivar 'Semi-plena', an ancient plant of Chinese temple gardens with flowers up to six inches in diameter. The species is so early in flower that even in gardens where it is hardy the flowers are often ruined by spring frost.

Next to flower are the cultivars of *C. japonica* and its hybrids which are numerous. This camellia is very hardy, being unharmed by more than thirty degrees of frost. It is a shrubby bush which in time may attain to twenty feet or more but is commonly smaller and in any case varies in stature from one kind to another. Some well tried cultivars are 'Adolphe Audusson' with crimson-scarlet flowers and a boss of prominent yellow stamens; 'Alba Simplex' a pure white single; 'Beni-wabisuki' with small crimson cup-shaped flowers and scarlet stamens; 'Elegans' which has an arching habit and anemone-centred rose-pink flowers; 'Lady Clare' an almost prostrate sprawling shrub with clear pink semi-double flowers; 'Pink Cup of Beauty', a form which has water-lily shaped flowers in a clear pink. There are many more but these are a few with which I am familiar.

In such gardens as the Peña Palace in Portugal and Dartington Hall near Totnes cultivars of *C. japonica* have reached an enormous size and are often so covered with flowers that, as they fall, the ground becomes ankle deep in petals. But good though these older kinds still are, it rather looks as if planting will, for some years, favour the newer *williamsii* hybrid, camellias Those originated at Caerhays Castle, one of the finest camellia gardens in the world and one where many camellias from the Far East were planted for the first time in the west and where much breeding of new ones was undertaken by that great gardener J. C. Williams. They are all crosses between *C. japonica* and *C. saluenensis.* The best, certainly the most popular, is supposed to be 'Donation', a fast-growing shrub with double silver-pink flowers. A very fine and very early single white is 'Cornish Snow'. 'J. C. Williams' is a single rose-pink, 'St. Ewe' a single rose-red, and 'Salutation' a large-flowered clear pink.

MECONOPSIS

For some time after *Meconopsis betonicifolia*, the sky-blue poppy so called, was introduced from Tibet in 1924—it was called *Meconopsis baileyi* in those days—it was the glamour plant of gardens. Where it could be grown it was loudly boasted of; and those who could not grow it envied those who could.

Its particular shade of blue is unique, it is true: but, from experience of this, it is very far from being the best of the blue 'poppies' from the Far East. Its faults as a garden plant are numerous. Unless a stock be carefully rogued over a number of years, it is not even reliably blue, the flowers often being a depressing shade of violet or mauve; and it is not reliably perennial, plants which flower in the year of their planting or the year after being raised from seed, nearly always die thereafter and it seems to me that this meconopsis is, in fact, a biennial and in any case monocarpic. It is true that in some gardens most of the plants or at least a fair proportion of them seem to be perennial; I have been told that if, in the first year of a plant's maturity, one removes the flower buds and prevents it from flowering, it will then become perennial. The R.H.S. *Dictionary of Gardening* says as much. I can only say that those I grew did not behave like that.

Contrast this with *M. grandis*, from Nepal and Tibet. It is not only perennial but plants increase rapidly to form large clumps which can be divided to increase the stock. As to the colour, if you get the right form, and that is very important indeed since the colour of this species is variable and can be a disagreeable purple, it is the most lovely deep, pure blue, the most intense blue that I know among flowers. If a blue can be fiery, this one is, and only the finest of the Oriental gentians can compare with it for colour. True, it is not the sky-blue of *M. betonicifolia* but, at least for my taste, a much more beautiful colour. The form to get is called 'Prain's'. It is presumably named after the Prain who was at one time Director of Kew Gardens and before that of the Calcutta Botanic Gardens. The only source of this form which I know is the Slieve Donard Nursery in Northern Ireland.

There is not much point in growing meconopsis excepting where the conditions suit them and in Britain they are better, on the whole, in Scotland than in England though they do very well in the West Country. They need a woodland type of soil, peaty if possible and with plenty of leaf mould; they will only grow well in high rainfall areas but good drainage is essential as well. In dry soils and atmospheres they fail or are very poor.

I have grown other meconopses. *M. regia* is a biennial which has to be raised from seed every year if you want it flowering in the garden every spring or summer. In the first year from seed it makes a very large and very beautiful rosette of hairy, silvery leaves and this persists throughout the winter and is one of the most lovely things in any winter border or shrubbery, so much so that I have heard good gardeners regret that these plants ever flower at all. In the second year the five foot flowering stem grows from the middle of the rosette. This branches symmetrically, its lower branches carrying several flowers, the upper ones only a single flower. The poppy-like flowers are clear yellow and have red anthers. These meconopses are very stately and handsome plants but out of place unless the scale of the garden is large to match.

M. napaulensis has the same biennial habit but is an even more stately plant, with a flower stem to eight feet. I only ever got one colour in my stock of this, possibly because I always raised seedlings from seed of my own plants; it was claret red. *M. napaulensis* has the same kind of beautiful silvery rosette of hairy leaves at the base, persisting all winter in great beauty. The best form of this is blue-flowered, but I have never even seen it.

An oddity of this genus is that all but one species come from the Far East, and that only exception from Wales, and some other parts of Europe. It is *M. cambrica*, a perennial with yellow or orange flowers and it was a weed in my Devon garden but one which was valued.

There are a number of other fine meconopses, some of them difficult to cultivate in gardens; *M. superba* has very lovely white flowers, *M. punicea* is a vivid red, *M. bella* either clear pink or sky blue. A lot of them were of earlier introduction to this country than *M. betonicifolia* and one or two even have pale blue flowers, yet none ever made quite the popular success of *M. betonicifolia*. I have never understood why. Publicity?

HONEY FUNGUS

You are walking with the owner round a great garden of trees and flowering shrubs on the moister and warmer side of Britain, admiring the garden and the plants. You come upon a great rhododendron or camellia, a myrtle or some other shrub or tree which is clearly dying; its leaves are dry and drooping, its whole bearing dismal. Or you notice a great gap in the planting: some large plant has been removed. You look inquiringly at your host who looks gloomy and says 'Honey Fungus' . . . And you sympathize, knowing that the fungus is sending out the shiny black cords of its rhizomorphs—the organs which give it its vernacular name of Bootlace Fungus—a few inches under the soles of your feet, reaching for another victim in your host's garden.

Armillaria mellea is an agaric living on dead tree stumps and other vegetable carrion, usually underground. But it does not, unfortunately, confine itself to such carrion. From its seat on dead wood it will reach out and attack the roots of living plants, usually trees or shrubs but sometimes even herbaceous plants and bulbs. Suppose a shrub to be dying for no apparent reason; the experienced gardener examines the trunk at the collar, just below and above soil level; he lifts the bark there and he finds the wood covered with fan-shaped networks of white mycelium. Well, that could be some other and less deadly fungus, perhaps; but when, from that nucleus of infection, the gardener finds those black cord-like strands growing outwards below the soil in search of other roots to fasten on, he knows the worst, unmistakably: Honey Fungus.

Are there any prophylactic measures which the gardener

can take to prevent this fungus from establishing itself among his plants? Consider, first, its method of self-propagation. From the dead wood the plant lives on at first it sends up fruit bodies, that is toadstools, in late autumn. The caps are honey-coloured (hence the epithet *mellea*, honey); the scales are brown; the stems are yellowish-brown and they have a ring round the upper quarter, not far below the cap. Sometimes these groups are very large, and in any case there will be several of the toadstools together. From the gills of the caps are released, in due course, millions of minute spores, each one a possible source of new plants. So that it is some use to destroy the toadstools as soon as you see them. True, the spores always germinate on vegetable carrion and never on a living plant, so that they are not immediately dangerous. But as we have seen, it is from the original settlement on carrion that the plants put out their 'bootlaces' to attack the roots of living green plants.

Probably the best prophylactic measure is strict garden hygiene; this means that all tree stumps have to be dug up with every bit of root and burnt; also all other dead wood; that the land must be sharply drained; that all stakes must be well-pitched or creosoted. By depriving the spores of the *Armillaria* of places to settle and grow, you limit its spread. But it is a difficult and laborious business in a time like ours when labour is scarce and dear. Worse, in great woodland gardens it is impossible, for the *Armillaria* can grow on the small decaying twigs which come down every year with the annual leaf fall.

Supposing that a tree or shrub or hedge is killed by the fungus, then what can one do to check or destroy the source of infection? First it is very necessary to get out every bit of the victim's roots, and to burn it; next to remove all the soil from its site to a depth of two feet and burn that; thirdly to water the surrounding soil, after thoroughly forking it over, with a strong solution of formalin. It may or may not work, but certainly you cannot sit back and do nothing. *Armillaria* attacked a peach tree in one of the hot-houses of a well-known firm of market-gardeners. Before it could be checked and because it was not recognized at once, it had infected every tree in that house and wiped out the lot.

There is, however, a considerable consolation. I know several gardens in which *Armillaria mellea* has killed one or two shrubs; why has it not killed many more? Why, in my own garden in Devonshire which was full of immovably enormous dead tree stumps and roots, did we get tremendous shows of Honey Fungus toadstools but never, with one doubtful exception, lose a plant to Honey Fungus? There is no question that it is possible to have this fungus in your garden and yet to lose no plants to it. One theory is that the fungus can only attack live plants which have damaged roots or are in poor health through, for example, bad drainage.

It is wise to do all you can to keep this fungus out of your garden or to destroy it if it be present. But it does not follow that its presence necessarily means disaster.

VINEYARDS

Since, in 1948, Mr Ray Barrington Brock working in Surrey and I, working in Kent, reintroduced viticulture to Britain, two or three small vineyards have been planted and are producing a little wine. In the right places and with the right kinds of grape-vines, it can be done and we now have enough experience to draw some tentative conclusions. Before coming to them, however, there are some other points to be recapitulated.

England, like most of Germany, is on the extreme periphery of the wine-vine's country. This means that the climate is seasonally but not permanently suitable for viticulture; success probably depends on the summer position of the big Azores anticyclone.

From about the ninth century until the nineteenth the vine advanced and retreated, advanced and retreated, under several influences; in Germany the expansion and contraction of viticulture can be related, fairly closely, to wheat prices. B. H. Slicher van Bath, in his *The Agrarian History of Western Europe A.D. 500–1850*,* established the correlation with beautiful clarity. When wheat prices rose above a certain critical figure, vineyards were grubbed and wheat grown; and when wheat was cheap, vineyards were planted far beyond the limits of present day German viticulture.

It is impossible to make this correlation for English farming in the Middle Ages, and all one can say is that there is some correlation between domestic viticulture and the costs of wine importing; it was only worth growing wine in Britain if and when imported wine was scarce or dear; when it became plentiful and cheap, domestic viticulture declined. From the eleventh century (with about forty vineyards listed in the Domesday Book), to about the middle of the fourteenth, vineyard planting increased, with Gloucestershire as probably the most important viticultural county. In his *De Pontificum Anglorum* (A.D. 1125) William of Malmesbury wrote of Gloucestershire:

'Regio plusquam alicae Angliae provinciae vinearum frequentior densior proventa uberior sapore jacundior. Vina enim ipsa bibentium ora tristi non torquent acredine, quippe parum debeat Gallicis dulcedine.'

(This county is planted more thickly with vineyards than any

* Trans. by Olive Ordish: Edward Arnold, London, 1963.

other in England, more plentiful in crops and more pleasant in flavour. For the wines do not offend the mouth with sharpness since they do not yield to the French in sweetness.)

After about 1350 viticulture in England declined. Two reasons for this are suggested. One is that there was a rather abrupt climatic change, with summers cooler and wetter; there is evidence for this. The other reason was doubtless economic: wine was reaching England from Gascony very cheap. Neither cause alone would have led to a serious decline; viticulture has great stability for it is more profitable than other branches of agriculture and horticulture. In periods of agricultural depression in the Middle Ages, vineyard rents never fell by more than 30 per cent when rents of arable fell by as much as 60 per cent. But two unfavourable influences at one time were too much for English viticulture. Still, some viticulture, sometimes more sometimes less, was practised into the seventeenth century. The thirteenth century Pershore Priory vineyard passing into lay hands at the Dissolution was still being cultivated as late as 1544. Viticulture was revived by one or two gentlemen landowners in the eighteenth, and again in the nineteenth century by the Marquis of Bute in Wales. Probably the thirty-four years separating the end of the big Welsh vineyard and the planting of Mr Brock's and my own, were the only years since some time in the third century when there were no vineyards of any kind in Britain.

I would say that the first condition for success is a warm, dry summer climate. That eliminates all but the coastal strips of the south-west and west, but means that those coastal strips, especially in Cornwall and Pembrokeshire, would be very suitable; also the south coast and the south-east and parts of the east. A study of weather statistics compared with those of the northernmost vineyards of Continental Europe, suggests that the ideal country for viticulture in England would be in the region of Eastbourne and on the Isle of Wight, but many other places would be quite as good as, for example, the Rhine Valley.

Winter climate does not matter; *Vitis vinifera* is ruggedly hardy.

If these are facts, why has viticulture been made profitable in the Rhineland but failed to persist in Sussex? The answer is that the Rhinelanders found a stable market for their wines in the countries all down the Rhine to its mouth from the eighth century; improved their wines; and so held on to their market. But Sussex could not compete with the London importers from Gascony.

The second condition for success is correct exposure: the vineyard should be on a slope or hillside, the steeper the better, facing between due south and south-east, with the rows of vines running due north and south. The nearer to the sea the better, provided the site is far enough inland to be safe from salt-spray in the wind.

The third condition for success is a light and preferably stony soil, very well drained. White wine is best grown on limestone or even chalk. The Champagne country is chalk. Vineyards are not likely to succeed in this country on heavy or even medium clay soils.

The fourth condition is right choice of plants. It is very likely that as experiment continues, if it does, vines more suitable than those we have hitherto chosen from the hundreds of varieties tried, will reach us from, for example, Germany and perhaps the USSR. Meanwhile, my own choice would be to make the vineyards with three varieties and the wine with all three kinds of grapes together. They are 'Riesling x Sylvaner' a pure *V. vinifera* hybrid of two famous varieties which is earlier and more fruitful than either parent; 'Seyve-Villard 5.276' a hybrid with more *vinifera* than American *Vitis* in its breeding and which has proved itself reliable and very fruitful here: and 'Seibel 13.053', another hybrid, this time with more American than European in its breeding, vigorous, very fruitful and yielding quite good wine if the grapes are perfectly ripe. The first would give the wine aroma and flavour; the second bulk and alcohol; the third would be an insurance against a bad year with the 'Seyve-Villard'. The wine could be made white; but it would tend to be a very faintly rose colour; it would be light and very dry, and its alcohol content would vary from year to year of course, but would not be less than 8 per cent or more than 10 per cent. It would be drinkable in one year from the vintage; and even in a very good year would not improve by keeping in bottle, for more than three years.

Probably the only thing which could make English wine commercially viable would be still higher prices for imported wine. No English grower could, as some importers can, market drinkable wine at 8*s.* or 9*s.* the bottle. There is one other helpful factor, however, the novelty of drinking English wine makes it possible to charge more for a bottle than the wine is worth.

As a means of exploiting poor soils in very good 'early' but topographically unploughable situations, and of giving a possibly profitable occupation to keen gardeners who have retired from their 'gainful' occupation, there is something to be said for viticulture in Britain.

SCIENTIFIC WATERING

Watering the garden has always been a pleasant occupation and has become more so than ever since cheap plastic hose and those ingenious 'Hozelock' devices made it possible to lay down an irrigation system of one's own without employing a plumber. The acts of freshening the foliage, turning the soil from dry grey to moist black or brown, and releasing a score of pleasant scents, are agreeable ones. But it is a hit-and-miss business; the gardener of judgement may get the quantity right; the majority do not, they water too much or, more often, too little. There must be something one can do to correct this; and in fact there is.

Plants take up moisture from the soil and transpire it through the leaves; this means that water is continually moving through them. If the water present in the soil is inadequate so that the plants cannot take up enough to make up the continuous loss by transpiration, then the plants flag and growth is checked until more water is provided, either by rain or by irrigation. But plants do not obviously and visibly flag immediately the water loss exceeds the water intake; they are, however, checked in growth before their distress is apparent to the gardener's eye. Therefore if you can maintain a soil-water condition such that your plants are never for a moment short of water you will get faster, steadier growth, bigger and healthier plants, larger crops of fruit, vegetables and flowers. This is not an opinion; it is a fact. On the other hand, if you waterlog the soil in an effort to keep the plants well supplied with water, you will defeat your own ends, because roots need air and will drown if water replaces the air in the soil. A soil is suitably moist when every particle composing it has a skin of water held in place by capillary attraction; it is waterlogged when the air between the particles is replaced by water.

This means that following rain or irrigation the soil should drain rapidly and that, provided it is good garden soil, soil of the correct texture and the correct mixture of mineral and vegetable particles, it will be in exactly the right condition to suit plants *immediately after a period of drainage following rain or irrigation.* This condition is used by irrigation specialists as a convenient level of moisture content from which changes can be reckoned and it is called 'field moisture capacity'. This is defined as 'the moisture content of soil when it is holding all the water it can against the force of gravity'. Another term coined by irrigation engineers for their and our convenience is 'soil moisture deficit'. The soil moisture deficit is defined as 'the amount of rain or irrigation necessary to restore the soil to field moisture capacity', i.e. to that condition so desirable for plants which immediately follows a period of drainage after rain.

These facts and findings, and the method by which irrigation need can be calculated are to be found in a useful and interesting HMSO booklet, Bulletin No. 4, Ministry of Agriculture and Fisheries, 1954, *The Calculation of Irrigation Need.* Very roughly it works like this: long-term averages for water loss by transpiration and evaporation from land planted with green crops have been established and tabulated. And so have averages for rainfall; both figures, of course, for the whole country but divided into regions, for they differ from place to place. Now, if the difference between water loss and water gain by rainfall be regularly made good by irrigation, the soil will be permanently maintained at field moisture capacity, that is in the ideal condition for your plants.

But averages are only averages and we need, for practical use, more specific and exact figures. And we can get them. By arrangement with the County Offices of the National Agriculture Advisory Service (NAAS) or the Meteorological Office, the horticulturist can be given the necessary corrections to the average figures, at the end of each month. How these are arrived at is not very important to the gardener, but in fact they are based on calculations made from the weather statistics for that month. If it has been exceptionally fine weather for the month, then the water loss by transpiration and evaporation will have been greater than average, the water gain by rainfall less; and if it has been wetter than usual, then water loss will have been less and gain more. What the farmer or gardener gets then is the figure, expressed in terms of inches of rain, of his soil moisture deficit. At this point he knows how much water, again in terms of rainfall in inches, his land needs or his garden needs to be restored to field moisture capacity.

His next problem is to turn that figure of rainfall in inches needed into one of volume of water, so that he can put on the correct amount by irrigation. The farmer or gardener pumping water from a stream or pond will have to do some arithmetic at this point, and the HMSO booklet I have referred to tells him how to do that. For the ordinary gardener the problem is much simpler: all he has to do is to learn to read the water meter which the local water authority will have installed by his standpipe, so that he can be charged for the water used in the garden.

When one inch of rain has fallen, how much water, in gallons, has fallen on your garden? One inch of rainfall is equal to 22,622 gallons per acre, which is 4½ gallons per square yard. So if your garden is, say, a quarter acre and your soil moisture deficit is one inch, then you must give 5,655 gallons of water, evenly distributed over the garden, to restore field moisture capacity. The problem of distribution is not very easy to solve correctly if you simply have one hose and walk round the garden holding it, or propping it on a fork which you move from time to time. The ideal is to lay down a system of polythene or alkathene pipes, with evenly spaced outlets, and then to use sprinklers.

The next step is to convert gallons required into terms of time. By this I mean that if you know that it takes one hour for one thousand gallons to flow through your irrigation system, and that your garden needs 5,000 gallons of water, then you know that all you need do is to turn on the tap and leave it on for five hours. The only way to arrive at this time figure is by experiment, for mains water pressures vary from place to place. Time the flow by watching the meter against your wrist-watch, for a quarter of an hour, and you have a figure accurate enough for practical purposes.

This is a very rough and ready account, then, of how irrigation need can be calculated instead of merely guessed. There is no question of its value; it has been thoroughly proved and I remember seeing Mr Roy Hay's garden at Hurtmore Farm in what was, I think, the first season of his watering it by calculation instead of by guesswork, and being amazed at the superiority of all kinds of crops and all kinds of ornamentals.

PROTEAS

I took it into my head some years ago to spend Christmas on the island of Tresco. I already knew the great Abbey Gardens but I had not seen them in mid-winter. And it was in those gardens where I spent the hours of daylight during a whole week, that, never having been to South Africa, I first saw Proteas in flower. And if I was impressed and taken with them on the bush, I was much more so when, having been invited to lunch by Commander Dorrien-Smith, I was able to see for myself how very beautiful the strange flowers of this genus are when cut and used in flower arrangements or, for that matter, simply stuck in a vase. I became determined to grow Proteas for myself; and finding from inquiries made of South African correspondents, that some of the species have to stand twelve or fourteen degrees of frost from time to time, I thought it not impossible that I could grow these curious but tender plants outdoors in Devon.

As it happens I was mistaken but one's failures in horticulture can sometimes be quite as interesting as one's successes.

There are about one hundred species of Proteas and they are confined to South Africa. The first European to describe and figure one was, of course, Clusius; the species *Protea nerifolia* and he thought it came from Madagascar; he called it a 'thistle' because the flower is something like a thistle flower in shape. The specimen he drew from must in fact have come from Table Mountain for its range is very limited. The thistle shape is due to the fact that the flowers, consisting of tubular perianth, stamens and styles, are packed densely into a thistle-shaped head which is perfectly regular and symmetrical; this inflorescence is surrounded and subtended by a series of imbricated bracts forming a cupped star, and usually vividly coloured.

Protea cynaroides, known in the vernacular as the King Protea, is a dwarf bush not exceeding three feet in height, but broader and sprawling in habit. The flowers are enormous, about nine inches across when open, the inflorescence proper being creamy yellow with a kind of silvery glitter, and the bracts flame red. Marianne North, the great flower painter whose eight hundred best paintings are at the Royal Botanic Gardens, Kew, is supposed to have 'screamed with joy' on first beholding this extraordinary shrub in flower. It is one of the hardiest grown at the Abbey Gardens, Tresco and is one of the proteas I tried and failed to grow in Devon; and have since been most impressed by in South Africa.

Another was *Protea barbigera*, the Woolly-bearded or Queen Protea. It has soft pink bracts, silvery white flowers and black anthers, and is an object of great beauty and greater strangeness. One or two others were likewise tried.

Two ways of growing the proteas were attempted. I imported seeds from various South African sources and planted them in pots of suitably acid compost in the greenhouse. And, despite warnings that proteas move very badly unless the soil ball is kept intact, I flew over young plants from South African whose roots had been washed clean to comply with phyto-sanitary regulations, but which had been sealed into polythene bags to retain moisture and therefore turgidity.

These plants, about eight inches tall, arrived in perfect condition and were very carefully and thoroughly planted out on a warm and sheltered terrace of soil which had been mixed especially to comply with suggestions made by the South African nursery which sold me the plants and who were extremely interested in what I was trying to do, and very helpful.

The proteas neither died nor grew, but remained exactly as they were throughout the spring, summer and autumn. I knew that proteas cannot stand a close atmosphere and should be exposed to winds and fresh air at all seasons; but I also knew that while *P. cynaroides* certainly, and *P. barbigera* possibly would stand frost of as much as ten or eleven degrees for short periods, and after being hardened by the hot South African summer, they are much less hardy as young than as old plants. So each plant was covered for the winter with a large individual cloche and the cloches were opened on every possible occasion. As a result the plants stood the winter very well, and were finally uncovered in May of the next year. They continued in exactly the same supine way as before, neither dying nor growing, throughout the spring and summer, but in early autumn the lower leaves began to turn red, and this reddening worked upwards until the whole plant was coloured. The leaves then withered and the plants died. This experiment was repeated with the same results. I think it likely that had I been allowed by the regulations to import the plants in their pots, it would have proved easy to establish them. But it seems clear that once protea roots have been washed clean of soil, they are very reluctant to take hold on a new soil.

My failure with seeds was certainly caused by want of skill and nothing else. Better gardeners would succeed. There was never the slightest difficulty in germinating the seed and raising the seedlings to a certain point, but of all the species tried only *P. cynaroides* and *Leucospermum conocarpum*, the 'Silver Tree' survived, and only a very few specimens of those, to a size such that they could be planted out of the greenhouse. The great majority of the seedlings of all species and several genera were killed by damping-off at a very early stage. Nothing seemed to prevent this; bottom watering, constant ventilation, dusting with captan, surfacing the soil with silver-sand, over they went just the same. The whole of the family of Proteacious plants is notorious in this respect, but good gardeners do raise them and many genera and species are established in America and Australasia. I really did try hard, but to very little purpose.

However, some seedlings were raised and grown on to a height of nearly a foot, and then planted out in conditions calculated and prepared at considerable labour and expense to suit them. Nevertheless, all behaved just like the plants imported from South Africa, as if they could not bear to put out a root into our soil and, after five years, I gave up trying, yet remained convinced that a sufficiently clever and patient gardener could grow proteas on the Cornish littoral and in one or two very warm corners of Devon, such as the Salcombe inlet.

The bushes themselves have no great beauty; the foliage is rather dull and the shape of the shrubs, their habit, seldom seems to be good. But the inflorescences are so extraordinary and in some cases so beautiful that it would be well worth growing them if one could.

WILD PAEONIES

I love all kinds of paeonies excepting the hybrid herbaceous ones which have been so developed that they are usually too tall and their flowers often blowsy. The moutans are among my favourite plants; and so are the botanical species paeonies which are as superior to the garden cultivars as are botanical species rhododendrons to the hardy hybrids, or some wild roses to most garden roses.

I have raised a number of species from seed. It is not difficult. As they like and perhaps need a period of cold before they will germinate well, I always sowed the seed, well-spaced, in boxes of John Innes compost, and then stood the boxes outside until late in March; I then brought them into the greenhouse, and they germinated evenly. In some boxes I have had 100 per cent germination but 80 per cent is about average. The seedlings were early pricked into small individual pots, grown-on on a bench outside the greenhouse, overwintered outside, brought in again, taken out in mid-summer for hardening off, and planted out in their second autumn. They are sufficiently hardy to stand that treatment in the west of England, but in the east some would need more care against cold in their youth.

Three favourites raised in this way were *Paeonia cambessedesii*; *P. mlokosewitschii*; and *P. peregrina*.

P. cambessedesii is a low, broad plant not more than eighteen inches high at its tallest point. The very handsome and much divided leaves are glaucous, almost blue in some lights and with metallic gleams. These leaves are handsomely displayed, held almost parallel with the soil surface and making excellent ground cover in shrubberies, for the plants, while they must have sun, like a measure of shade at noon or thereabouts and like to grow in the light and partial shade of tall shrubs. There is another reason for planting this paeony among shrubs: it comes from the Balearic Islands and is not perfectly hardy, and the shrubs afford some protection. However, it cannot be called tender and can be grown in most English gardens. The flowers are single, of course, cupped, a deep rose-pink in colour, their stamen filaments a deep red, but the anthers yellow, a delightful colour scheme.

The Caucasian paeony *P. mlokosewitschii* is very hardy. It

was introduced to Britain from Russia about sixty years ago. It makes a widely spreading, ground-covering plant of large leaves rarely exceeding eighteen inches in height. They are a smooth blue-green on the upper face, a hairy and paler glaucous green on the under side, the margins and veins being red. The flowers are flat, broad cups about five inches across and with the petals curved in at the edges. The petals are, in the typical case, a clear yellow, so are the filaments but the stigma, which is thick and prominent, is a rich violet. The colour is very variable; from a batch of seedlings you will usually get some pure yellow ones, but others will be apricot; others, again, pale primrose yellow. But all are pretty colours and a planting of a dozen of these paeonies in a shrubbery where they get sun most of the day but some broken shade during the hottest hours, makes a magnificent feature.

P. peregrina is a taller plant, the flower stems sometimes attaining about thirty inches. It comes from the Balkans and it is hardy. The very large leaves are much divided, some of the main divisions being themselves almost pinnate. They are pure shiny green on the upper surface, paler and hairy on the underside. The single flowers are four-inch cups and both the very concave petals and the many stamen filaments are deep red, the latter with a waxy look. This paeony flowers in May.

These three are among the most beautiful wild flowers in the world and in any garden where they can be seen they seem to me to put the bigger, blowsy hybrids to shame. Good, although not so good, is a white-flowered paeony from Siberia and north China, *P. obovata*. The leaves are large, glaucous, the stature about eighteen inches, and the single, cupped white flowers have faintly rose-pink filaments. This paeony was introduced from China in 1915 but is not common in gardens here.

Paeonies will grow in any good, fertile soil. They are equally good on limestone or chalk and peaty soils. Of the four named, *P. peregrina* is the most tolerant of shade, in fact it does best in woodland conditions. When planting any herbaceous paeony, be sure that you have the site right from the beginning; they dislike being moved once they are established and take years to recover from the check of a move—very unlike the shrubby paeonies which move readily and suffer no such check.

Among other wild paeonies I have grown is our own native one, now confined in the wild to Steep Holme Island. (It may be naturalized rather than native, but at all events it grows wild there.) This is *P. mascula*. It is worth growing if you prefer the simplicity and distinction of the wild flower to the elaboration and flamboyance of the hybrid.

FRANK KINGDON-WARD AND THE MANIPUR LILY

The most recent addition to the lily garden, from the wild, I mean, not from the plant breeders, is the Manipur Lily, *L. macklinae.*

Between India and China there is a vast region of mountainous country covered with jungle, broken by rivers running in deep gorges—the Irrawaddy, the Salween and the Mekong are three of them—and subject to wild and stormy weather including fogs, torrential rain and thunderstorms. This country had for many years been explored by Frank Kingdon-Ward in search of new plants. During the later years of the last world war the United States Air Force flew many thousands of tons of military equipment and stores over this region, vulgarly known as the Hump, from India to Kumming; and some hundreds of aircraft were lost in the atrocious weather. In his *Pilgrimage for Plants* (Harrap, London, 1960) Kingdon-Ward says:

'It now fell to the lot of the American air force to pick up the remains. All crashes had been located as nearly as possible and marked on the map. Teams were sent out to find them, and in some cases to learn where their crews and passengers had been buried. As I was free just then I volunteered to help in the hunt, and was taken on by the Air Force. Several planes lost between Assam and Burma were assigned to me, and accompanied by two G.I.'s I set out for Manipur State.'

The English plant-hunter and his American companions went by jeep to Ukhrul and then took to their feet, crossed a valley to a village from which, across another deep valley they could see the summit of Sirhoi Kashong (8,445 feet). Kingdon-Ward climbed to a ridge behind the village to survey the country.

'At about seven thousand feet or a little higher I found myself on a limestone slope covered with short crisp turf. The track skirted a scree which lay at the foot of the razor-edged ridge above, then worked its way up to the crest farther along. It was winter, and the slope was very bare; yet it was just the sort of ground I would carefully cast my eyes over in the hope of noticing some unusual plant. I did so, and presently—not a little to my surprise—I saw the open capsule of a dwarf iris. It was almost certainly *Iris kamaonensis*, a widespread species; but I was delighted to see it because it evoked happy memories and also suggested greater possibilities. I redoubled my efforts as I went along. It was getting dark; I must hurry up if I wanted to find anything more. I scrambled up the steep face above the scree, which brought the ground closer to my eyes, and near the top I found more iris, and traces of other plants, but nothing outstanding.

'We had already finished our work on the plane which had crashed in the pine forest not far from here, and by this time were on our way back to Ukhrul. The direct route was by a track which crossed the deep valley to the Sirhoi ridge. With my two companions I set out next morning. It was a warm January day, the path was steep, and the distance farther than it looked. Towards evening, having crossed the valley, we found ourselves on the ridge which led to the top of Sirhoi, with the village, still some distance away but in the opposite direction. I was tired myself; my young companions seemed almost at their last gasp. Men accustomed to going everywhere on wheels tire quickly on foot; to have to toil up and down steep hillsides by a scarcely visible track, on a hot day, was not their idea of Army life. They lagged behind. However, we eventually reached a rest-house beyond the village, ate our evening meal out of a tin, and flung ourselves on our bedding-rolls to sleep.'

On the next day, as the two young Americans were finding the elderly Englishman's pace a bit too much for them, he sent them back to Ukhrul and the jeep to wait for him, while he set out to get to the top of Sirhoi; he claims that this was to make sure that there was no aeroplane wreckage up there; one suspects he had other, and partly botanical reasons. I need not follow him in detail. He says:

'But I now found something far more exciting. This was another trilocular top-shaped capsule, which could only be that of a lily (or possibly, I thought a Nomocharis, which may be briefly described as an alpine lily). Yet it was almost too low down for a Nomocharis; there was nothing really alpine about this mountain, in spite of turf and scree. The plant was barely six inches high, and it bore a solitary terminal capsule about the size of *Nomocharis pardanthina*. I dug it up—a difficult job in that hard rocky soil—and three inches below the surface I found a small whitish bulb. The dry crumbling fruit, and several others on plants growing near by, contained a few leather-brown seeds which the wind had failed to dislodge. They would probably remain till the thin walls of the capsule were soaked and rotted by the summer rain, to be incorporated with the mould; or they might germinate within the capsule itself.

'As I expected, the plant was more abundant higher up, and I found a fair number, very few of which contained seeds. But I gathered enough to have a good chance of raising it, for the seeds were plump and obviously fertile. I also dug up a few bulbs to send to my friend the Political Agent for Manipur State in Imphal, who was a keen gardener. It would be asking a lot of this lily—if it was a lily—to grow in the Residency garden on the hot plains five thousand feet below, but at any rate it was worth trying . . . .'

Other seeds went to the Royal Horticultural Society. From his gardener friends in Imphal and Shillong reports of the new plant were discouraging: the flower was insignificant and it was 'dirty white'. Kingdon-Ward rejected that description with indignation; he was certain that his new plant was a lily, and no lily would be dirty white. Back in England he heard from Dr Turrill of Kew that the seedlings raised from his seed had done well and that one had flowered. What had it been like? Not very impressive. Colour? Well, a sort of dingy white. Kingdon-Ward was disappointed yet he could not so easily give up his Manipur Lily. Perhaps, seen flowering in the wild, it would redeem itself. He would soon know; he had undertaken to collect plants for the New York Botanic Garden and had arranged to begin in Manipur. By the end of February 1948 he, this time accompanied by his wife, was back in Ukhrul. In April they went back over his traces of the year before and there found the new lily coming up near thickets of the fragrant-flowered *Rhododendron johnstoneanum*. They transferred a few bulbs to the fenced nursery garden of their cottage in Ukhrul.

In May they were away, climbing Khayam Bum in search of new rhododendrons. Here is what Kingdon-Ward says of their return:

'The long pull of three miles up the last hill to the Ukhrul ridge was behind us; we almost ran along the level path to the cottage, and went straight to the tiny strip of prepared soil by the entrance. This had been fenced against marauding pigs; cattle, however, put their heads over the fence and browsed the tops off any plants they fancied. The lilies were in flower—or rather, had flowered—but were more than half over; only one complete flower and several fragmentary ones remained. They were not tall enough to be eaten by cattle, but heavy raindrops had made little craters in the soil and spattered the plants with mud from head to foot. They looked bedraggled, homesick, woe-begone and cheap. Their colour? Well—muddy white describes it!

'I was shocked and disappointed, but I rallied later. The final test was still to come: the Manipur Lily, growing on its own ground in its own time.

'Could excuses be found for our Ukhrul plants too? The weather?—but it had been no better on Sirhoi, which had been smothered in cloud for five weeks. Twelve or fifteen hundred feet difference of altitude?—negligible! Well then, the sour, unappetizing village soil and the juvenile plants?—but the bulbs had been carried down in the clods of Sirhoi turf that originally enclosed them?

'Whatever the reason, I *still* felt that these miserable lilies were not the real thing. What seemed certain was that it was now in full bloom on Sirhoi, and that if we wanted to see the lily at its best we must go soon.'

They did so; and, of course, Kingdon-Ward was vindicated:

'A few hundred feet higher we found the first flower, and stood before it spellbound. I could have laughed aloud, but it would have been sacrilege, like laughing in church. Dirty white? dingy white? What rubbish! The half-nodding bell was a delicate shell-pink outside, like dawn in June, with the sheen of watered silk; inside it was like faintly flushed alabaster. The points of the petals curled back, but towards the base clasped one another closely. The stamens too were beautiful; the anthers, with their deep honey-orange pollen, are so nicely balanced on the needle-tips of the filaments that they tremble at a touch. We sang, we shouted with joy; then moved on, up the hill, up the hill, up the hill, till we found ourselves surrounded by pink lilies in bud, lilies half open, lilies in full bloom. There were stems with two, with three, flowers; and as we approached the summit, where in sheltered hollows the grass grew longer, we found them as much as three feet high, each stem bearing six or eight flowers. The long pointed damask-rose buds added a special charm. When a breeze swept through the meadow, hundreds of lilies bowed their heads and swung their bells to and fro, the whole slope twinkling and dancing joyfully.'

The lily was named for Mrs Kingdon-Ward *L. macklinae* (her name was Jean Macklin). I acquired some bulbs in the early 'sixties and grew them in the shade of some dwarf rhododendrons low enough for the lilies to grow through. They came up every year and they flowered earlier than any other lily, in May, but they did not do what I should call well in Devonshire, for if they survived and increased a little in size, they did not increase in number and of six I lost one. They set plenty of seed and seedlings were raised. This lily is not difficult and though unspectacular it is one of the most charming I have grown.

One wonders, what in due course, the lily breeders will do to strengthen the Manipur Lily or use its charm in combination with that of other lilies. But up to now, as Mr Jan de Graaff tells me, they have not succeeded in crossing it with any other. It looks less like a lily of the genus *Lilium* than a lily of the genus *Nomocharis* and perhaps it is nearer to that genus. But it is a great acquisition for its own sake; and because of the circumstances in which it was found, it makes a sort of memorial to the American airmen who gave their lives in getting supplies to their Chinese allies.

SOURCES

I think that the French were the first to study the ancient origins of cultivated plants and the Russians, notably in the person of N. I. Vavilov, to make a science of it.

Vavilov claims that the earliest centre for the distribution of plants of economic importance was Chinese. It seems likely that Anatolia and Palestine may have been earlier. The oldest centres of relatively sophisticated farming were not necessarily ancient sources of new plants; it would depend upon the richness or poverty of their flora. But I doubt whether that statement would be supported by the findings of archaeology since his work was done in the 'twenties and 'thirties. Setting aside the plants of agriculture, those of horticulture, from this Chinese centre, include radish, turnips, a number of cabbages, rhubarb, Spanish onion, apricot, quinces of the *Chaenomeles* group, oranges, lemons, and persimmons, mulberry, the opium poppy, and many scores more. It is a list chiefly remarkable for fruits and vegetables. Vavilov was not interested in ornamentals, but then the distribution of ornamental plants, plants grown for their beauty, is a very late development. It is true that one finds in his Chinese list such plants as Morning Glory and Tiger Lily. But the first had a medicinal use; and as for the second, the Chinese cultivated the Tiger Lily for its edible bulbs, not for its pretty flowers, a practice which led to its naturalization in many Chinese colonies remote from the original range of this lily.

The list of plants distributed from the centres of ancient Indian cultivation contains few items of interest to us; most of the plants are confined to the tropics. However, this list does include the aubergine and, more important, some cucumbers. A number of the Citrus fruits were originally wild in India as well as in parts of China, and were either independently domesticated there, or brought into Indian cultivation after Indians had taken a hint from the plants cultivated in and introduced from China. The first cultivation of many useful trees and other plants goes back so far in time that it is probably impossible to be sure of the first cultivators' identity. But apparently the myrobalan plum, so important as a stock for the better kinds of plums and gages, came originally from India. Black pepper, marihuana, and indigo are Indian plants. Indigo is no longer of economic importance but marihuana, Indian Hemp (*Cannabis sativa*) has been distributed to every continent both as a fibre plant and a source of the drug.

'India', says Vavilov, 'is undoubtedly the birthplace of rice, sugar cane, a large number of legumes, and many tropical fruit plants including the mango and numerous citrus plants (e.g. the orange, lemon, some species of tangerine). Assam, in particular, is most remarkable for its citrus plants.'

Probably by far the most important contribution from the Indo–Malayan source, as Vavilov calls it, was the banana which has become of such value in the sub-tropical and tropical parts of every continent. The claim that it was also native to Central and South America is not supported by evidence.

Central Asia was a source of the most important of all agricultural plants, wheat. Among garden plants it yielded cantaloupe melons, carrots, onions, garlic and spinach. This does not mean that these vegetables came only from there; or those attributed to other sources only from those sources; it means that cultivars contributing to our modern cultivars as parents crossed with their kind from other sources, came from that centre. The same is true for fruits. For example there are wild almonds growing in several of the ancient centres of agriculture; and a modern almond tree derives from several and perhaps all of them, as a modern orange or apple tree contains genes contributed by several rather than by one of the ancient centres where it can be found wild.

Once the idea of taking a particular plant into cultivation reaches a primitive farming people, they may begin with an imported cultivar but they will also turn their attention to the same or a related species found wild in their own country. That this was so is to be deduced, I believe, from the way in which the sixteenth- and seventeenth-century European settlers in the Americas dealt with the esculent plants in the wild. They begin with the European cultivars, of the grape for example; and only later did they bring the wild relatives of those cultivars, when they found them, into their gardens. Even in the case of ornamental plants, this is true.

The Near-Eastern centre is chiefly important for its grain plants, including many wheats; and for forage plants, above all alfalfa which even the Chinese introduced from Iran, in 128 B.C. They did so because they were, at the time, looking in Iran for better horses for their cavalry than they had at home; they found the horses they wanted in Iran and introduced alfalfa at the same time, realizing that these superior animals needed superior fodder. As an interesting 'extra' their official horse-buyer, General Chan k'ien sent home seeds of *Vitis vinifera*, the wine vine of history, and some other useful plants.

Also from the Near-Eastern centres came a variety of vegetables and salads, including lettuce, a number of melons and cucumbers, all the stone fruits, nuts, apples and pears.

A principal source of the garden roses is, of course, Iran (Persia). The original lilacs were Near-Eastern plants; lavender, laurel and the Damask rose are from the Eastern Mediterranean. So too are most of the culinary herbs.

Zea mays, Indian Corn, now one of the most important staples all over the world, and an important kitchen-garden plant, came from Central or perhaps Central-South America. So did a very large number of the beans of the climbing type (haricots). From the same source or from the South American source we had the tomato, tobacco, chocolate, the avocado pear, and, most important of all, the potato.

Although cultivars continue to be distributed from one part of the world to all the rest, a continuous and reciprocal exchange, it is probable that in the field of esculent plants the work is finished; it is not very likely that any esculent plant of importance remains still to be distributed from a centre of origin to the other agricultural countries of the world. But for ornamentals, the case is different. A large number of important flowering plants were distributed from the seventeenth to the mid-nineteenth centuries; but the peak period for distribution of such plants was from about 1850 to about 1920. It was in that period that Europe, Asia and America exchanged their native lilies and began to cross-breed them; that literally hundreds of rhododendron species and scores of camellia cultivars and species came from Asia to Europe and America; that South Africa and Australia sent their hundreds of flowering plants to suitable climates in the other continents; that the flowering trees, shrubs and herbaceous plants of the Andes reached European and North American gardens and spread into parts of Asia and the Far East.

For seven or eight thousand years men were too busy bringing food plants, fibre plants, dye plants, medicinal and drug plants from alien sources, and sending their own to the foreigners, to pay much attention to ornamentals. The ancient civilizations of Iran, China and Japan were the ones which were early rich enough to spend resources on plants which pleased the eye and the nose, but did not make them materially richer. It is very likely that of all our garden ornamentals the three which were earliest in some kind of commerce simply because men wanted plants of beauty as well as plants of use, and could afford to pay for them, were the rose, the paeony and the camellia, the first in Iran and the Near East, the other two in the Far East.

There are doubtless still hundreds and perhaps thousands of ornamental plants still to be found, domesticated and distributed; thereafter to be cross-bred with their kind from other sources, to yield more garden hybrids. But perhaps even in this field the best part of the work has been done, and the best species of every plant genus have been carried by men to every place where they can grow.

FLOWER SCENTS

When I describe a flower in print which I very often have to do, I can, by the use of a mixture of botanical and common terms convey a pretty exact idea of what the flower is like: I can convey its shape, its texture and its colours in the words which we have for expressing those attributes. What I cannot do is to convey the smell, because there are no words for smells. It is curious that it should be so for it must be the case that at the time when language was being invented smells were of much greater importance to mankind than they are now; men were probably still making use of their noses in the same way, if not to the same extent or so effectively, as animals do. And since words were invented to convey colours and tastes, it is surely odd that they were not invented to convey smells. It could be that such words formerly existed and that we have lost them; but that seems improbable. Another reason might be that smells are more specific than colours: by this I mean that whereas there are hundreds of objects in any landscape which are green, or red or blue, so that the word can be used in describing many things, the smell of, say, fox is specific to the fox and since very few things smell like fox, even to our inefficient noses, and perhaps nothing quite like it to a nose still being used in the natural struggle for existence, there would be no point in having a word of general use for the smell of fox; one need only say 'smell of fox'.

Not that scents are absolutely specific. Roy Bedichek, in *The Sense of Smell* (Michael Joseph, London, 1960) says, for example, that the scent of *Sophora secundiflora* in flower is identical with the scent of a newly opened box of Concord grapes. Even more oddly, the scent of the familiar American Currant bush on a warm, wet day is, to my nose, identical with the smell of goat. But supposing we had a word—I will coin one, *smar*, for the smell of goat, then although I might write 'these flowers are tubular, the tube opening into five segments which are reflexed; they are red and smar', whereas I should have frequent occasion to use all the other adjectives in that sentence, I should so rarely have a use for smar that it would hardly be worth having.

Whatever the reason for our want of words to describe scents, it has bothered writers for centuries. Theophrastus, in *Enquiry into Plants*, wrote that:

'. . . the various kinds of good or evil odour, although they exhibit considerable differences, have not received further distinguishing names, marking off one particular kind of bitterness or sweetness from another; we speak of an odour as pungent, faint, sweet or heavy, though some of these descriptions apply to evil-smelling things as well as those which have a good odour.'

Note that when we are forced to use words to describe scents, the words we use are borrowed from the terminology of taste or some other sense: a thing smells sweet or sour or pungent—though perhaps pungent belongs as much to the sense of smell as to the sense of taste. Moreover though the same sense of taste has a richer vocabulary, it is still not made of specific words in the sense that red, or more closely defined, scarlet, are specific.

Because he thought that it would make his classification of plants more exact and detailed, Linnaeus proposed to give specific meanings, in botany, to certain scents; his words are *aromatic*; *fragrant*; *ambrosiac*; *alliaceous*, *hircine*; *foul*; *nauseous*. It will be amusing to see whether we agree about the meanings of these words, and I will now write down without thinking what plants they suggest to me—Rue; rose; *Lilium auratum*; onions; black currant; henbane; none, I cannot think of any plant which smells *nauseous* although there may well be some—are there not some aroids which stink of decaying meat? And I have read somewhere that that, also, is the scent of the ripe durian fruit*. Your own list will probably be quite different, whereas unless one of us is colour blind we could not disagree about the colours of that list of plants. In short, Linnaeus's scheme would not have worked unless some way could have been found to make everyone with a normal sense of smell agree about the meanings of the terms to be used.

In the case of other senses we have inherited agreement on the meanings of descriptive words. If you and I stand and look at a rose and both call its colour crimson, it does not follow that we are seeing the same thing. If we invented words for scents, we should only have to issue a set of rules going something like this: 'The olfactory sensation experienced in the presence of a goat will in future be called smar.'

I suggest another game: gather, in the height of the flowering season, as many scented flowers as your garden afford, having invited in a few friends for drinks. Blindfold your friends and let them try to identify the flowers each by its scent. I think that most people will get some things right: I am sure of, for example, violets and primroses and tea roses. But I am prepared to lay a large bet that not one gardener in ten thousand would fail, on having a truss of *Rhododendron johnstoneanum* or

* Since this was written I have been in Indonesia. Ripe durian smells of dustbins in hot weather.

Rhododendron fragrantissimum flowers held under his nose while he was blindfolded, to identify one of the lilies, probably *regale*. The scent of lilac is specific; the scent of philadelphus is not. Lily-of-the-valley is specific; but are you perfectly certain you could pick it out of a dozen other flower smells, blindfold?

But granted all this, it remains odd that we have no words for scents, because as well as having been very important to man at about the time when language was coming into existence, they are far more important to infants than any other sensations, at least for some days or weeks after birth. Babies find the nipple with their noses, not their eyes. And among animals—this must once have been true among human beings also—the dam knows her own young, the young creature its dam, by smell. Come to think of it, however, if that is so then it is a reinforcement of my explanation for want of terms, that smells are too specific. If every individual human being has a different scent, as he does to a dog, it would seem to be out of the question to have a word for every scent.

This suggests something else, however, that living creatures, plants or animals, emit what is in fact a complex of smells in a certain combination, and not just a simple scent. It is, in fact, inconceivable that every human being should have a different simple scent, but very easily conceivable that there are enough possible combinations of, say, a dozen primary scents for every human being to smell differently from every other human being to the canine nose.

I do not think that the primary chemistry of this subject has been well studied. We know that the scent of a flower is in fact a stream of molecules to which the olfactory nerve ends are sensitive. But as far as I know we do not make such a clear statement as what follows:

'The scent of this rose is composed of the esters A, B and C. In the case of the variety *lutea* C is absent. However, when the variety *lutea* is crossed with the type, ester C is restored to the hybrid, and a fourth, formerly supposed by Jones to be an intimate mixture of A and B, has been shown by Cohen to be a new ester, which he has called D, due to a mutation of the gene controlling scent.'

What I am suggesting here, of course, is that flowers, as well as men and beasts, emit compound scents composed of two or more of the limited number of primary scents. I have borrowed the word 'esters' because it is in bodies so called that the aroma and flavour of wines, and for all I know, foods, reside.

Perhaps, if there is ever a world-language spoken by all the members of the human race, it may include words for primary scents. We shall first have to discover what they are. There is no reason why we should not; after all, for most of man's history he did not know that all but the primary colours are mixtures of two or more of those primary colours.

CHINESE LANDSCAPE GARDENING

It is a significant fact brought out by the historian of Chinese painting, Osvald Siren, in his remarkable treatise *Gardens of China* (The Ronald Press Co., New York) that the makers of the greatest Chinese gardens were master painters. From a period which antedates our own art of landscape gardening by at least a thousand years and probably much more, gardening in China as in eighteenth-century England was to a considerable extent a manifestation of landscape painting, using natural objects instead of paint, a piece of ground instead of a piece of silk.

In Italy, and for a long time in Japan, the art most closely associated with that of gardening was that of poetry; thus in Italy the garden is a formal pattern made according to strict rules, like classical poetry; and in Japan it is a lyrical restatement of myths in terms of a limited number of recognizable symbols. In China the case is very different.

The Chinese had a love of nature like that of the English. In their town gardens they created natural landscapes in miniature. But, to quote Siren:

'The Chinese garden, considered as a special type of landscape gardening, may with more reason than most other types of parks and gardens be characterized as a work of the creative imagination or, in other words, as something corresponding to the demands which must be made upon a work of art. It is not a direct imitation of Nature, slavishly dependent upon given types of scenery or landscape motifs, nor is it the result of an abstract, schematizing activity which does violence to the natural elements of composition; rather is it an expression of artistic ideas and conceptions that have emerged from an intimate feeling for Nature. It is distinguished by surprising charm, and the picturesque beauty of an imaginative creation, though it may also degenerate to artificial intricacy and an almost bewildering lack of unifying plan. At its best it lives with the infectious rhythm of a spontaneous work of art.'

There is, however, one way in which the Chinese garden more nearly resembles the Japanese garden and even the Humanist gardens of Tuscany, than the English landscape garden, and that is in its intimate connection with the house. Large or small, simple or complex, the garden was an extension of the house; or, rather house and garden were designed in one piece as an integral dwelling place. Not only did the principal building merge with the artificial landscape, but the whole garden was composed about the pavilions from which the several parts of it could be enjoyed.

'These pavilions and verandas offer relative isolation and protection while at the same time giving one the feeling of being out in the open air, in a fanciful landscape to which the twittering of birds and the chirping of the cicadas sometimes also gives a voice.' (Siren)

This analysis is borne out by the *Yüan Yeh*, a treatise on gardening much quoted by Siren: the reader is therein urged to make his garden in a quiet corner of the town—town gardens were always much more important than country gardens in China—and he is told that in such a garden:

'A single mountain may give rise to many effects, a small stone may evoke many feelings. The shadow from the dry leaves of the banana tree is beautifully outlined on the paper of the window. The roots of the pine force their way through the hollow crevices of the stones. . . . If one can find stillness in the midst of the city turmoil, why should one then forego such an easily accessible spot and seek a more distant one?'

What is meant, here, by 'mountain'? A very important element of the Chinese garden is natural stones and these were often used to represent mountains. In Siren's opinion,

'. . . it must nevertheless be admitted that the 'mountains', i.e. the hollowed and furrowed blocks of stone, have played a still more prominent role in Chinese gardens.* They are without doubt the most original and most specifically Chinese of all the elements constituting the peculiar character of these gardens. Ponds, pavilions and winding paths of all kinds are to be found in pleasure gardens in many lands, but hollowed out rocks assembled in the form of mountains and grottoes occur only in China or in gardens that have been planned according to Chinese models. In their irregular and surprising forms is

* i.e. a more prominent role even than water.

reflected the special temper of Chinese garden art. At their best they contribute more than any other compositional element to bring out what I will call the expressionistic element of this picturesque art.'

From the evidence of Chinese landscape painting it is clear that the Chinese gave much importance to these great stones eroded by time, wind and water; and that they were taken as symbols of the awe-inspiring forces of Nature. The *Yüan Yeh* also makes this point, emphasizing that the rocks used by the gardener must, like those painted in ink on silk or paper by the landscape artist, look wild and fantastic. Siren, who was perhaps not acquainted with English literature, misses a point of interest here; surely there is more than a touch of precisely the romantic spirit which led English gardeners to build stony grottoes which also had to look wild and fantastic; and hermitages inhabited by professional hermits, or persons posing as such. In short, in both the Chinese and the English cultures Nature had ceased to be alarming and hostile and civilization had progressed to the point that both peoples could afford to admire and play with what they had formerly feared. Siren quotes from the seventeenth-century novel *Hung Lu Mên* a description of a garden in which the characters walk among '. . . rugged rocks looking either like goblins or resembling savage beasts, lying crossways or in horizontal or in vertical positions, on the surface of which grew moss and lichen with mottled lines or parasitic plants which screened off the light. . . .'

Where did these garden boulders come from? The best were water-eroded limestone and they were taken from lakes and streams. The man who searched the mountains for a good stone, found it, got it out of the lake or river bed, brought it to town and set it up in a garden, was honoured as an artist just as if he had made the stone himself. The finest of these stones, which might be as tall as a man and very bulky, were extremely valuable. The

Yüan Yeh, which was written and published in the seventeenth century of our era, says that such stones had been collected since time immemorial but had become very rare. Not all of them were large: size itself was not a merit. In the Sung period, miniature gardens were fashionable; they were made in bowls or pans of porcelain or metal, and there would be an island in water, the island composed of stones, shells and dwarfed trees. The whole *objet d'art* was kept on one's study table. The island gardens in this miniature form were 'auspicious' and it seems clear that they, and the Japanese Horai islands, have a common derivation. Really good stones for these tiny gardens were extraordinarily dear: for example, at about the time when the reign of William the Conqueror was nearing its end in England, the Chinese poet and statesman Su Tung-p'o bought such a stone, called the Nine Peaked One, for one hundred pieces of gold. Reverting to the big stones for the outdoor garden, the ancient ones were called *T'ai hu* and they were even more costly; consequently, and like any other antiques, they were often copied by antique-fakers and such copies were so good that although, apparently, the fakes were sometimes exposed, to our eyes they are indistinguishable from the real thing.

In all this there is an interesting anticipation of the European *objets trouvés* school of art, in the honouring of the finder of the stones, in the fact that certain stones became famous and valuable and were celebrated by poets and discussed learnedly by art critics. The social importance of such stones, their reputation, were really very extraordinary. The best of them were almost deified; the greatest painters of the Sung, Yüan and Ming periods painted portraits of them; and such paintings later had an enormous influence on Japanese gardening.

'It is related of Mi Fei the celebrated painter and very acute art critic of the early twelfth century that he was in the habit of bowing to a wonderful garden rock and greeting it reverently as his elder brother.

All Chinese gardens were walled and the walls splendidly coped with brightly coloured glazed tiles. Other architectural elements were canals and pavilions with curved roofs and ornamental balustrades. Such pavilions are, to the European eye, the most recognizable characters of Chinese garden art, if only because of the familiar Willow Pattern china but also because they were much imitated in the Chinoiserie period of European gardening. They were for use, of course, and always so placed that a particular aspect of the garden could be enjoyed from them. Some were closed rooms; others were open to the air in the manner of a veranda. The glazed tile roofs were blue, green or yellow so that there was more colour in them than in European garden architecture. The ornamental balustrades were made according to one of many established, almost 'classical' patterns; but from the seventeenth century onwards strict rules were not always kept and several patterns might be combined. It seems that such mixing of styles was not always approved: the *Yüan Yeh* illustrates the primary patterns and says, or rather its author says:

'I have been collecting patterns for many years; some are quite intricate, others are simple and in good style. These patterns I have arranged in a series according to their variations. From this you can take your choice. . . . Nowadays balustrades are sometimes made with ornaments of seal-characters, but these are not distinguished by uniformity and they do not express any coherent meaning.'

Pavilion windows were of fanciful shapes and their paper 'panes' were sometimes painted.

Garden paths were made with ornamental paving and they were carried over water on the characteristic arched bridges copied by us in our own Chinoiserie gardens. Path mosaics often reproduced the ornaments and patterns used in the garden buildings. Men of taste, like the author of the *Yüan Yeh*, apparently preferred abstract to realistic patterns in their paths.

'Some use stone as large as goose-eggs to produce the patterns but such patterns . . . tend to produce a vulgar effect. . . . It is best to use larger and smaller ones but I fear the workmen do not understand this. In between the stones one may use roofing tiles with which to form patterns representing herons, deer, lions with globes, and so on, but they make a ridiculous impression.' (*Yüan Yeh*)

The layout of a Chinese garden was elaborate. The paths were serpentine, dividing the whole into an irregular maze. Straight lines were anathema since they are not in Nature. The rule of the uneven held good in the vertical plane also, for the skyline of the garden was to be kept as nearly as possible like the jagged crest of a mountain range, though it would be softened by trees.

Flowers were more important than in Japanese gardens, less important than in our own. An author of the Ming Period, Yüan Chung-lang, says in his *Ping Shih*:

'. . . in former times flower lovers set off on long excursions over high mountains and through deep ravines to find one or another rare variety. . . .'

These people were the forerunners of our own Fortunes and Forrests, Wilsons and Kingdon-Wards and it is very curious that the most distinguished of modern Chinese plant-collectors, Dr Hu Hsen-hsu and Dr Cheng Wan-chun, served their apprenticeship under European collectors. These old Chinese plant collectors must have been the men to whom we owe camellias, paeonies and many other of our best garden plants. Yüan

Chung-lang continues that when some outstandingly beautiful tree or shrub was about to flower, the real flower-lover,

'. . . moved his bed out of doors in order to be near it and able to observe how the flowers developed from childhood to maturity and finally faded and died. Others planted masses of flowers in their gardens in order to study all the variants or introduced a few into their dwellings to observe their habits more closely. Some could deduce the size of the flowers from the smell of the leaves, others could judge from the roots what colours the flowers had. These people were real flower-lovers, and cherished a deep feeling for flowers.'*

They did indeed: there is much writing by such flower-lovers which is as absurdly sentimental and ridiculously anthropomorphic as the worst which some of our own more 'charming' writers on gardening have perpetrated. Here, for example, is a piece, again by Yüan Chung-lang:

'When they stand in the sun and their sensitive bodies are protected against the wind, they are happy. When they look intoxicated or silent or weary, and the day is foggy, then the flowers feel sad. When the bloom-laden branches droop and are not able to draw themselves up, it is as if the flowers were dreaming in their sleep. When they seem to smile and look around with a gleam in their eyes, the flowers have awakened from their slumbers.'

To judge both from garden writings and from the very long series of flower paintings in the Chinese art, the garden flowers and trees of importance were Oriental and Opium poppies; plum-blossom, i.e. plum-trees grown as ornamentals; bamboos in great variety; orchids; moutans; hibiscus; roses; water-lilies; chrysanthemums; orange-trees; pomegranate trees; and other

* The translation is Lin Yu-tang's.

fruit-trees grown for their blossom rather than for their fruit. It is said that during the Sung period over one hundred species of bamboos were in cultivation in gardens or on farms. Pine trees were important in Chinese as in Japanese gardens. Camellias were cultivated and a careful selection made of good cultivars at an early date. It is surely very curious that rhododendrons other than azaleas, in which China is very rich, do not seem to have been cultivated at all. Some lilies were grown and from descriptions they seem to have been *Lilium regale*; so were species of narcissus, iris, gentian, hydrangea and magnolia. *Juniperus chinensis* and *Thuja orientalis* were the commonest of garden conifers but *Cupressus funebris* was much planted.

But the Chinese gardeners although admiring flowers for their own sake were not 'plantsmen' making collections but artists using plants as material for compositions and believing in an ancient lore of associations which enriched the life of the garden:

'By planting flowers one invites butterflies . . . by planting pines one invites the winds . . . by planting banana trees one invites rain and by planting willow trees one invites cicadas.'

CHANCE HYBRIDS

When I see a good shrubbery or woodland garden being weeded by hoeing and not by hand, I never fail to wonder whether some excellent new garden plant is not being unwittingly exterminated. From time to time a chance hybrid occurs, offspring of two species of one genus, brought together in the garden. The number of these in garden commerce is not large but would be much larger if weeding were done only by hand and by gardeners able to recognize an interesting shrub in infancy.

Daphne burkwoodii which would, I suppose be more correctly written by the latest rules *Daphne* x 'Burkwoodii', appeared as a chance hybrid and was fortunately noticed as such in Burkwood and Skipworth's nursery at Kingston-upon-Thames. Its parents were *Daphne caucasica* and the 'Garland Flower' *D. cneorum*. From the latter the hybrid inherits its evergreen habit and free, fragrant flowering; from the former its stature and erectness. It won an R.H.S. Award of Merit in 1937 and is one of the best daphnes for the garden.

Such hybrids have not always been found as seedlings among the weeds. There is the different case of *Mahonia* x 'Charity': seeds of *M. bealei* were gathered from a plant in the Slieve Donard nursery for the raising of seedlings. A whole box of the seedlings turned out to be untypical of *M. bealei* and an examination of characters revealed that the pollen parent must have been *M. lomariifolia*. The hybrid is the best of the hardy, winter-flowering mahonias.

Over a century ago Messrs Fisher & Holmes had *Berberis darwinii* and *B. empetrifolia* growing side by side in their nursery. A seedling barberry found growing nearby turned out to be a hybrid between them. With all the flower beauty of *darwinii*, the hardiness of *empetrifolia* and a grace all its own, this hybrid seedling turned out to be a better garden plant than either parent. We know it now as *Berberis stenophylla*.

The lovely *Eucryphia* x 'Nymansay', a cross between the tender, evergreen *E. cordifolia* and the hardy, deciduous *E. glutinosa* has occurred twice as a chance hybrid seedling: in 1915 at Nymans, Sussex and again later, at Mount Usher in County Wicklow. *E.* x 'Mount Usher' like *E.* x 'Nymansay' is vigorous, evergreen, relatively hardy and, like *E. cordifolia* and unlike *E. glutinosa*, lime-tolerant. I have grown both hybrids and cannot tell t'other from which. We have one other hybrid *Eucryphia* in our gardens and that, too, was a chance seedling. This one was found growing in Rostrevor gardens, County Down and turned out to be a cross between *E. glutinosa* and *E. lucida*. It is an evergreen, delicate, slender little tree and could never have occurred in the wild because *E. glutinosa* is a Chilean, *E. lucida* an Australian. The hybrid is *E.* x 'Intermedia' and is not very hardy.

Probably the most important of chance hybrids commonly grown is the London plane-tree *Platanus acerifolia*. The origin of this magnificent tree which has been distributed to every part of the world and is so remarkable for its tolerance of air-pollution, is not absolutely known. But on the authority of that great dendrologist and plant collector, Professor Augustine Henry, backed by that of W. J. Bean, we can say that the London plane originated as a chance hybrid between *Platanus occidentalis* and *P. orientalis* near Oxford in about 1670.

A tree of less importance to citizens but of much more importance to gardeners, x *Cupressocyparis leylandii*, the fastest growing hardy conifer and incomparably the best windbreak tree, occurred as a chance hybrid but in the manner of *Mahonia* x 'Charity', i.e. the seeds from a cone of *Chamaecyparis nootkatensis* were deliberately sown to raise seedlings of that species but turned out untypical. The young plants were clearly partly *Cupressus macrocarpa* and the explanation is that pollen from that cypress was wind-borne to the other parent. That was in 1888. In 1911 the reverse process occurred, again by chance, in the same place, Leighton Hall, near Welshpool: wind-blown pollen from *nootkatensis* fertilized flowers of *macrocarpa* whose seeds yielded a hybrid indistinguishable from the first one.

In all these instances the chance hybridization has occurred between plants in cultivation and could not have happened otherwise since the species concerned do not grow, in nature, within wind- or bee-range of each other. The intervention of man was necessary though the hybridization was not deliberately done. Do such chance hybrids ever occur in the wild? The answer is that in a few genera, they do; the genus *Cistus* is a good case in point. *Cistus* x *purpureus* is a hybrid, found in nature between *C. villosus* and *C. ladaniferus* and *C.* x *cyprius* is another such natural hybrid.

Valuable chance hybrids have enriched the orchard and fruit garden as well as the flower garden. The first of the large-fruited strawberries was a natural hybrid, raised in France, between *Fragaria virginiana* and *F. chiloensis*. The apple 'Cox's Orange Pippin', now of enormous economic importance, derives from a seed of Ribston Pippin whose flowers had presumably been pollinated by some other variety and by chance. Another apple, 'Crawley Beauty', was found as a chance seedling and so was the apple 'Granny Smith'.

FROM SEED

As the growing of annuals declines, and even of vegetables, gardeners become less accustomed to growing their plants from seed. Yet it is in some ways the most rewarding way of doing one's garden propagating. It is well worth while raising shrubs, bulbs and herbaceous perennials from seed; and especially so if you take seed from the plants in your own or your friends' gardens, or subscribe to the R.H.S. and share in the annual seed distribution; or buy seed of uncommon species from foreign seed-collecting agencies.

Some seeds germinate best when perfectly fresh: all kinds of primulas and meconopsis belong to this class. In such cases the best source of seed is your own garden and the seed should be sown as soon as it is ripe enough to gather. I have even found that if you can collect primula, including polyanthus, seed when it is already mature but still green, germination is much better. Primula, meconopsis and other plants from high rainfall areas drop their seeds in permanently moist soil and it is difficult to germinate in dry conditions: if you have a mist propagation unit such seeds will do well under mist, with the cuttings.

At the other extreme are seeds intended to resist great heat and drought. I wanted to raise several kinds of Acacias from seed obtained from Australia. I failed to germinate any of the first batch and when obtaining a second asked, at the same time for advice. I was told that the seeds of acacia have a very hard *testa*, the outer skin, and that something should be done to help the embryo break through, i.e. to let in water. The method recommended was to scrumple up some newspapers on the concrete floor of a shed, put the seed into a fine gauge wire gauze sieve, set fire to the newspapers and pass the sieve back and forth through the tips of the flames until some of the seeds began to jump like pop-corn. *Acacia* seeds of several species germinated quickly and well after such treatment. Acacias are, of course, leguminous and the seeds of this family are famous for their toughness: some have been kept in liquid air or hydrogen (—250°C. or about 450°F. of frost) for many weeks without any loss of viability.

Some seeds will germinate only after a period of freezing cold; the seeds of some lilies belong to this class. Lily seeds need understanding before one undertakes the propagation of lilies from seed. First of all there is a group of species whose seeds germinate *underground*: they do this while the soil is still warm, producing a tiny rootlet and two leaflets on a minute stem. The food stored in the seed feeds the stem, swelling it into a miniature bulb. At this point in the process of what is called *hypogeal* germination, one of two things happens: those lilies which belong to the class of *immediate hypogeal* germination species, begin to grow at once from the bulblet. But others belonging to the *delayed hypogeal* class, go into a resting period and do not continue to grow until a certain degree of cold has been experienced for a certain period of time. The first leaves may appear above the soil in the spring after sowing; but if the winter be very mild they may not show a leaf for another year, so that visible germination may take two years.

Other lilies belong to the category of those having *epigeal germination* and here again it may be immediate or delayed, i.e. leaves may show one month after sowing or not for six months. Epigeal germinators differ from hypogeal in that they do not form a bulb until after the leaf has appeared.

The stony seeds of many shrubs such as roses, hawthorns, hollies, have a *testa* relatively impervious to water although not as hard as *Acacia* seeds, germinate better if 'stratified'. They should be put in layers in a heap of damp sand at a temperature between freezing point and about 40°F., for three or four months: then sorted out and sown. An acquaintance of mine was exceptionally successful in raising hawthorns from seed: he fed the berries to half a dozen hens kept in a pen, collected and 'sowed' their droppings, and—I do not know why—got unusually fast and full germination.

Then there is the process known as 'vernalization'; the following is from Sir E. J. Salisbury's (formerly Director of Kew) *The Living Garden*:

'The effect of temperature on germinating seeds is then, not only dependent upon the duration of warmth or cold, but apparently also on the fluctuations. Quite a number of seeds germinate more readily in a germinator that is subjected to changes of temperature than in one where the temperature is constant. Earlier development and earlier maturation can be induced in some plants by subjecting the soaked seeds to a low temperature (from 1°–3°C.) for about a fortnight. Wheat treated in this way will develop ears a fortnight earlier than a crop raised from untreated seed. The method, which is known as "vernalization", is applicable to seeds that are not to be sown immediately, as if, after treatment, the seeds be dried off, they can be stored and sown later, when the accelerating action will still be exhibited.'

The same author points out that the first man to experiment with the pre-treatment of seeds was Francis Bacon and that though he got no results from steeping seeds in wine, he got quicker germination from seeds steeped in manure water.

Certain seeds which are rich in oils have a short viable life: magnolias are a case in point and so are camellias; the germination rate falls steeply for every day they are kept before planting and bought seeds, which cannot be really fresh, germinate poorly. I have also found it best to plant paeony seeds as soon as they are ripe but to leave the seed boxes out of doors all winter; when the boxes are brought into the greenhouses in spring, the seeds germinate readily.

Seeds vary in size, of course, enormously: the smallest are like a superfine dust—those of orchids for example; at the other extreme are coconuts and even larger seeds. A good rule to follow with all seeds is to cover them with a compost as deep as their own diameter. In the case of very small seeds it is often impractical to cover them at all, in which case the boxes must be shaded until germination has taken place.

Some of the smallest seeds I have ever sown were those of *Callistemons.* As they also had a high germination rate the seedlings were difficult to handle if the seed was sown too thickly. I learned to mix such seed very thoroughly with four or five times their own volume of silver-sand and to sow the mixture uncovered. This distributes the seedlings widely in the box. Rhododendron seeds are best sown in that way and those of some heathers. The boxes or pans of all such minute seeds must never be watered from above; the seed, washed into the soil, fails to germinate. The compost being sufficiently moist at the time of sowing, the boxes are best sealed into polythene bags so that no watering is required for many weeks. Another way of germinating such seeds is to shake them up with some moist sphagnum moss in a glass flask and then cork the flask. It should be kept in deep shade and in warmth. Germination occurs and the seedlings are, in due course, sorted from the moss, pricked into boxes, and weaned in a close case.

Some seeds seem to germinate best in conditions one would think inauspicious. Seeds of *Pittosporum tenuifolium* in my Devon garden used to germinate well when they fell on to the coarse limestone chips of the drive, but not when they fell on to good soil; so did those of *Hellebores*.

MAGNOLIAS

I have grown about a dozen species of magnolias and become deeply interested in that extraordinary genus of primitives. There is a very remarkable collection of species at Caerhays in Cornwall and some very fine magnolias at Dartington Hall. Though their range in Britain is wide they do best in the West Country.

The most impressive of the genus is *Magnolia campbellii*, a deciduous tree which may reach to 150 feet in height and comes from the Sikkimese Himalaya, growing there at altitudes of up to 10,000 feet. This means that it is hardy; but as it flowers in late February, March and early April, its flowers are apt to be spoiled by frost in all but the most favourable sites. There is a very old specimen of this species at Overbecks, a National Trust garden near Salcombe, Devon which is as big as a well-grown oak and when in flower, perhaps the most spectacularly beautiful flowering tree in Britain. The flowers, borne on the still leafless branches, are cupped, about ten inches across when wide open, very sweet scented and in colour from deep rose-pink to crimson. But this species does not flower until it is twenty-five years old and should, therefore, be planted when the gardener is still young. Its foliage, with pointed, oval velvety green and bronze leaves to nine inches long, is lovely.

There are three evergreen species of this genus but I have grown only two of them, *M. grandiflora* is the familiar one, with shining green leaves, felted red on the reverse side and fragrant nine-inch creamy flowers. It is an American native but fairly hardy here, though it dislikes cold winds. The most pleasing specimens are to be seen in the great tree nurseries about Pistoia, in North Italy, where they have a beautifully regular, columnar, very fastigiate form, and another, pyramidal. Altogether, this is one of the noblest evergreens in cultivation. So, in its different way, is *M. delavayi*, a native of Yunnan and not nearly as hardy as *grandiflora*. Its leaves are oval, up to fourteen by eight inches, tough and leathery. The creamy flowers tend to open at night and scent the gloaming of spring evenings.

The Yulan, *M. denudata*, has been cultivated by the Chinese for about 1,500 years. It is a rounded, broad, much ramified tree to forty feet. It is hardy. Following mild winters it often flowers in March; otherwise in May. My own specimen flowered at four years old. Its thick-petalled flowers are pure white and about six inches in diameter when open wide.

For the small garden the best of this genus is *M. stellata*, a hardy, deciduous shrub up to twelve feet tall with silvery-haired overwintering flower-buds. It is easily raised from cuttings, flowers when young and when mature, flowers lavishly. I found it intolerant of lime but otherwise very easy.

In some ways the most charming magnolias for gardens are *M. sieboldii* and *M. sinensis* which are alike but the latter, especially its variety, *grandiflora* is the finer. It is a shrub to twenty feet with rounded six-inch leaves, glaucous to bright green, velvety beneath. The beautifully cupped white flowers with rich purple centres are held facing outwards, freely borne after the seventh or eighth year, and they are fragrant. In this as in other magnolias the scarlet fruits are decorative.

M. wilsonii has an unusual and very attractive way of carrying its flowers. It is a fast-growing tree to twenty feet or so; my own attained eight feet in six years from seed. It flowers young. The foliage is handsome. The flowers are saucer-shaped, four inches across, opening in May or June, white with a purple centre. They are pendulous on long stalks, so that their beauty is most evident if one can arrange to look upwards into them. To that end the species should be discouraged from growing shrub-like by suppressing all but the main trunk, and all side shoots, until it is seven feet tall, when a head is allowed to develop.

For those willing to wait for flowers but preferring rose-pink to white or cream, there are, in addition to the mighty *M. campbellii*, three others. They are as follows:

M. sprengeri x 'Diva' is a tree to thirty feet with large broadly oval leaves. It flowers on the leafless branches in April and the flowers are like those of *campbellii* but a deeper pink on the outside than within.

M. sargentiana robusta is a West Chinese species growing fast to well over fifty feet, flowering in April on the bare shoots: the flowers are shaped like water-lilies, deep carmine pink on the outside, paler pink inside, and up to a foot in diameter.

M. veitchii is a tree to forty feet. Its leaves are bronze in youth, deep green and up to a foot by seven inches at maturity. The blush-pink flowers in April are very large. Although this magnolia has a specific name it is a *campbellii* x *denudata* hybrid and flowers at about ten years of age.

The commonest magnolias in gardens are cultivars of the x *soulangiana* complex. All are bushes, broader than tall, with tough robust foliage and erect goblet-shaped flowers. These flowers are white more or less stained with inky purple, according to variety. Deriving from a *denudata* x *liliflora* cross, they have little of the distinction of the other magnolias but they are easy, hardy and vigorous.

Magnolias like a deep, preferably rather peaty loam, permanently moist but well-drained. And protection from strong, especially cold, winds.

HYBRIDS, AND F_1 HYBRIDS AND HARDINESS

If, when the pollen from the male organs of a flower is put on to the female organs of a similar flower—of the same species and form—fertilization takes place, and the nucleus of the pollen tube fuses with the nucleus of the egg, the plant which grows from the resultant seed will be identical with its parents.

But if the pollen comes from one species, while the egg belongs to another, that is if pollen from species A lights on a stigma of species B, the plant growing from the resultant seed will combine the characters of both parents. If it does so in such a way that the characters exhibited by it make it a better garden plant than either parent, it is clearly desirable to keep and propagate it. But if it is the kind of plant which we want to grow from seed, this may be difficult.

This first generation of such a crossing of two wild species is called the F_1 generation (F = *filia*, daughter, I believe). But supposing, in order to obtain seed in quantity of this new garden plant, the gardener 'selfs' it, i.e. fertilizes the female parts with pollen from its own male parts, a phenomenon called the 'segration of characters' defeats his aim. For of the resulting offspring, some will resemble one, others the other, of the original wild parents, and only a proportion of the seedlings of this F_2 generation will resemble the F_1 generation. In short, the desirable new plant will not 'come true' from seed. It may be of a kind which we cannot grow any other way, that is an annual vegetable like sweetcorn—a typical case—or carrots. But if its qualities are such that it is well worth the trouble involved, it can still be put into garden commerce: the seed producer repeats the original cross, every season and on a mass scale. All the seed he sells is thus that of an F_1 hybridization and the kind of plant in question is thus known as an F_1 hybrid.

In the case of plants like herbaceous perennials and shrubs which can be propagated vegetatively, whether by cuttings, layering or root-cuttings or by the new technique of 'meristem propagation', there is no need to have recourse to F_1 hybrids, i.e. to repeating the cross on a mass, seed-producing, scale year after year. Vegetative propagation reproduces the attributes of the mother plant identically.

Hybridization has been resorted to in order to combine, in the hybrid offspring of species, their best qualities, not only of flower form and flower colour, but of habit, disease resistance and, for example, hardiness. One species of a genus may be very good for colour and form, but tender. By crossing it with a hardy species of that genus, the plant-breeder may get a hybrid nearly as good—sometimes quite as good or even better—for colour and form, and hardier than the tender parent. *Eucryphia* x 'Nymansay' has the evergreen attribute of the *cordifolia* parent yet it is as hardy as the deciduous *glutinosa* parent. Many of the hardy hybrid rhododendrons have one parent which is tender.

In certain genetical conditions a hybrid may, in one or more of its characters, transcend *both* parents: if two tender species have, recessive in their genetical make up, the characters of hardiness, it may be released by crossing them and the hybrid will then be hardier than either of its parents.

Geneticists hold that the genetical make up of a species is not affected by environment. There are some horticulturists who have reservations about this. They know that, for example, rhododendrons collected at an altitude of 10,000 feet are hardier than rhododendrons of the same species collected at 2,000 feet. The hardiness is transmitted to seedlings: must there not, then, be a genetical difference? Probably, yes, but it may have occurred as a mutation and thus made possible the survival of the species, in its mutant form at the higher altitude. In short, the environment has not produced the hardiness; the newly emerged hardiness made possible a change of environment.

Fruit growers know that, for example, 'Cox's Orange Pippin' apples grown grafted on a dwarfing stock are not quite identical with the same apples grown on a vigorous stock. But, say the geneticist, this is not a genetical change, and if the apple came true from seed, there would be no difference between seedlings from the pips of apples on dwarfing stock and those of apples on vigorous stocks.

The hardiness, and other good qualities, of a hybrid, depend, for perpetuation, on reproducing the hybrid exactly—from seed by using F_1 seed only and repeating the cross every season; or by vegetative propagation in the case of perennial or woody plants.

BARBERRIES

Some English gardeners are plant collectors. There is no harm in this if the collecting mania is not allowed to ruin the design of the garden. And perhaps the best way to satisfy the collectors' craving in horticultural terms, is to collect a genus which is large and diverse enough to remain interesting for years, preferably for a lifetime; but not so large as to be overwhelming. *Rhododendron* is an example of an unsuitable genus, with over a thousand species. It might suit a millionaire, of course, but not you and me. A very suitable genus would be *Berberis*.

Separated from *Mahonia*, as it should be, *Berberis* includes about 200 species but a minority—say between fifty and seventy-five—are really interesting. Although some of the deciduous species are interesting, my own taste is for evergreens, many of which are perfectly hardy.

There was at one time an attempt made to exterminate our native *B. vulgaris* though it is a handsome shrub which, as W. J. Bean very rightly says, is 'more beautiful than many rarer things'. The reason for this attempt, which made this barberry rare in the wild, is that the corn mildew, a fungus disease of wheat, passes its first stage as a parasite on *Berberis*, specifically on *B. vulgaris*.

Those species which I have grown and favour include the following:

B. darwinii—of course: it makes a dense and many-stemmed and much-branched shrub to about twelve feet tall. It was discovered by Charles Darwin in 1835 and introduced by the plant collector William Lobb in 1849. The source, like that of so many other fine garden plants, was the island of Chiloë. Its vividly green foliage, red-tinged orange flowers and blue fruits all make it a superb ornamental shrub. Its hybrid with *B. empetrifolia*, *B. stenophylla*, has the advantage of being as beautiful as *darwinii* but even hardier and like *darwinii* bears its golden flowers in innumerable racemes.

Its other parent *empetrifolia*, is another Chilean evergreen with narrow reflexed leaves, but it is a dwarf and bears its flower singly or in pairs.

In 1924 F. Kingdon-Ward discovered a new evergreen barberry in Tibet, *B. calliantha*, a dwarf to three feet with triple spines. This has quite large leaves, some of them over two inches long, waxy white on the lower surface but shining green above. For a barberry its flowers are very large, about an inch in diameter and creamy yellow. Kingdon-Ward was also responsible for introducing another evergreen barberry from Tibet, again a dwarf of good habit and flower, *B. chrysosphaera*.

To return to barberry species of more imposing stature, but still evergreen, *B. gagnepainii* attains eight feet. Its taper-pointed, narrowly lanceolate leaves are as much as four inches long and the half-inch bright yellow flowers are freely borne in clusters of six or twelve.

One of the most interesting of all the thirty-odd evergreen barberries I have grown is called *B. hypokerina*, usually a rather dwarf shrub of stiff and even awkward habit but with remarkable leaves. Stout and leathery, they are green above, milky-white beneath, six inches long, the margins wavy and set with ferocious spines. The crowded clusters of flowers are pale yellow.

For colour, a richer orange than *darwinii*, the best species of the genus is *B. linearifolia*. It is another Chilean and was introduced forty years ago. The flowers, larger than those of *darwinii*, are deep orange inside, and apricot on the outside; but they are in clusters at the joints, not in racemes.

I found many splendidly flowering natural hybrids of this with *B. darwinii* in woods on the shores of Lake Nahuel Huapi in Argentina. *B. wilsoniae*, another beauty, is partially evergreen. It grows to four or five feet, but more in diameter, hemispherical, remarkably symmetrical, the very numerous branches gracefully arched, and the pale yellow flowers borne in short racemes which are very numerous.

A number of barberries are much more ornamental as berrying than as flowering shrubs. Three outstanding in this respect bear the cultivar names 'Barbarossa', 'Bountiful' and 'Buccaneer'. Another is called 'Pirate King'. In all the best fruiting barberries the fruits are coral, apricot or scarlet and in the finest they are translucent.

Formerly classed with *Berberis* but now with a genus of their own, *Mahonia* can be crossed with *Berberis* and there is an interesting and decorative inter-generic hybrid *Mahoberberis* with leaves half-way between *Mahonia aquifolium* and *Berberis vulgaris*.

The tallest and most graceful of the evergreen barberries make fine specimen shrubs; the shorter ones are best planted in groups or to clothe banks; the very dwarf kinds make good rock-garden plants.

NOMENCLATURE

I confess to being irritated by people who, visiting one's garden, asking the name of a plant and being answered, then complain about Latin names and ask if there isn't an 'ordinary' name. Very often there is not; or not in English. And thousands of plants introduced since 1700 have never been given vernacular names.

Nor are vernacular names as good and valid as botanical names, for whereas the botanical names tell you something about the plant, the vernacular name does not and is even, very often, misleading—lily-of-the-valley is not a lily; rose-of-sharon is not a rose.

The naming of plants is governed by rules and those rules are based on two principles; that a plant has only one valid name; and that that name is the earliest given to it which conforms to the rules of nomenclature.

The names of wild plants are invariably in two parts and sometimes in three: one, genus; two, species; three, variety. The first, or generic, name is *invariably* written with a capital initial letter and printed in *italic*. The second, or specific, name is the earliest specific epithet given to it by Linnaeus in his *Species Plantarum* (1753), or subsequently by a qualified botanist according to the rules. Note the words 'specific epithet': the specific name is often a descriptive epithet; thus, *vulgaris* = common; *officinalis* = officinal; *esculentum* = edible; *europaeum* = European; *nigra* = black and so on. But the specific, like the generic name often does honour to a person or even a place: *wilsonae, henryi* (*or henryana*) are cases in point, where the names of persons have been used as specific names; *Bougainvillea* is a case where a generic name derives from a proper name. It was formerly the case that if the specific name was that of a person or place, it was spelt with a capital letter, though printed, like the generic name, in *italics*. This is now incorrect, and the specific name is invariably written and printed with a small letter.

Botanists only recognize a plant name as valid if it has been published with an adequate description which must be written in Latin, and a figure.

In addition to its generic and specific name, a wild plant may bear a third, or varietal, name, usually in one word but sometimes in several. This varietal name is preceded by the contraction var. for variety, in Roman letters, but is itself printed in italics. So, up to now, we have:

Generic name: *Rhododendron*
Specific name: *ponticum*
Varietal name: *album*
= *Rhododendron ponticum* var. *album.*

Gender of specific and varietal names agrees with that of the generic name. A varietal name may be doubled or trebled if necessary to describe the variety: for example, a variety may be both dwarf and variegated, and the varietal name could then be *nana variegata*; or fastigiate and purple leaved, giving *fastigiata purpurea.* Strictly, the second epithet should be preceded by the Latin word forma in Roman type.

These, very briefly—and there are reservations and complications—are the principal rules for wild plants.

Coming now to cultivated plants. It was formerly the case that a garden variety produced by selection or in some other way, could be given a Latin varietal epithet as if it were wild. Supposing you had an especially vivid form of *Lobelia fulgens* and wished to name it so as to distinguish its quality, you might in the past, have called it *Lobelia fulgens brilliantissima.* This is no longer correct. The rule now is that you must give your plant a name in the vernacular, not in Latin; and put it between single inverted commas: so it becomes *Lobelia fulgens* 'Brilliant'. To be pedantic, you should put the contraction cv. (for cultivar) before 'Brilliant'—so, *Lobelia fulgens* cv. 'Brilliant'.

There are some other rules: if you want to name a plant to honour your wife or your mistress, you should not call it 'Mrs Mary Jones' or 'Miss Jane Smith', but 'Mary Jones' or 'Jane Smith'.

When we come to hybrids, the rules are simple. Intergeneric hybrids are indicated by the multiplication sign in front of a compound composed of elements of the two parental generic names, e.g. x *Cupressocyparis* (*Cupressus* x *Chamaecyparis*) or x *Mahoberberis* (*Mahonia* x *Berberis*). Interspecific hybrids bear the name of the genus to which both parent species belong, followed by the names of those species separated by a multiplication sign, or by a multiplication sign followed by a 'specific' name, e.g. *Berberis darwinii* x *empetrifolia* or *Berberis* x *stenophylla*.

If you wish to be very correct in your naming of plants you will go further than this. You cross *Rhododendron sinogrande* as the pollen parent with *Rhododendron falconeri* as the seed parent, and correctly written, your seedling should be described thus:

Rhododendron sinogrande ♂ x *Rhododendron falconeri* ♀
cv. 'So-and-so'

But in practice you would write:
Rhododendron x 'So-and-so'

The point I want to make is that very often the correct Latin names of plants are (a) beautiful, (b) descriptive of the plant's special quality and (c) evocative of the plant's history and (d) exact and precise. And to avoid or deform these names is mere laziness which deprives the gardener of a considerable pleasure. A distinguished expert in rhododendrons was called in to identify a plant in a great garden. For some time the expert gazed at the bush in glorious flower until the gardener asked,

'Well, sir, is it *Rhododendron cinnabarinum roylei?*'

'Sir', replied the expert, 'I name this plant *Rhododendron cinnabarinum roylei magnificum.*'

Pompousness? Pedantry? No, poetry, and of the best kind, the kind with a respect for identity.

ROOT-CUTTINGS

One of the ways of propagating, vegetatively, certain garden plants, is by means of root-cuttings. This is by no means true of all plants: but just as many plants are capable of forming, on bits of their stems or even their leaves, adventitious roots and so making a whole new plant, so certain plants have the power to make adventitious shoots on bits of their root, achieving the same result by the reverse process.

There is no difficulty about using this method of propagation. But there is one important rule which must not be overlooked. The shoot-growth buds always develop on that end of the root-cutting which was nearer to the stem; the new roots, on the other hand, develop on the end furthest from the stem. In a sense this does not concern the gardener because this will happen even if he plants the cutting upside down and the new plant will show him by its behaviour which way up to plant it. But it is expedient to plant some root-cuttings vertically and in that case they should be planted with the root-producing end downwards and the shoot-producing end upwards, of course. So, when making the root-cutting of thick-rooted plants, cut the end nearest the stem square across, the end furthest from the stem on the slant. This makes no difference whatever to growth and merely serves to identify the ends correctly.

An ordinary propagating case can be used for root cuttings as for stem cuttings. The compost can be pure silver-sand, sandy loam or sand and peat; or a sterile medium such as vermiculite. It must be kept moist, of course. Thick root cuttings, such as those of some anchusas, oriental poppies and, in the kitchen garden, sea-kale, are planted vertically, like stem cuttings: about two or three inches is the correct length.

Thin root-cuttings such as those of *Phlox decussata*, gaillardias, romneyas, and some other plants are treated rather differently: they should be only an inch long and laid flat on the surface of the propagating compost. They are then thinly covered with compost, almost as if they were long seeds.

An interesting aside touching the propagation of *Phlox* by this method. Healthy plants can be grown from mother plants afflicted by eel-worm: the eel-worms all being in the stems at the end of the season, and overwintering in the remains of the stems, the roots are free from these pests and root cuttings will produce plants free from eel-worm.

SOME HEBES

Hebe is the correct generic name of the woody or shrubby, as distinct from herbaceous, veronicas. With a single exception they are all—there are about seventy species—natives of and peculiar to New Zealand. Nearly all of them have opposite leaves arranged in very symmetrical rows, whether those leaves be tiny and scale-like, or large and lanceolate. And all bear their flowers in pyramidal panicles, some terminal but others axillary.

Unfortunately relatively few *Hebes* are perfectly hardy in our average climate. However, many are hardy near to the sea, and a few inland. All are valuable garden plants, especially for their habit of flowering in late summer and autumn when most of our own flowering shrubs are over. I shall mention here only a few of which I have personal experience, but the genus is worthy of more attention than it commonly receives from English gardeners.

I must give priority to the *Hebe* called 'Bowles Hybrid'. I do not know its breeding but its quality is superlative. It is a slender-branched, arching, low shrub rarely more than two feet tall and as much through, with narrow, pointed leaves. In early summer it bears masses of long, symmetrical racemes of pale mauve flowers. It is one of the prettiest small shrubs one can grow and, like all *Hebes*, extremely easy to raise from cuttings. When flowering is over, you clip the plant all over with shears to prevent seed being formed. It at once starts growing vigorously again and, in early autumn, is again covered with flowers. It is just hardy inland in the south, but better near the coast. A plant of this in a garden of mine sported a branch bearing pure white flowers with chocolate anthers.

Going to the other extreme of stature, there is a group of magnificent hybrids of *H. speciosa* derivation. They are, as I have grown them, vigorous shrubs to eight feet, but commonly not more than six, with glossy, pointed leaves about five inches long. In 'Alicia Amherst' the flowers are almost royal blue; in 'La Séduisante' they are a rich pink, and in 'Purple Queen', deep purple, the colour being apparent even in the young stems and the leaves. Unfortunately none of these cultivars is really hardy inland and they are, in practice, confined to the south and west coasts.

Some of the *H. salicifolia* hybrids are excellent; unlike the *H. speciosa* kinds which are stiff and erect, these are arching and graceful shrubs, often to five or six feet and spreading quite wide. In *H.* x *andersonii* the large lavender-blue flower spikes fade to white as the flowers go over and in its form 'Variegata' the leaves are marked and margined creamy white. One of the most handsome of the *speciosa* hybrids is even more strikingly variegated, the leaves being green, cream and deep rose-pink, young stems and flowers rose pink. It is, however, tender.

'Autumn Glory' is a good representative of yet another group of *Hebes*, with rounded, glaucous , fleshy leaves and richly purple flowers all summer and autumn. There are many similar cultivars with fancy names. They are rather like small versions of the *Hebe* (? *H.* x 'Latifolia') used as a hedging plant in Ireland and the Scillies.

A curious *Hebe* of no great beauty but worth having as one of those plants which look like a totally different genus and make a good talking point in the garden, is H. *cupressoides* which, with glaucous, scale-like, closely adpressed leaves, nearly resembles a small cypress.

By far the most beautiful *Hebe* in cultivation and, in my experience, by far the most difficult to grow, is *H. hulkeana.* It has slender, soft-wooded branches which need support; in any case this lovely but tender shrub should be grown, in most of Britain, on a wall facing south or west. Its glossy leaves are rounded and quite large. Its flowers are lavender and borne in superb panicles up to a foot long. This *Hebe* is not easy to establish and is very easy to lose.

Very different from all the above is a favourite rock garden shrub of mine, *H. pimeleoides* 'Glauco-coerulea'. It is a small, prostrate shrub with glaucous leaves, and lavender-blue flowers. A form I had bore flowers which were blue and white on the same spike.

Provided winters are not too cold *Hebes* will survive exposure, especially on the sea coast, tolerating salt-spray as very few other good flowering shrubs will do. They are not fussy about soil and they seem never to be attacked by pests or diseases.

INDEX OF PLANTS

GENERAL INDEX

INDEX

INDEX

INDEX

INDEX

INDEX